EDUCATIONAL CHANGE IN INTERNATIONAL EARLY CHILDHOOD CONTEXTS

Copublished with the Association for Childhood Education International (ACEI), *Educational Change in International Early Childhood Contexts: Crossing Borders of Reflection* examines the role of teacher reflection in a variety of educational contexts worldwide. Using a case study approach that integrates research, theory, policy, and practice, international contributors show how, in some settings, local traditions and values are honored, whereas in others, international educational ideas and programs become modified to suit local needs. Cases from Japan, China, Palestine, South Africa, Kenya, Finland, Italy, and New Zealand are discussed, as well as models from the United States.

Through its thorough investigation into teacher reflection practices throughout the world, *Educational Change in International Early Childhood Contexts: Crossing Borders of Reflection* focuses on the transformative value of these practices to promote change in early childhood education. Framing commentary from Linda R. Kroll and Daniel R. Meier provides context and places the case studies in conversation with one another, allowing for productive international comparisons in this dynamic collection.

Linda R. Kroll is Professor of Early Childhood Education at Mills College.

Daniel R. Meier is Professor of Elementary Education at San Francisco State University.

EDUCATIONAL CHANGE IN INTERNATIONAL EARLY CHILDHOOD CONTEXTS

Crossing Borders of Reflection

Edited by
Linda R. Kroll
Daniel R. Meier

Routledge
Taylor & Francis Group

NEW YORK AND LONDON

Association for
Childhood Education
International™

First published 2015
by Routledge
711 Third Avenue, New York, NY 10017

and by Routledge
2 Park Square, Milton Park, Abingdon, Oxon OX14 4RN

Routledge is an imprint of the Taylor & Francis Group, an informa business

Library of Congress Cataloging in Publication Data
    Educational change in international early childhood contexts : crossing borders
    of reflection / edited by Linda R. Kroll, Daniel R. Meier.
        pages cm – (International perspectives on early childhood education)
    Includes bibliographical references and index.
    1. Reflective teaching—Case studies.
    2. Culturally relevant pedagogy—Case studies. 3. Early childhood education—
    Case studies. I. Kroll, Linda Ruth.
    LB1025.3.E3346 2014
    372.21—dc23   2014013334

ISBN: 978-0-415-73262-8 (hbk)
ISBN: 978-0-415-73263-5 (pbk)
ISBN: 978-1-315-84894-5 (ebk)

Typeset in 10/12 Bembo
by codeMantra

for Hazelle
—Daniel R. Meier

for Dennis
—Linda R. Kroll

CONTENTS

FOREWORD

Joseph Tobin

The essays in this book collectively demonstrate the value of bringing an international perspective to thinking about key issues in early childhood education. They make a case for overcoming the North American/European ethnocentrism that characterizes much scholarship and policy in the field. The United States and England are among the countries that have a history of exporting theories and practices for the education and care of young children to Asia, Africa, Latin America, and the Pacific Islands. Ironically, although the United States continues to struggle to develop a comprehensive system of early childhood education and care and is domestically divided by acrimonious, politicized debates about the proper balance of play and academics in the preschool curriculum, it packages preschool curricula for export overseas, often with underwriting from U.S.-based foundations and NGOs.

I'm suggesting that something is amiss here and that what is needed is a more symmetric exchange among countries of ideas about early childhood education. What is also needed are studies, like those in this book, that contribute to greater appreciation for the need for preschools to be responsive to their local contexts and that argue for the value of a global diversity of approaches. These projects are more worthwhile than attempts to come up with a universal definition of best practices for early childhood education. By presenting us with an assortment of studies from around the world, this edited collection makes a useful contribution to making the field less parochial and ethnocentric.

I see great value in early childhood practitioners and scholars learning about approaches from other countries. But I am not suggesting that the primary pay-off of being exposed to ideas from abroad is to provide models for us to import and to put in place of our own. What I am suggesting instead is that encountering national and cultural differences can change domestic practices in less linear ways, by presenting us with evidence and perspectives that work to question taken-for-granted assumptions and expand the repertoire of the possible. To give two examples from my Preschool in Three Cultures studies: if it works for Japanese preschool teachers to hold back from intervening quickly in children's fights, perhaps teachers elsewhere needn't intervene as quickly and aggressively as they think they must. If Chinese four-year-olds can give and receive critical feedback on their storytelling without tears, perhaps our notions of the fragility of children's self-esteem should be rethought. The implications of such reports from preschools far away are not that these practices would necessarily work in our domestic contexts, but rather that once such previously unfamiliar practices have been introduced to us and have been shown to have sense and meaning, we no longer have the luxury of not considering them as options.

The other core feature of this book is its focus on reflection. Most international work in the field of early childhood education looks primarily at policy (how national systems of ECEC are organized and funded) and at curriculum (goals, standards, and pedagogical practices as laid out in performance standards and guidelines). The essays in this collection take another approach, as they share a focus on the role of reflection in early childhood educational practice. Instead of reporting primarily on the official and planned aspects of ECEC, the essays here look at the power of reflection in practice. Collectively, the essays argue that much of the difference between just teaching and teaching well lies in the practice of reflection. No lesson plan, whether copied directly from a curriculum guide or written by a classroom teacher, ever goes exactly as planned. What makes preschool classrooms so fascinating is their endless capacity to surprise and sometimes confound even experienced practitioners. Linda Kroll, in her introductory chapter, refers to this as the "uncertainty" of preschool classrooms. The educational psychologist Rand Spiro suggests that such uncertainty is characteristic of "ill-structured domains," by which he means not sloppily planned and run operations, but instead, contexts such as emergency rooms, battlefields, and, I would add, preschool classrooms, where contingencies and uncertainties play such a dominating role that practitioners must be intuitive, spontaneous, and creative rather than governed primarily by rules, customs, and habits.

This is where reflection comes in. Some of this reflection happens in "real time" as, in the midst of morning opening, reading a story, conducting a science lesson, or monitoring action on the playground, something a child says or does suddenly makes the event veer off in an unexpected direction. The practitioner must then respond quickly, but this does not mean that the response lacks reflection. Perhaps the defining characteristic of the expert early childhood educational practitioner is the ability to accelerate the process of reflection so that it happens in the blink of an eye. The expert teacher acts in such situations not by following fixed rules, but by considering many factors all at once—factors that may include the meanings of the initiating child's words or action; the mood and reactions of classmates; the children's previous patterns of behaving and feeling in similar (but never identical) situations; the teacher's goals for these children, both short-term (in the next ten minutes) and much longer-term (for the day, the week, the year, or these children's future lives). Teachers' decisions must be made on the fly, so quickly that there isn't time for an orderly progression through a list of steps on a decision tree. These decisions happen so fast that, as Maurice Bloch (1991) suggests, there isn't time for them to follow linguistic reasoning. Expert teachers, like expert practitioners of other fields, are able to notice, consider, take account of (which is to say, to reflect on) more factors than their less expert counterparts in their field.

The kind of reflection most discussed in this book is not this thoughtfulness that takes place in a blink of an eye in the midst of action, but instead the thoughtfulness that characterizes skilled practice that takes place away from the action, as teachers write journal entries at the end of the day, replay events of the day in their head as they drive home or cook dinner, and discuss classroom events with colleagues in the teachers' lounge or in professional development workshops.

I like that the essays in this book focus on reflection as a collaborative rather than an individual enterprise. Although it must be true that skilled preschool teachers do a lot of reflection alone, silently, in their heads and sometimes in journal writing as well, these chapters suggest that a characteristic of quality preschool programs is that their staff engage in systematic, collegial practices of reflection. These include, for example, the "lesson studies" (discussed in this book in Chapter 10) that are organized by many Japanese preschool teachers, where lesson plans are brainstormed and lessons are piloted, observed, documented, and sometimes videotaped and then collaboratively analyzed and modified. Systematic reflection also includes reflection not only on how teachers taught but also on how children learned, as most famously embodied in Reggio's notion of documentation, which refers not only to the collection of artifacts of children's learning but also and more importantly to an ongoing process of reflection on these artifacts. The authors of this collection connect reflective practice to professional development and emphasize that professional development is a process of career-long learning.

The other key theme of this collection is globalization. The world, including the world of early childhood education and care, is increasingly caught up in the global circulation of people, goods, and ideas. In his chapter, Daniel Meier uses the term *time-space compression* to refer to these processes, which have both positive and negative impacts on early childhood education and care settings. A positive but challenging effect of this shrinking of the world is that ECEC settings in many countries are increasingly diverse in the children and families they serve and in their staff, as my colleagues Angela Arzubiaga and Jennifer Adair and I discuss in our 2013 book *Children Crossing Borders*. This compression also means that practitioners can draw on ideas from a wider range of sources. Negatively, globalization can have the opposite effect, leading to a global homogenization of practices and a wiping out of approaches characteristic of particular cultures, a loss of diversity in approaches to early childhood education akin to the loss of biological diversity.

Space-time compression also is an apt description of the acceleration of pressure to reform preschools. A corollary of this acceleration is what I call the myth of never-ending progress, the idea that in early childhood education, as in other fields, we are and need to be continually making progress (Tobin, 2005). Notions of quality in ECEC change from generation to generation. What was taken for best practice a generation or two ago we now see as lacking. I suggest that the quality standards of earlier eras were not worse, just different. To believe otherwise is to suffer from progressivism, the unwarranted belief that the standards and practices of every generation are better than those that came before. The myth of progress fuels demands for never-ending reform and the implementation of the latest "state-of-the-art" approaches, with the unfortunate consequence that local, contextual, time-tested approaches are under constant threat.

The essays in this collection, by showing the impacts of time-space compression on early childhood education, make an argument for appreciating the value of the local and the cultural in ECEC and therefore for resisting the relentless pressure to reform and rationalize. If there is a single conclusion to be drawn from these essays it is that quality ECEC programs remain sensitive to their local context.

References

Bloch, M. (1991). Language, anthropology and cognitive science. *Man, 26(2)*, 183–198.

Tobin, J. (2005). Quality in early childhood education: An anthropologist's perspective. *Early Education and Development, 16(4)*, 422–434.

Tobin, J., Arzubiaga, A., & Adair, J. (2013). *Children crossing borders: Immigrant parents and teacher perspectives on preschool for children of immigrants*. New York, NY: Russell Sage Foundation.

Tobin, J., Hsueh, Y., & Karasawa, M. (2009). *Preschools in three cultures revisited*. Chicago, IL: University of Chicago Press.

ACKNOWLEDGMENTS

We first thank all of the contributors to this volume on reflection and inquiry in international early childhood who wrote such innovative and enlightening chapters. They all passionately believe in the power of reflection for empowering teachers and improving children's lives on a global scale. We also thank the children and adults featured in this volume for helping to make the book a powerful portrait of new possibilities for teaching and learning. We acknowledge, too, those individuals who took the time to review and comment on sections of this volume—Nodelyn Abayan, Ali Borjian, David Hemphill, Ros Marshall, Divya Vyas, and Maria Zavala. We also thank Alex Masulis, our editor, for enthusiastically supporting this book and Daniel Schwartz for always answering our production queries.

I (Daniel) would like thank my coeditor, Linda R. Kroll, for joining me in this endeavor and for her patient and careful editing and support of this joint creation. She's been a fantastic colleague to work with on this project. I also thank the San Francisco State University MA early childhood students who have enrolled in my international education course and have helped inspire me to work on this book. Last, a big shout-out goes to Hazelle, Kaili, and Toby for their joy and commitment to broadening international horizons.

I (Linda) would like to thank my coeditor, Daniel Meier, for inviting me to join him in this work and for his patience, editing, and support in this joint book. I also want to thank him for welcoming me into his International Early Childhood Education class, where I learned so much about the possibilities for and of cross-national work. He, too, is a fantastic colleague and I look forward to future coauthored projects. And a big thank-you to Dennis, Condy, and Dana for their loving and unending support.

CONTRIBUTORS

Brenda Fyfe is Dean of the School of Education at Webster University, an international university based in St. Louis, Missouri, with residential campuses in eight countries and five continents. Dr. Fyfe has been working in collaboration with Carlina Rinaldi and her colleagues from Reggio Emilia for over 25 years and has authored many publications on the Reggio approach to early education. She holds leadership positions on the boards of national organizations such as the Association for Constructivist Teaching and the North American Reggio Emilia Alliance and has been a consultant/evaluator for the Higher Learning Commission for over 20 years.

Dr. Kyoko Iwatate is Professor of Early Childhood Education at Tokyo Gakugei University (TGU) which is one of the Japan's leading universities of education. The focus of her research is assessment and evaluation in early childhood education. For 28 years, she has been working on ECE teacher education at TGU. She is involved in the training program for inservice teachers organized by the board of education and visits preschools to give advice to teachers on their in-house research projects. She is also one of the members of the subcommittee for Teacher Education in the committee of Elementary and Secondary Education, the Central Council for Education in MEXT.

Kaisa Kopisto, MA (Education) has worked as a lecturer and researcher in kindergarten and early childhood education programs at the Department of Teacher Education University of Helsinki. Currently she works as a Coordinator for the Omnischool research and development project funded by the Finnish government. Her work in research and development projects has focused on the development of evaluation in early childhood, the effectiveness of preprimary education as well as the transitions from preprimary to primary education. Recently her research interest has been in studying children's everyday experiences with relation to pedagogy and learning environments.

Buad Mohamed Khales is Assistant Professor and Head of the Department for Elementary and Kindergarten education at Al Quds University in the West Bank, Palestine. She is a consultant to the Ministry of Education on developing a strategic plan for early childhood education and has participated in constructing early childhood policy and a framework for early childhood education in Palestine. She is a teacher educator for early childhood through middle school teachers and has worked on such projects as teacher education in Palestine, the implementation of children's rights, and new ways of teaching in kindergarten. She is the author of articles and book chapters focusing on reflective teaching, inquiry into teaching practice, and project learning for children's science education.

Leena Krokfors is Professor of Teacher Education and Vice Dean of Academic affairs at the Faculty of Behavioral Sciences at the University of Helsinki. She is a director of the Research Unit of Teaching and Learning at the Department of Teacher Education. Her research interests are in the paradigms of teacher education, especially the theory of research-based teacher education, teachers' pedagogical thinking, and reflective learning. Recently, her research work has concentrated on methodological questions in the analysis of formal education and informal learning, collaborative interaction and social knowledge creation in multimedia-enriched learning environments, and the use of digital video technology in educational settings.

Dr. Linda R. Kroll is Professor of Early Childhood Education at Mills College, Oakland, California. She has published and lectured both in the United States and around the world and teaches early childhood courses on child development and cognition, language and literacy, curriculum and reflection, and qualitative research. Dr. Kroll is the author of a number of publications, including her most recent book, *Self-Study and Inquiry into Practice: Learning to Teach for Equity and Social Justice in the Elementary School Classroom* (Routledge, 2012).

Lasse Lipponen is a professor of education, with special reference to Early Childhood Education, at the Department of Teacher Education, University of Helsinki. His research work is directed toward children's learning at the intersection of formal and informal learning environments, understanding children's experiences and perceptions in their life-world with digital documentation and participatory research methods, and teacher education.

> Karen Anne Liley, BEd (Hons)
> Ko Tararua ngā maunga
> Ko Waikawa te awa
> Ko Tainui te waka
> Ko Wehiwehi te marae
> Ko Ngati Wehiwehi, ko Ngati Tukorehe, ko Ngati Rangitawhia oku iwi
> Ko Karen Liley ahau

Karen Anne Liley is Kaiwhakahaere (Manager/Supervisor) of Te Puna Kōhungahunga and Te Kohanga Reo o Hineteiwaiwa at the University of Auckland, Faculty of Education Aotearoa/New Zealand. Her previous occupation was a physiotherapist. After the birth of her tamariki (children), she became involved in early childhood education through the Auckland Playcentre Association, a parent-led organization. She then earned her early childhood teacher qualification. She has been an early childhood teacher for the past 13 years and most of that time has been in Māori-medium early childhood centres where te reo and tīkanga Māori are used throughout the curriculum.

Daniel R. Meier is Professor of Elementary Education at San Francisco State University. Meier teaches in the MA Program in Early Childhood Education and the EdD Program in Educational Leadership. He teaches courses in reading/language arts, narrative inquiry and memoir, educational research, international education, first and second language development, and families and communities. He received his BA from Wesleyan University, EdM from Harvard University, and PhD from the University of California at Berkeley. He has written numerous articles and several books on teaching and learning, language and literacy, and reflective practice and teacher research. His current work focuses on early childhood teacher research groups in the San Francisco Bay area and reflective practice in early childhood teacher education in the West Bank/Palestine.

Dr. Amasa Philip Ndofirepi holds a PhD degree in Philosophy of Education awarded by the University of the Witwatersrand (Wits), South Africa, and whose thesis is Philosophy for Children: The Quest for an African Perspective. He has extensive experience in teacher education (in Zimbabwe and South Africa) and has research interests in philosophy for children, African philosophy, African philosophy of education, critical thinking, and childhood issues. He also has published articles in internationally acclaimed, peer-reviewed journals and presented papers to national and international conferences around these themes. He is currently a Postdoctoral Research Fellow in the Faculty of Education, University of Johannesburg.

Lesley Pohio, MEd, DipArtEd, AdvDipTchg, DipNZFKU, CertMgEC, is a senior tutor in the School of Arts, Languages and Literacies at the University of Auckland, Faculty of Education. Lesley's main areas of teaching with early childhood teacher education student teachers are the visual arts in the early years and early years movement. Her teaching and research interests include the notion of making learning visible, the position of the visual arts in early childhood education, and the pedagogy of place. Prior to teaching at the university, Lesley taught at Unitec New Zealand in the early childhood teacher education program. Lesley has extensive experience in a range of early childhood settings and was previously the head teacher at Akarana Avenue kindergarten, a large multicultural early childhood centre in Auckland.

Carlina Rinaldi is the president of Reggio Children, professor at the University of Modena and Reggio, former director of the municipal early childhood centers in Reggio Emilia, and successor to Loris Malaguzzi (one of the leading pedagogical thinkers of the 20th century). She has an international reputation in early years education; has spoken on the topic around the world; and has authored and edited many books, articles, and media publications on the Reggio Emilia approach.

Laura Salo, MA (Education), works as a project designer at the Department of Teacher Education, University of Helsinki. Her research interests are in developing pedagogy and especially assessment. Mrs. Salo has worked in several research and development projects regarding assessing and using ICT in education as well as expanding learning environments.

Adrienne Sansom (PhD) is a senior lecturer in the School of Curriculum and Pedagogy (Te Kura o te Marautanga me te Ako) at the University of Auckland. She teaches dance/drama education and early years pedagogy. Current research focuses on the body and embodied knowing and cultural identity primarily through the art forms of dance and drama. Recent publications include her book *Movement and Dance in Young Children's Lives: Crossing the Divide* published by Peter Lang; "Mindful Pedagogy in Dance: Honoring the Life of the Child" for *Research in Dance Education*; "Daring to Dance: Making a Case for the Place of Dance in Children's and Teachers' Lives" in F. McArdle and G. Boldt (Eds.), *Young Children, Pedagogy and the Arts*; "My Body, My Life, and Dance" in S. Shapiro (Ed.), *Dance in a World of Change: Reflections on Global and Cultural Difference*, Human Kinetics; and "Dance with Connections to Moving and Playing in the Early Years" in B. Clark, A. Grey, and L. Terreni (Eds.), *Kia Tipu te Wairua Toi—Fostering the Creative Spirit: Arts in Early Childhood Education*.

Fengyuan (Sarah) Sun began her position as the Program Specialist at Kai Ming Head Start in San Francisco, California, in November 2011. She was born and raised in China and completed her graduate level work in the United States. She has a Master of Social Work degree with a concentration in Nonprofit and Public Management and an emphasis in Children and Family, which she completed in 2009 at Rutgers, the State University of New Jersey, New Brunswick. In 2011, Sarah received her second master's degree in Early Childhood Education from San Francisco State University with the Distinguished Achievement Award. She has extensive experience working with infants, toddlers, and preschoolers and holds a California Child Development Program Director Permit. Her primary focus as a Head Start early childhood education and social service professional is improving program quality through research-based efforts.

Mikiko Tabu is a professor in Early Childhood Education (ECE) at Seitoku University, which has produced the largest number of ECE practitioners in Japan over the last five years. She teaches Issues in Education in Modern Japan and Theory and Practice in ECE and visits various types of preschools to supervise students' internship and fieldwork. Her current research interests include the history of ECE, the qualification system, and the professional education of ECE practitioners with intercultural perspectives. She has conducted several Japanese Government Grants-in-Aid for Scientific Research projects, such as "On Strategies of Mobilization of Private Resources for Expanding Early Years Provisions—England and Japan" and "New Aims and Functions of ECE Teacher Education under the Anticipated Renewal and Graded Qualification System; Comparative Considerations on the Californian Licensing System and Workplace-Management."

Trevor Valentino has worked in the early child education field for the last 12 years. He has taught at Cow Hollow School in San Francisco since 2007 and has since been promoted to Assistant Director. Trevor received his BA in African American Studies (honors) and English at the University of California, Berkeley. He later received an MA in early child education from San Francisco State University, where he wrote about his collaborative experience with teachers in Kenya. He comes from a strong constructivist perspective, which endorses an emergent curriculum and a child-centered approach to education. He is currently studying how to support teacher collaboration within early child education settings. Trevor has presented at CAEYC, Awareness without Anxiety: Nature and Young Children, and the Innovative Teacher Project series, where he copresented a two-year study on children's creative thinking through graphic expressions.

Molly Van Houten received her master's degree in Early Childhood Education from San Francisco State University. Interested in international and multicultural education, she spent seven years living and working in Guatemala. Molly currently lives in Almaty, Kazakhstan, where she teaches kindergarten at an international school.

INTRODUCTION

Linda R. Kroll and Daniel R. Meier

Teaching well is a lifelong learning endeavor. Although this perspective is not necessarily universally acknowledged, all teachers know that one can never know enough about how to teach the children in one's charge well. Good teaching for the youngest members of our global societies is essential for their success both in the moment and in their future educational lives. These young children need the best teachers to help them realize this success and to be lifelong learners. Teachers, too, need to be lifelong learners. *Reflective practice*, *reflection*, *inquiry*, and *investigating one's own practice* are all terms for ways to continue learning about one's teaching practice.

In thinking about reflective practice and inquiry, we focus on the learning of the students, the teachers, and to some extent the families and communities of those students and teachers. Teacher reflection and inquiry as a vehicle for teacher development and educational reform has been identified as one essential aspect of improving the lives of children and their families internationally. However, there are multiple ways for these practices to occur, depending on the teaching context, the teacher's level of preparation, and the opportunities for continued professional development. In addition, the actualization of these practices depends on social and cultural values and beliefs, traditions around socialization, and concepts of what counts as knowledge.

How reflective practice can be enacted and how it works to support lifelong learning to teach in different global contexts is the topic of this book. We examine the forms and functions of reflection and inquiry on early childhood education in a variety of global contexts. Taking a case study approach, we specifically look at what the role of teacher reflection is in educational change and how local traditions and values are honored and continued in a particular country or region, as well as how educational ideas and programs from other countries and regions are adapted and modified. Early childhood teacher educators, early childhood teachers, and early childhood researchers have written the chapters, representing a multitude of ways to think about the process.

As we wrote alongside the authors of the nine chapters, we discovered that reflection and inquiry on the part of teachers is often accompanied by reflection and inquiry on the part of their young students. We also discovered that reflection and inquiry take on multiple guises and definitions, depending on the context in which they are applied. However, no matter how reflection is enacted, the focus it provides on improving and changing practice, on learning from others, and on empowering those practicing is evident. We intend teachers, policy makers, researchers, and others to take note of the power of reflection and inquiry to spur educational change at the global as well as the local level.

Multiple definitions and meanings for words that we share in this discussion emerged as we read and reread the chapters. Each chapter has its own interpretation of what it means to be a reflective practitioner and what inquiry into one's own practice looks like. In an illuminating treatise on cultural differences in the definition of the learner, of learning, and of what it means to know and the value of learning, Jin Li (2012) describes different cultural definitions of what it means to be a learner, and (for us) this discussion reverberated in our thinking about what it means to be a reflective and inquiring teacher. Inquiry itself is a Western traditional concept (Li, 2012), deriving from the notion of the importance of curiosity about the world as essential to learning. Curiosity about one's practice is at the heart of reflection and inquiry into teaching. On the other hand, Eastern tradition values learning for oneself, to perfect oneself, to better serve the world (Li, 2012). Thus, while the purpose of learning in each context may seem to contain philosophical differences, inquiry and understanding are essential aspects of the learning process, East and West. In the chapters that follow, we will see how these processes are used and applied across early childhood classrooms, teacher education contexts, and communities of practice.

The book is organized into four sections. Part I contains two chapters, one by Linda R. Kroll and the other by Daniel Meier, the editors of this volume. These chapters set the stage for thinking about the big ideas in this text—that of reflection and inquiry as means for teacher development and learning and the global context of early childhood education, identifying both strengths and challenges of addressing and learning from an international body of early childhood educators.

Part II reflects the perspectives of cross-national teacher education and teaching. In Chapter 3, Trevor Valentino writes about his experience working with teachers in Kenya, what happened during his summer there, and what he learned about collaboration in particular that he was able to bring back to his own practice in the United States. In Chapter 4, Fengyuan Sun discusses her experiences growing up and attending schools in China and then teaching early childhood in the United States, contrasting her own cultural beliefs and experiences with those of the children and families with whom she works. This contrast provides us with insight into the reciprocal opportunities that such a cross-national experience provides for both the teacher and the families with whom she works. In Chapter 5, Molly Van Houten describes her experiences as a U.S.-educated early childhood practitioner teaching in Guatemala, learning to acknowledge and appreciate the Guatemalan and indigenous views of the teacher and reconciling it with her own understandings of what can lead to powerful teacher learning.

Part III presents international views on the practice of reflection and inquiry among teachers and their students and between teachers, students, and the communities they serve. In Chapter 6, Amasa Ndoferepi discusses the implementation of philosophical discussions for young children that takes place in South Africa. In Chapter 7, Lesley Pohio, Adrienne Sansom, and Karen Liley describe how teachers and children together engage in reflection and spiritual inquiry through engagement with place in New Zealand. In Chapter 8, Brenda Fyfe and Carlina Rinaldi describe the process of documentation that engages children and teachers in the schools in Reggio Emilia, Italy, and in St. Louis, Missouri.

Finally, Part IV addresses the question of professional learning, professional growth, and professional development among teachers. In Chapter 9, Kaisa Kopisto, Laura Salo, Lasse Lipponen, and Leena Krokfors describe the policies and changes occurring in early childhood teacher preparation in Finland and the role of reflective practice in the Finnish model. In Chapter 10, Kyoko Iwatate and Mikiko Tabu describe the system of early care and education in Japan and the preparation of teachers for different contexts. Finally, in Chapter 11, Buad Khales describes preservice and inservice teacher preparation through reflection and story in the West Bank, Palestine.

Each chapter gives a particular view of how reflection and inquiry can support teachers' and children's learning in multiple ways. In different global contexts, we are asking similar questions about how to best serve young children and the teachers who work with them. The glimpses we have into these different contexts open up new possibilities for cross-national and international learning and development for all of us.

References

Li, J. (2012). *Cultural foundations of learning: East and west.* New York, NY: Cambridge University Press.

PART I

Inquiry, Reflection, and International Early Childhood Education

1

INQUIRY AND REFLECTION TO PROMOTE SOCIAL JUSTICE AND INTERNATIONAL UNDERSTANDING

Linda R. Kroll

In her first year of teaching in a privately owned preschool, Rachel was teaching toddlers for the first time. At this school, teachers looped with their children, meaning that Rachel had three more years to look forward to teaching this group of children. She was particularly puzzled and challenged by one little girl. Sari would sometimes be very attached to Rachel and sometimes be angry with her. Rachel could not attribute these sudden mood changes to any particular context, so she decided to put the inquiry and reflective skills she had learned in graduate school to work and try to understand what was happening in her interactions with Sari. Rachel wrote in a journal daily, focusing her reflections on what the child had done during the day and how she and the child had interacted. She also took photos throughout the day of what children (including Sari) were doing with each other and with the other two teachers in the classroom. As Rachel thought, wrote, and examined her photos, she realized that it was not the little girl who was having difficulty, but that she, for some reason, was looking for approval from this child and that she was having difficulty developing a strong relationship with Sari.

This realization came about mostly because Rachel was using different media as tools for reflection about what was happening. In addition, this understanding was supported by her participation in discussions with fellow graduates and faculty of her Masters in Early Childhood Education program in a series of meetings organized to examine how documentation and inquiry were influencing their practice. Rachel's experience is a good example of how inquiry, reflection, and collaboration around practice can provide support for early childhood educators and encourage improved teaching and greater satisfaction among them.

Reflection, reflective practice, and inquiry into teaching are common terms among teacher educators, among professional development institutions, and within a growing number of international educational institutions. Zeichner (1994) and Zeichner and Liston (2014) describe the growth of the international movement that has burgeoned over the last 25 years under the title of reflection as the result of a reaction against the view of teachers as technicians who enact prescribed methods and curricula. Loughran (2002) traces the genesis of reflective practice and notes the importance of the identification of a problem in enacting effective reflection that will lead to better practice and, simultaneously, help support the teacher's ongoing curiosity and passion about his or her practice. He examines "the value of reflection as a meaningful way of approaching learning about teaching" (Loughran, 2002, p. 33). He defines effective reflective practice in this way: "Effective reflective practice is drawn from the ability to frame and reframe the practice setting, to develop and respond to this framing through action so that the practitioner's wisdom-in-action is enhanced and, as a particular outcome, articulation of professional knowledge is encouraged" (Loughran, 2002, p. 42). Thus, reflection can lead to learning and professional knowledge, contributing to other practitioners' and researchers' understanding of the teaching and learning process.

In this chapter, following on these giants of reflective practice, we consider why inquiry and reflection can promote effective teaching practice in early childhood settings. Next, we look at how a reflective stance helps teachers manage the uncertainty of teaching amidst a context where the myth of certainty dominates recommendations for practice. We then examine how reflective practice is enhanced by and enhances collegiality among teachers, parents, and communities. The chapter proposes that teaching is research and, thus, that inquiry and reflection should contribute to educational theory, practice, and public policy. Next, the chapter suggests that such a stance can enable the creation of a democratic forum where the building of sound local educational practice is discussed among all stakeholders, extending the power and efficacy of educators and the families they serve and influencing governance and policy around early childhood education on a local and global basis. Finally, we look at reflective practice from a global perspective to consider how inquiry and reflection contribute to an international research conversation on early education.

Why Inquiry and Reflection are Good Practice

Although most of these authors (e.g. Loughran, Zeichner & Liston) are writing about K-12 teacher reflection, the use of inquiry in early childhood settings is well known and supported in many international contexts (as illustrated in this book). Early childhood educators come to the field with a variety of educational backgrounds and experiences. In California, for example, they have educational backgrounds that range from minimal training to advanced degrees (Whitebook, Kipnis, & Bellm, 2008). Yet, no matter how much "training" they have had, they will not know exactly what to do in every context and in every circumstance. Although the outside world promotes a myth of certainty that a quality education is made up of the *right* curriculum and the *right* teaching methods, in reality questions, puzzles, and required instant decision making make the act of teaching one of disequilibrium and imbalance. Unlike some professions where one can learn to solve problems by following a set of guidelines or procedures, the road map for teaching is strewn with byroads, boulders, lane changes, dead ends, and other unexpected events. Thus, the stance that early childhood educators must adopt has to include a questioning curiosity and acceptance of this stance in their work. Using inquiry and questioning about his or her own practice allows a teacher to have a system for addressing the problems inevitably raised on a daily basis.

A stance that encourages such a perspective, that allows one to step back from one's practice and think about what one is seeing in a systematic and organized way, gives one greater control of what one is doing. Thus, when a teacher wonders why something she[1] does may or may not work, she is beginning to develop an attitude that is beyond the minimal "I'm effective" or "I'm not effective." This development allows her to go beyond a set of routines or methods to begin thinking about what things are working (or not) in certain circumstances. She begins to develop some generalizations about her practice in her own particular context with her own group of students. It allows her to begin to develop a personal set of theories about teaching and learning informed explicitly by personal practice and experience. Because inquiry is systematic and reflective, the teacher is not reacting at a holistic or gut level or an emotional level (although what your instinct tells you is very important). By employing a systematic look at her practice, she begins to develop habits or routines or schema that allow her to make connections across contexts. Korthagen and Kessels (1999) describe this process of teacher learning as "level reduction," with three particular stages of development that are constantly renewed by and the result of systematic inquiry and reflection.

Rachel, for example, employed several inquiry and reflection processes to make sense of her question. The impetus behind her questioning was not simply that she was puzzled by the child she was working with. Rather, the opportunity to engage in discussion with her former classmates and instructors inspired her to think about a problem that, until the chance presented itself, had gone "under the radar." Her frustration with herself and this child was manifesting itself in doubt about her efficacy as a teacher, particularly as one for toddlers. As she put it, she had "never worked with little ones before," despite her previous two years of experience in the College laboratory school with children aged 2–5 and her two years of experience in an international preschool before attending graduate school. The chance to participate once again in an organized inquiry and reflection process gave her the support she needed as a beginning teacher to look at her practice from an inquiry stance.

The Uncertainty in Teaching

Teaching is filled with uncertainty. Being an early childhood educator involves juggling many aspects of classroom and center life. These include working with young children who may not be very communicative about their needs; working alongside other teachers; ensuring that everyone's (children's and teachers') needs are met some of the time and that no one's needs are neglected all of the time; negotiating with families, other teachers, and other children in the center; dealing with the demands of site directors and program directors; and handling constraints placed on early childhood educators by laws, regulations, and policy makers. Each classroom, center, program, or neighborhood constitutes its own culture, which is created by those who participate in each of the contexts. The uncertainties created by these constraints are common to every teaching position at nearly every level of education. Teaching in early care settings involves particular kinds of uncertainty as early childhood education and care are managed by numerous agencies at both the state and federal level in the United States. Depending on the nature of the program, there can be special funds that must be allocated, more diverse populations that have their attendant diverse strengths and needs, and more likelihood that the students and their teacher will not share a common culture. These factors contribute to greater uncertainty, which is inherent in schools in any case.

How teachers regard the existence of uncertainty and manage it is instrumental in determining whether and how they remain in the profession. Gu and Day (2007) discuss resilience and the factors that lead to teachers in the K–12 arena to stay in teaching. They found that "the nature of resilience is determined by the *interaction* [italics in the original] between the internal assets of the individual and the external environments in which the individual lives and grows (or does not grow)" (p. 1314). Thus, the uncertainty factors that lie in the teachers' work context as well as personal context have a great effect on whether they stay in the teaching profession.

Helsing (2007) writes about uncertainty in teachers, attributing the uncertainty to "its lack of a knowledge base or technical culture" (p. 1317). She implies that the lack of consensus about the goals or methods of good teaching is the result of this missing knowledge base. She continues, "Teachers also experience uncertainties due to the complex nature of their work, which is centered on human relationships and involves predicting, interpreting, and assessing others' thoughts, emotions, and behavior" (p. 1317–18). The juxtaposition of a lack of knowledge base with a context that is centered on human relationships (and the changing uncertainty of such a context) demonstrates the complexity that uncertainty contributes to the profession. The requirement for "a knowledge base" implies that there is yet to be found the right way to teach, one that will work in most circumstances, a positivist and prescriptive belief. Such an implication contradicts our understanding that human relationships are highly idiosyncratic and depend entirely on the individuals involved in the cultural context in which the relationship exists. Thus, looking for a knowledge base in a context that will prove particular is unrealistic and probably quite unproductive. Helsing (2007) discusses further the different characteristics of uncertainty. On the one hand, there is uncertainty that disables the teacher, causing anxiety, frustration, and burnout because the conflicts and dilemmas that confront the teacher seem unable to be reconciled. On the other hand, there is uncertainty about whose recognition can lead to improved practice; accepting the existence of uncertainty and using the questions and dilemmas its existence raises to improve practice is a more positive outcome. This kind of uncertainty does contribute to a knowledge base on how to enact and improve practice.

Early childhood teachers are familiar with the uncertainties that underlie both their classroom practice and their working contexts. In the United States, for instance, public early childhood programs have a variety of funding streams that are regulated and controlled by different agencies, including in some cases the federal government's Department of Education and Department of Health and Human Services, the particular state department of education, and the local county or municipal health and human services agencies. The uncertainty in funding can leave centers and the families that need the care scrambling for financial support. But in addition to financial uncertainty, early care and education centers are subject to changes in standards, the continual development of new standards, and expectations, mostly without much input from the teachers or even the directors. Thus, in addition to the daily uncertainty of working in a situation where human relationships are at the core, teachers and directors are subject to political and social uncertainties that are outside much of their control. Such circumstances mitigate against the establishment of a community of teachers, children, and families together investigating their own learning and establishing a reflective community.

Despite the clear existence of uncertainty, a dominant myth of certainty surrounds the profession. The search for quality early childhood education implies that there is one right way that, if we could only discover it, would ensure that we would know exactly what to do in our classrooms. In the media, effective early childhood education is being touted as the most efficient path to reducing the achievement gap between different socioeconomic status (SES) and ethnic groups in the United States. Again, the notion of "effective" early childhood education (ECE) implies that there is one right way that will solve the identified problem.

Hilda Borko's presidential address at the American Educational Research Association in 2004 gives us a way of thinking about the uncertainty of teaching and classroom practice by using a *situative perspective* to understand what happens in classrooms (Borko, 2004). She shows us clearly how teachers become the experts on their classrooms. Learning can be conceptualized as "changes in participation in socially organized activities, and individuals' use of knowledge as an aspect of their participation in social practices" (p. 4). The situated nature of learning in classrooms applies to teachers and students alike. As Paul Cobb explained it, "[L]earning should be viewed as both a process of active individual construction and a process of enculturation into the … practices of wider society." (Cobb, 1994, p. 13, as quoted in Borko, 2004, p. 4). Therefore, teachers' learning and their expertise are developed in multiple contexts through multiple methods. However, teachers must have a stance of curiosity about their practice to find such uncertainty inspiring rather than daunting. As Ball and Cohen (1999) point out,

"Teachers have to learn how to frame and explore conjectures, how to bring evidence to bear on them, how to weigh the often-conflicting information they get, to make well-supported judgments" (p.16). Learning to learn in particular contexts with many uncertainties is essential to building one's knowledge as a teacher. Those teachers who welcome this opportunity thrive in a context of uncertainty. Learning to welcome disequilibrium and to use this sense of imbalance to explore one's practice is essential to enacting an inquiry and reflective stance. Rachel's participation in the discussion with fellow teachers and her willingness to openly explore that which she found confusing illustrates such a stance.

How Inquiry is Supported by Collegiality

Rachel's experience demonstrates how, working together, teachers can inspire inquiry into one another's practice. This principle of collegiality to promote the learning of all involved is complicated. In many contexts, teachers, on the one hand, feel the need to appear as experts in their fields—and indeed they *are* experts. But, on the other hand, they need to consider multiple perspectives on their practice to understand more fully what is occurring and what questions might be raised. With a few notable exceptions, teachers are rarely regarded as experts. Instead, they are seen as recipients of the more important knowledge developed by researchers; education experts in policy; and, often, the general public, who believe that having experienced school (as they all have), they are experts in it. In thinking about the education of the youngest members of society, outside agencies frequently focus on safety and care as the most important aspects of early childhood education, often ignoring the educational possibilities and potential of young children.

Collegiality promotes discussion about the uncertain aspects of the classroom. Collegiality among teachers in a classroom or center supports the education and development of the children enrolled. Teachers can share impressions of children's learning and well-being and support one another in finding possible solutions to identified problems. Teachers can share curriculum and mentor one another about ways to support children's learning. In a context where reflection and inquiry are supported by organizational structures, teachers can find many ways to support the children they care for and each other as they work together.

Collegiality among teachers and children can be supported by reflection and inquiry, as children and teachers together reflect on and discuss their interests and their learning. Promoting open forums for discussion of interesting problems supports a metacognitive stance among all participants. By taking on an inquiry stance, teachers model for children the sense of wonder about the world and about what they are learning. Children can learn to articulate in many forms of representation the questions and wonder they have. By working together, teachers and children promote each other's learning. Thus, inquiry and reflection can support good working relations and collegiality can support inquiry and reflection for children and teacher learning (Project Zero, 2000).

Another arena for collegial relations in supporting children's learning and an inquiry stance is collegial relations between teachers and parents and between teachers, parents, and children. In the same discussion where Rachel presented her dilemma, several other teachers discussed how they tried to use documentation and inquiry to support parent participation and an understanding of what was happening in their school. The challenge they found was that although parents were interested in the documentation of *their own child's work*, they were not particularly interested or intrigued by the work of the group or the goals of the whole class. The challenge for these teachers was how to create collegial relations among parents and teachers, such that these relationships were more inclusive and more than the teacher reporting to the parent about his or her child's activity and learning. In the course of their meetings over several months, teachers found multiple ways to engage with parents and to promote an inquiry stance that fostered discussion about the children's learning and the projects occurring in the classroom (Kroll et al., 2013).

Developing collegiality with parents is particularly important for family childcare workers, where they may be the only adult or one of two adults working with a small group of children in a home setting. Here, although there is clearly a shared goal for the child to be happy and well-cared-for, parents often believe they are purchasing a service rather than participating *with* the teacher in planning and caring for the children in the family childcare. As family childcare workers participate in inquiry and documentation about their work, they invite the families to join with them and the children in understanding what interests the children and to contribute to the children's continuing learning. Thus, there are multiple ways that teachers, parents, and children can collaborate around the children's learning, and most of these involve reflection and inquiry into what is occurring in the family childcare setting.

Collaboration, then, is an essential component of effective reflective practice. It can take many guises and involve multiple participants, but it is most important that teachers, children, and their families be involved in the process in an equitable way such that they all understand their roles and responsibilities in crafting and contributing to a vibrant educational setting for all participants.

Teaching as Research

Inquiry into the learning and teaching in one's classroom or center is research. Inquiry is helpful in the immediate teaching situation, but it also invites the opportunity and possibility for teachers to contribute to each other's understanding and to the wider world of educational research. Going public with one's inquiry provides professional stature to the teacher and simultaneously challenges the teacher to take responsibility for what he does with his students. When our investigations remain private, we may think that we do not need to justify or question what we find. The responsibilities inherent in going public include deep respect for our students and careful reporting about and reflection on what we think we have found. For inquiry to be seen as research, it must become public. Teachers can make their inquiry public in many ways, and in doing so, they begin to take their findings beyond their classrooms—into the greater teaching and research community. Going public is essential if teachers' voices are to be heard in the larger world of education. Teachers' voices are essential to this world, but for the most part, they have been silenced. Teachers have been seen as the consumers of educational research rather than as contributors to the field. However, teaching well and conducting research on teaching are excellent partners (Cochran-Smith & Lytle, 1993). In early childhood education, this recognition as experts is even more important, as early childhood educators have been marginalized even more thoroughly than K-12 teachers (Meier & Henderson, 2007).

Teaching well is a juggling act. As one teaches, one has to pay attention to how one's students are understanding and making sense of what one is teaching. Thus, teaching is learning and instructing simultaneously. If one teaches consciously, paying attention to the results of one's teaching, then teaching becomes a form of research about learning, both one's *own* learning and the learning of one's students. When teachers treat their practice as research, they formalize their practical understanding about teaching and learning. Learning how to ask good questions and then to systematically investigate those questions is the essence of research, but it is also the essence of good teaching. The beginning of inquiry and reflection is learning to ask good questions about practice. As teachers conduct investigations, they will be empowered to continue to investigate and understand their own practice and their students' learning and their work will remain interesting and novel as they work in what may be one of the most difficult professions in which to do well and to stay interested.

In addition, treating teaching as research empowers early childhood educators to be seen as the experts in their field, as indeed they should be. Thus, in collaboration with curriculum developers, policy makers, and educational psychologists, early childhood teachers can contribute to finding the most effective ways to teach children within the myriad of cultures, languages, and resources that are available in the United States. Rather than being the consumer of educational knowledge, teachers can contribute mightily to that education knowledge bank. Teachers have a special perspective in this educational community. They know the daily routine, practice, and life of the classroom. In using inquiry to understand that daily life, they can build knowledge that others can use. Cochran-Smith and Lytle (1993) put it well: "The unique feature of the questions that prompt teacher research is that they emanate from neither theory nor practice alone but from critical reflection on the intersection of the two" (p.15). Teacher research, therefore, can contribute uniquely to knowledge about teaching, learning, and education. As the importance of early education becomes recognized internationally, the role of the teacher as investigator and expert is more essential.

There is also a moral component to treating teaching as a research endeavor. Teachers are determined to do the best for the students they teach. Their goals should be to help those students actualize their potential to be competent individuals who contribute to the lives of their families and to greater society. But teachers can only do this if they continually examine whether they are meeting their own best potentials and making contributions toward this end. Much of the public does not understand the critical learning that occurs during the early childhood years. This endeavor cannot be measured in test score results or through assessment tools required for many early childhood centers, which do not tell us very much about how students will do in the future. Rather, teachers must document the learning of their students as well as their own learning; systematic exploration of their practice and its results can provide that documentation.

In preservice and inservice teacher education, there is a recent tradition of involving teachers in inquiry through professional development, graduate programs, and workshops. In spite of the acceptance of practitioner research at many levels of teacher education, teacher research still must earn the approbation and respect of the larger educational community. Teacher research still must be recognized as the tremendous contribution it is and can be. Instead, the teaching profession has recently been subject to pressures from policy makers to produce as in a market economy (Cochran-Smith, 2008). How well teachers produce students who can achieve good test results is the criterion by which they and their educational systems are judged. Such criteria put the teacher in the role of consumer and directed worker rather than that of a professional using his or her own professional knowledge and judgment to teach students. Research on their own practice gives teachers the professional knowledge and, in the end, the moral authority to decide what is best for their students' learning and development. In some teacher research communities, an important part of the research is concerned with finding ways to promote social justice and powerful education settings for all students. One such context is the Mills Teachers Scholars, a group of teachers who work closely with one another in a professional development setting in their schools and at Mills College in Oakland, California, to investigate how their practices contribute to the enhancement of their diverse population of students' learning (http://millsscholars.org). Although these teachers come primarily from K-12 settings, early childhood educators have participated and their views and perspectives are welcomed. Here, the focus is inquiry and collaboration around issues of social justice, with each teacher going public at the end of the school year and research cycle.

In spite of the fact that teaching is a relationship-oriented, people-populated profession, it is paradoxically isolating. Teachers work in their own classrooms with their students (sometimes as their partners), but rarely with their colleagues as partners. Teacher research provides an opportunity for teachers to collaborate and develop inquiring contexts for themselves and their colleagues and to collaborate with their students, thus democratizing the inquiry or research process. With their students, teachers can investigate the learning occurring within classrooms and make these findings public. Sharing investigations can enhance reflection and inquiry across an early childhood center or school. At the Mills College laboratory school, for example, teachers post daily reports with photos, quotations from the children, and children's work, demonstrating what questions children are investigating and opening the conversation about the classroom work to observers, families, and other teachers and student teachers in the school. By sharing one's inquiry and student results, a teacher is going public with her research. The importance and significance of one's work is enhanced by the actual act of sharing it.

Teacher research is and has been an important part of educational research in classrooms. John Dewey (1938) saw teachers as central to the enterprise because they came to the research tradition from guiding, monitoring, and reflecting on their students' learning (Meier & Henderson, 2007). Because of the observational, continually evolving nature of teacher inquiry questions and research, a qualitative research design is often most appropriate. Qualitative research has a respected tradition in anthropology, psychology, and social science. However, in education, a *positivist* tradition of research has been emphasized, where useful research is seen as being restricted to formal, objective methods, typically using large sets of quantitative data (Meier & Henderson, 2007). This "evidence-based scientific research" is what policy makers often request or demand, and it effectively shuts out the use of qualitative research that focuses on the details and the context rather than the broadest outlines. Although both forms of research are important for understanding and improving educational opportunities for students, Berliner (2002) points out how complex educational settings are and how this complexity leads to the difficulty of doing good research that is limited in method. "Educational researchers have to accept the embeddedness of educational phenomena in social life, which results in the myriad interactions that complicate our science" (p. 3). Teacher research on the actual unfolding of classroom interactions and learning has the potential to contribute knowledge about what actually happens in classrooms. Such knowledge and evidence can lead to new understanding about how to provide the opportunities for excellent education outcomes for all students and better teaching situations for their teachers.

Creating a Democratic Educational Forum for Enacting Effective ECE Practice

Knowledge that is constructed by both participants and researchers on early childhood educational practice can contribute to the creation of better policies and more democratic decision making with regard to policy. Currently, public policy and regulation regarding the education of young children in the United States rests in multiple official departments (e.g., education and health and human services), indicating that there is a sense of community obligation for this responsibility. However, what community responsibility and family participation mean in action varies widely. This variation is in large part due to the acknowledged purpose(s) of early childhood education. Unlike K–12 public education, which is seen as a right of the child, early education can be seen in two ways depending on the population it serves. One view of early education is economic; children need to be cared for while their parents are working. Thus, early childhood care is for the benefit of society and the parents and only peripherally and conveniently for the child's development. The other view is educational and pedagogical. From this perspective, early childhood education is for the benefit of the child, as much a right as K–12 public education. Of course, both views can be held simultaneously. Many families choose to put their young children in care because they believe in the benefit of the experience for their children and because they need it so that they can work. Because ECE is not part of public education in many states, not all children are able to participate. Only the poorest and the richest ends of society have it available. Those who are identified as living in poverty have access to state and federal preschool programs that vary widely in quality; those who can afford preschool have access to excellent private preschool programs. Families that do not qualify for subsidized care and cannot afford private care make do with care that may not satisfy either the educational needs of the child or the economic needs of the adult family members (Polakow, 2007).

Clearly, the issues of the purpose of care, the support for care that meets the needs of all constituents, and the basic human right of a free and excellent education for all members of society are central to thinking about the role of the community in early childhood education. Dahlberg, Moss, and Pence (2007) propose that early childhood institutions could serve as fora in civil society "where children and adults engage in projects of social, cultural, political and economic significance" (Dahlberg et al., 2007, p. 62). Included centrally in this engagement is reflection on the learning that occurs for adults and children through participation in the forum and the development of further inquiry into how to continually maximize the efficacy of these fora. Gonzalez, Moll, and Amanti (2005) propose that the funds of knowledge of the local community be seen as a resource for children's learning. Their research (while centered in elementary school settings with preservice and practicing teachers) provides an actualization in the United States of how communities and schools can come together around the education of the children of the community. Inquiry and documentation of the learning and teaching occurring in the early childhood settings can serve as a jumping-off place for informed community conversations about what constitutes a quality early childhood program that serves all its participants, thus contributing to a better educational context for all. International examples of effective community school collaboration and conversation—for example, the municipal infant toddler centers and preschools in Reggio Emilia and Pistoia, Italy—can be instructive to other communities striving to build conversations across the various constituencies who both use and support the existence of early childhood care centers and schools.

Inquiry and Reflective Practice in Early Childhood in International Settings

Reflection on teaching and learning in early childhood settings can occur in multiple ways. Teachers throughout the world have many opportunities to reflect on their practice, and in some cases, they have the opportunity to go public and do more substantial inquiry into their teaching and their children's learning. What constitutes reflective practice can look different in different cultural contexts and settings. In the chapters in this text, specific examples of reflective practice are described and highlighted by those who work and do research in those settings. However, before we embark on those chapters, we might consider some ideas that are potentially unifying around the question of reflection in a global context.

Reflection occurs when teachers are curious about their practice—when they question what they are doing and seeing on a regular basis. Some contexts provide support for reflection and questioning, whereas in other settings, reflection and questioning may occur in spite of constraints. Because of the serendipitous and uncertain nature of the teaching–learning relationship and situation, good early childhood teachers are continually wondering about their students, their learning, their well-being, and their school context. In spite of many rules, regulations, and "quality control," each early childhood site is unique and draws on the contributions of the individual teachers, the particular children at that site, and the children's families.

A well-known example of effective reflection and inquiry is the pedagogical documentation process used in the Italian municipal schools in Reggio Emilia and Pistoia. This process supports teachers that reflect on their practice and their students' learning on a daily basis. Their work has become internationally famous, and they have influenced many early childhood educators throughout the world, including in Sweden, the United States, Singapore, the United Kingdom, and New Zealand. In one school in New Zealand, for example, Gould and Pohio (2006) describe how different representations of practice, including video, photographs, and stories, invite parents, children, and teachers to reflect on and share their expertise in the service of enhancing everyone's learning. This particular example adds two further questions to our investigations in this text: (1) What possible multiple pathways for reflection and inquiry can lead to early childhood programs particular to the context in which they reside? (2) What variety of opportunities are available for the teachers, children, and families to learn from one another?

Dahlberg, Moss, and Pence (2007) describe in detail a joint project between an indigenous First Nation community and a Canadian university (University of Victoria) to develop early childhood institutions on the reservation for the community members. The report of this endeavor demonstrates how, through a process of inquiry, knowledge of an appropriate institution and curriculum were developed together, with the Tribal Council leading the way and the University as a supportive and curious partner (Dahlberg et al., 2007). This example demonstrates how the power of inquiry and the establishment of a community comprised of different perspectives (tribal leaders, university researchers) can create a program of post-secondary preparation for Early Childhood professionals through the combination of community knowledge and academic knowledge. The basis of collaboration was the recognition of the importance of the stance of "not knowing"—that this stance represented the acceptance of "*the powerful potential of not knowing* [italics in the original]" (Dahlberg et al, p. 170). Through inquiry and reflection, collaboration, and joint investigation, a new view of the potential of the intersection between indigenous and conventional practices was born.

In this text, we show how an investigation of reflective practices, as they are manifested in different ways in different global contexts, can inform all of us on how to build stronger, more effective early childhood education. However, before exploring inquiry and learning in a variety of international contexts, we need to articulate a view of the global condition of early care and education. What are some of the issues and conditions internationally impacting the welfare and education of young children? Once we have considered these factors, we must remember that inquiry and reflection can take on many different guises—that each context will dictate how reflection and inquiry might be manifest and how it will be useful. Although we are asking questions that have universal importance, the answers will be contextually constructed and contextually understood.

References

Ball, D. & Cohen, D. (1999). Developing practice, developing practitioners: Toward a practice-based theory of professional education. In L. Darling-Hammond & G. Sykes (Eds.), *Teaching as the learning profession: Handbook of policy and practice* (pp. 3–32). San Francisco, CA: Jossey-Bass.

Berliner, D. (2002). Educational research: The hardest science of all. *Educational Researcher, 31(8)*, 18–20. doi: 10.3102/0013189X031008018

Borko, H. (2004). Professional development and teacher learning: Mapping the terrain. *Educational Researcher, 33(8)*, 3–15.

Cobb, P. (1994). Where is the mind? Constructivist and sociocultural perspectives on mathematical development. *Educational Researcher, 23(7)*, 13–20.

Cochran-Smith, M. (2008). The new teacher education in the United States: Directions forward. *Teachers and Teaching, 14(4)*, 271–282.

Cochran-Smith, M. & Lytle, S. (1993). *Inside/outside: Teacher research and knowledge*. New York, NY: Teachers College Press.

Dahlberg, G., Moss, P., & Pence, A. (2007). *Beyond quality in early childhood education and care: Languages of evaluation* (2nd ed.). New York, NY: Routledge.

Dewey, J. (1938/1963). *Experience and education*. New York, NY: Macmillan Publishing.

Gonzalez, N., Moll, L. C., & Amanti, C. (2005). *Funds of knowledge: Theorizing practices in households, communities, and classrooms*. Mahwah, NJ: Lawrence Erlbaum.

Gould, K. & Pohio, L. (2006). Stories from Aotearoa/New Zealand. In S. Fleet, C. Patterson, & J. Robertson (Eds.), *Insights: Behind early childhood pedagogical documentation* (pp. 78–86). Sydney, Australia: Pademelon Press.

Gu, Q. & Day, C. (2007). Teachers resilience: A necessary condition for effectiveness. *Teaching and Teacher Education, 23*, 1302–1316. doi: 10.1016/j.tate.2006.06.006

Handal, G. & Vaage, S. (1994). *Teachers' minds and actions: Research on teachers' thinking and practice* (pp. 9–24). London, England: Routledge.

Helsing, D. (2007). Regarding uncertainty in teachers and teaching. *Teaching and Teacher Education, 23*, 1317–1333. doi: 10.1016/j.tate.2006.06.007

Korthagen, F. & Kessels, J. (1999). Linking theory and practice: Changing the pedagogy of teacher education. *Educational Researcher, 28(4)*, 4–17.

Kroll, L., Baumgart, N., Buel, P., Carducci, C., Clark, N., Flynn, N., ... Knowlton, E. (2013, April). *Documentation in Action: Using Documentation for Reflection, Research and Practice.* Presented at the Invisible College pre-AERA conference. San Francisco, CA.

Loughran, J. (2002). Effective reflective practice: In search of meaning in learning about teaching. *Journal of Teacher Education, 53*, 33–43.

Meier, D. & Henderson, B. (2007). *Learning from young children in the classroom: The art and science of teacher research.* New York, NY: Teachers College Press.

Polakow, V. (2007). *Who cares for our children: The child care crisis in the other America.* New York, NY: Teachers College Press.

Project Zero. (2001). *Making learning visible: Children as individual and group learners.* Reggio Emilia, Italy: Reggio Children Publishers.

Whitebook, M., Kipnis, F., & Bellm, D. (2008, November). *Diversity and stratification in California's early care and education workforce* (Research brief). Center for the Study of Child Care Employment, University of California, Berkeley.

Zeichner, K. (1994). Research on teacher thinking and different views of reflective practice in teaching and teacher education. In I. Carlgren, G. Handal, & S. Vaage (Eds.) *Teachers' Minds and Actions: Research on teachers' thinking and practice* (pp. 9–28). London: The Falmer Press.

Zeichner, K. & Liston, D.P. (2014). *Reflective Teaching: An Introduction.* (2nd ed.) New York: Routledge.

Endnote

1 Early childhood teachers are both men and women. To underline this phenomenon, the text refers to a teacher as both he and she. The use of the single personal pronoun *he* or *she* will be alternated throughout this chapter.

2

INTERNATIONAL EARLY CHILDHOOD EDUCATION: UNSETTLED ISSUES, NEW POSSIBILITIES

Daniel R. Meier

In the current global educational arena, teacher reflection and inquiry can play a pivotal role in strengthening early childhood education on an international scale. In this chapter, I highlight several unsettled issues and new possibilities that provide a historical, theoretical, and pedagogical backdrop for this volume's upcoming chapters on reflection and inquiry in particular social, cultural, and educational settings. First, I discuss persistent global inequalities in children's overall well-being and the protections enacted at policy levels designed to improve children's health, rights, and educational opportunities. Second, I look at the effects and benefits of globalization and focus particularly on issues of time, space, and development. Third, I discuss aspects of knowledge construction and look at ideas associated with global childhood and the education of indigenous peoples. I then discuss the role and image of international early childhood educators by presenting the experiences and views of three global educators. Last, I conclude with a personal story about the transformative possibilities of international early childhood education.

Global Inequalities, Global Protections

Globalization has raised awareness of persistent inequalities in children's social, physical, and academic lives. There remain critical inequalities in educational access and achievement both within and across countries and regions around the globe. These inequalities and challenges continue to impede educational change and the creation of frameworks and environments conducive to nurturing teacher inquiry and reflection as part of professional practice. Indeed, as argued in Chapter 1 by Linda Kroll, it is the very power and promise of reflection and inquiry that can help change inequitable and status quo educational systems and practices.

Disparities in Wealth and Resources—Across and Within Countries and Regions

In wealthier countries and regions, unsettled issues at the macro level still persist in the form of rigid system hierarchies, high teacher turnover, disparate educational goals, under-resourced preservice and inservice teacher education, inequitable distribution of resources, challenges to family involvement, and inappropriate assessment measures. In some of these countries and areas, relatively "new" challenges have also arisen as policy makers and educators try to understand and meet the needs of linguistically diverse children, children with special needs, highly mobile migrant children, immigrant children, binational children, displaced children from war and conflict, and children of political asylum and refugee status.

In these countries and regions, although teacher reflection and inquiry has taken root and flourished in certain contexts, critical issues at the micro level persist in the need for increased teacher collaboration and dialogue, documentation of children's learning, involvement of families in assessment, and the intricacies of curricular planning and instruction. There are also political and philosophical tensions between what is often conceived of as grassroots movements for teacher reflection and the more established top-down and system-mandated standards and assessments for standardizing children's learning and teacher effectiveness. In general, in these contexts, although many teachers are working in contexts with ample material resources and infrastructure, they continue to confront challenges to teacher agency and creativity that impede a more robust growth for teacher inquiry and reflection.

In countries and regions with fewer resources and means of support, even with recent positive changes in global economic development and growth, an alarming number of children still lack basic human rights, access to health care, clean water and sanitation facilities, basic nutrition, safe and secure living conditions, access to free schooling, and adequate educational resources and materials. Economic and educational conditions for adults also remain critical in these countries and regions, and a disproportionate number of women and female youth lack access to prenatal care, family planning, employment, adequate food sources, and educational opportunities.

Although extreme poverty has decreased globally, 1.2 billion people remain in extreme poverty worldwide, and in Sub-Saharan Africa alone, about 50% of the population lives on less than $1.25 per day (*Millenium Development Goals Report*, p. 7). Additional factors contributing to disparities in children's health and well-being include environmental disasters due to deforestation and global warming; the recent global economic recession; and violence from war, terrorism, and intractable conflict. These and other factors result in children's unstable home lives, the uprooting of families and communities, emotional stress and trauma, anti-social behaviors, children's general uncertainty for the future and their safety, difficulty enrolling and attending school, and an overall lack of adequate educational achievement and development across their lifespans.

Although certain areas of the world have undergone historic economic growth and development, millions of young children continue to lack access to early childhood and primary grade schooling. In certain rural areas, there are few schools for children to attend and they are often a great distance from children's homes and communities. In areas with schools, the physical facilities may lack adequate space for large classes of children, inviting and effective learning environments, and appropriate learning materials. In both rural and urban contexts, early childhood teachers are likely to have received minimal preservice teacher training, little in the way of professional development and support, and low salaries. Girls are more likely than boys not to attend schools during the early grades, and this gender disparity increases in high school (*Millenium Development Goals Report*, p. 16). Although literacy rates and other traditional indicators of educational achievement have increased in a number of these regions, the levels of achievement still lag far behind children's counterparts in wealthier countries and regions. This is not to say, though, that children in contexts with more resources and materials all fare well. The educational, economic, and health gaps and disparities between certain groups of children and families are a tremendous challenge in these countries as well.

Children's Rights and Protections

Over the last 30 years or so, and particularly in the last 10 years, governments and international organizations have moved to improve young children's social, physical, and educational well-being and future on a global scale. These policies, measures, and actions have focused on the reduction and eradication of attitudes, politics, conditions, policies, and environments that have harmed and deprived (and continue to harm and deprive) children of their inalienable human rights to health, self-determination, and education. These policies, documents, and goals are the result of both large-scale nongovernmental agencies and sub-agencies such as the United Nations (UN), the United Nations International Children's Emergency Fund (UNICEF), the United Nations Educational, Scientific and Cultural Organization (UNESCO), nongovernmental international organizations such as the Association for Childhood Education International (ACEI), and other groups at a more local level, as well as governments and local authorities in particular countries and regions.

In 1981 (and entered into force in 1986), the *African Charter on Human and People's Rights* focused on issues of human rights and freedoms as convened by African states in the Organization of African Unity. Although children are infrequently mentioned, several of the charter's 62 articles focus on ensuring "the protection of rights of the woman and the child as stipulated in international declarations and conventions" and call for the establishment of a Commission on Human and Peoples' Rights to ensure human rights protection in Africa.

The 1989 UNICEF Convention on the Rights of the Child in New York City resulted in the first legally binding international agreement (by ratification or acceding of 193 countries) on children's rights. The convention's 54 articles focused on four main areas of children's rights: right to survival, to reach maximum development, to be protected from harmful influences and exploitation, and to be respected for their perspectives and voices.

In 1990, UNESCO convened the first World Conference on Education for All (EFA) in Jomtien, Thailand. As many as 155 countries and an even larger number of organizations set six goals to be reached by the year 2000, which included universal access to learning, a focus on equity, and improved learning environments. The 2000 UNESCO's World Education Forum in Dakar, Senegal, produced the *Dakar Framework for Action, Education for All: Meeting Our Collective Commitments* and featured six regional plans for action on a global scale. The framework carries on the work of the 1990 Jomtien, Thailand, conference by arguing that "education, starting with the care and education of young children and continuing through lifelong learning, is central to individual empowerment, the elimination of poverty at household and community level, and broader social and economic development" (Strategies, article 51).

Special studies also serve to highlight the urgency of a particular issue or problem concerning children's rights and protections. The *Machel Study, 10-Year Strategic Review* (2009) published by UNICEF chronicled the horrors of war and conflict on a global scale, an effort set in motion by Graca Machel's 1996 study on children and conflict. The *Strategic Review* recounts recent changes in zones of armed conflict, highlights principles and approaches to safeguard children's physical and social well-being and futures, and outlines recommendations and key actions to improve the lives of children in conflict zones worldwide.

Annual reports also play a policy role in promoting the protection of human and educational rights for children on a global scale. The 2012 UNICEF Annual Report argues for a "more equitable world for children" and highlights its goals, programs, and partnerships for improving basic health care, access to education, and inclusive education for all children "regardless of gender, income, location, religion, ethnicity, disability or other factors" (p. 14). The 2013 UN Millenium Development Goals (MDGs) Report delineates eight main goals: eradicating extreme poverty and hunger, achieving universal primary education, achieving gender equality and empowering women, reducing child mortality, improving maternal health, combatting HIV/AIDS and other diseases, ensuring environmental sustainability, and developing a global partnership for development.

Globalization has also focused attention generally on issues of human rights and specifically on the needs and rights of indigenous peoples. There is an increased emphasis on viewing indigenous peoples as "global citizens" rather than "national citizens" (Coleman & Sajed, 2013, p. 68), and a number of policy and action efforts have tried to preserve indigenous languages and cultures, protect local environments, hold governmental agencies responsible for equitable distribution of funding and resources, and specify certain goals and timetables in educational policy documents and programs.

Globalization

While forms of globalization have occurred in earlier historical times (Hemphill & Blakely, 2014), the current global marketplace of educational ideas and frameworks (Tobin, Hsueh, & Karasawa, 2009) has created an unprecedented level of new information, ideas, practices, and materials to influence early childhood education on an international scale. But given the persistent inequalities in educational access and opportunity, educational change and transformation on a global scale must include an equitable distribution of growth and development. This change will bring about greater freedoms and choices. As the great economist Sir Arthur Lewis from St. Lucia noted some 60 years ago, growth and development confer "a certain freedom that comes from a wider range of choices" (Henry, 2013, p. 175). Lewis (1955) also argued that growth comes about through the creation of new knowledge and new ideas, but also cautions that all new ideas may not be "appropriate" and that the "rate at which a new idea is received depends partly upon the idea itself" (p. 178). The key challenge in the current globalization flux is to understand and increase awareness of historical and global forces on educational equity and change. In the following two sections, I discuss the relevancy of time–space compression and modernity versus development for highlighting historical antecedents and influences on recent global tensions and possibilities in education.

Time-Space Compression

Social, political, and economic changes due to globalization have continued and will continue to influence the potential for teacher reflection and educational change to transform the social, cultural, and educational lives of teachers, children, and their families. The Internet and other forms of technological change have dramatically increased the amount and speed of access to international early childhood ideas and practices. It is now easier than ever in many regions and contexts to access information about a country's or region's educational traditions and organization. Underlying this phenomenon of global information access and transfer is the idea of a *time-space compression* in communication and information across the globe (Harvey, 2011; Hemphill & Blakely, 2014; Mignolo, 2011). Time-space compression can impede an equitable spread of education knowledge and practices internationally and discourage local collaboration and decision making based on local needs and talents. In short, it can stand in the way of needed efforts and changes to democratize early childhood education and create more transformative structures, ideas, and practices.

Certain economic, political, and social forces of globalization have resulted in a new kind of emphasis internationally on exchange and consumption (Harvey, 2011). One of the key trends in consumption is a movement away from the consumption of goods to the consumption of *services*, which includes education

(Harvey, 2011, p. 6). This new form of consumption is characterized by a shorter time period or span of engagement and experience that results in a *compression of time* devoted to the particular form of consumption. In the use of technology in education, for example, educational webinars and other forms of global Internet access can be seen as a form of relatively short-term engagement by educators. Many of these experiences last only a few hours, although the unstated expectation is often that a webinar will have powerful and lasting long-term effects on educational thinking and practice.

Globalization can also be characterized by an associated *compression of space* constraints due to such technological changes as satellite communication systems, which results in increased temporal simultaneity of events and experiences at the global level (Harvey, 2011). For example, participation in a webinar or access to an online video can easily occur simultaneously for educators in different geographic areas across the globe.

Spatial compression, though, does not so much flatten and connect the world as it *localizes* it due to certain economic forces and interests—"Heightened competition under conditions of crisis has coerced capitalists into paying much closer attention to relative locational advantages" and as "spatial barriers diminish we become much more sensitized to what the world's spaces contain" (Harvey, 2011, p. 8). In a potentially harmful result, this superlocalization can make it possible for the "people and powers that command those spaces to alter them in such a way as to be more rather than less attractive to high mobile capital" (p. 9). This process, then, can work against local control and collaboration in local education contexts and encourage the global disbursement and placement of whichever ideas, policies, and practices that particular "people and powers" deem effective or successful.

Global space compression can also result in local educational contexts that are "differentiated in ways attractive to capital" (p. 9), or to whichever educational systems and approaches are in vogue or held as the gold standard globally. One critical result of this differentiation has been "the production of fragmentation, insecurity, and ephemeral uneven development within a highly unified global space economy of capital flows" (p. 9). In international education, this can lead to the tendency for early childhood settings to become competitive in local settings and to specialize and stand out as being unique so that they attract children, families, resources, and funding. Further, time-space compression "exacts its toll on our capacity to grapple with the realities unfolding around us" (p. 17)—the allure of and pressure to adopt particular global standards and approaches can detract from the complicated local process of addressing local needs and realities.

Modernity and Development

Along with time-space compression, for international education to become more transformative and equitable, it must come to terms with how aspects of time, culture, and modernity are linked with the social, political, and economic effects of coloniality (Mignolo, 2011). Cycles of coloniality over the last several hundred years in many areas of the world have influenced national, regional, and community beliefs and traditions regarding connections between time, experience, the environment, socialization, and learning. Over time, Western and European powers and societies promoted the ideological frameworks and concepts of science, history, and modernity. This view of time and history came to dominate and position cultures and worldviews along one prescribed continuum—"history as 'time' entered the picture to place societies in an imaginary chronological time going from nature to culture, from barbarism to civilization following a progressive destination toward some point of arrival" (Mignolo, 2011, p. 151).

The idea of time, then, became a prism through which to separate out and distinguish the "natural and the less civilized" from the "modern and the cultural." "Time was transformed into a colonizing device" (p. 152) to demarcate and categorize cultures and histories into certain time periods and to contrast the modern (in present time) with the traditional (in the past). This dichotomy resulted in part in the "subalterization of knowledges" (p. 153) of traditional societies and peoples and created a hierarchy of what counted as valid and acceptable knowledge and understanding. In essence, time became "a fundamental concept in building the imaginary of the modern/colonial world and an instrument for both controlling knowledge and for advancing a vision of society based on progress and development" (p. 161).

Understanding the history and evolution of dominant conceptions of development and knowledge are critical for expanding varied global views and approaches to reflection and inquiry in early childhood education. Dominant forms of educational discourse at the global level continue to prize certain "modern" and "superior" ideas and forms of knowledge as the most valuable and effective. These approaches and ideas are seen as forward-moving and are designed to achieve certain developmental and historical endpoints (Smith, 1999). These supposedly superior forms of knowledge are associated with the presupposition that "history is about development" (Smith, 1999, p. 30) and that the forward movement of societies and institutions indicates and ensures progress and achievement.

One danger, though, is that the "dominant narrative" of what constitutes progress and development can contribute to a "naive acquiescence to the institutionalism of certain approaches" and "a universalistic mindset" that not only marginalizes other forms of early childhood education but "also fails to recognise a child's right to his or her own culture and identity" (Pence & Nsamenang, 2008, p. 35). This oversimplification of what constitutes the accurate and authentic montage of all children's social, cultural, and intellectual lives also "suggests both an ignorance of the other heritages and also the belief that others are incapable of producing a healthy childhood" (Pence & Nsamenang, 2008, p. 21).

Learning and Knowledge—Multiple Pathways

As we consider in this volume how inquiry and reflection can have an expanded role in transformative early childhood education at the global level, the field must value multifarious pathways toward acceptable forms of knowledge, learning, and development. This will broaden the acceptable forms of teaching and practice for educators and open up increased possibilities for reflection and inquiry to play a role in this process of transformation.

Global Childhood

Historically, the forms of teaching and learning with the greatest policy influence and status have been linked to Western-based scientific thought and "organized around the idea of disciplines and fields of knowledge" and classification systems (Smith, 1999, p. 65). In educational contexts primarily in the West, although increasingly in other areas of the world, educational systems and policies have elevated certain beliefs and assumptions about childhood and education. These "gold standard" early childhood education ideas are linked to a range of ideas including the very notion of childhood as a distinct time period, the idea of a single cohesive global childhood, the view that children learn best through play and exploration, the idea that children learn best by constructing their knowledge of the world, the value of curriculum standards and goals, and the idea of effective instruction based on teacher assessment and evaluation.

The rapid changes in the global economy and the educational marketplace have "shaped ideas and concepts associated with global childhood … and the recognition of childhood as a construct shaped by cultural and social practices" (Ebrahim, 2012, p. 81). While the concept of a global childhood has benefits— a common set of ideas and goals, potential for a more equitable distribution of resources, and the recognition of children's need as similar (Ebrahim, 2012)— there are a number of drawbacks and challenges.

The dominant ideas and practices traditionally associated with global childhood can inhibit the proliferation of certain educational philosophies, traditions, and beliefs from less traditionally powerful and influential societies, countries, regions, and groups. For instance, ideas associated with global childhood usually privilege formal school-based learning, which can discount time-honored and valued local practices and "home-grown models" (Ebrahim, 2012, p. 82) in Africa and other international contexts where children also learn in informal community-based settings with grandparents and teenagers.

For transformative education to take root and flourish globally, international early childhood education must account for the more fluid "cultural blending, shifting, and overlapping" at the global level (Hemphill & Blakely, 2014, p. 21). The concept of *hybridity* (Bhabha, 1994; Hemphill & Blakely, 2014; Mabardi, 2000) argues for recognizing the ever-changing interrelationships between people, regions, traditions, and worldviews. These relationships are evident externally as cultural markers of behavior, dress, and technology across physical borders. These blurred relationships are also seen internally in the blending and hybridity of ideas, languages, imaginations, experiences, and reflections.

Indigenous Ways of Teaching and Learning

An appreciation for and understanding of the educational traditions and values of indigenous peoples can help deepen and broaden ideas and practices associated with global childhood. The inclusion of indigenous ideas and practices also serves as a political and ethical commitment to preserving multiple pathways for conceptualizing modern early childhood education. The traditions and worldviews of indigenous peoples can bring to consciousness "new" possibilities for global teaching and learning based on enduring, time-honored relationships with other humans, the earth and nature, community, and the spiritual world (Madjidi & Restoule, 2008). Indigenous worldviews of our relationship with the earth, for instance, can reconnect children to the earth's resources—"we are only just beginning to understand the sophistication and the level of true understanding" and "innate wisdom" that indigenous communities have about natural environments (Cajete, 1994, p. 114).

Forms of indigenous teaching and learning, in rural and urban as well as institutional and community contexts, are embedded in the time and space dimensions of daily practices, rituals, and an intimate and sacred sense of and relationship to place. The conceptualization of what constitutes education and learning is both "life-wide and life-long" (Madjidi & Restoule, 2008, p. 84) and integrates learning holistically in formal and informal settings across the human life span. Teaching and learning are less tied to Western-based "ages and stages" and developmental milestones than to the dynamic cycles of natural time, change, and continuity. There is also a sacred linking between rites of passage and human development and self-actualization—"when these times of transition are marked, ritualized, witnessed, and supported, it creates a kind of experiential map of self-development" (Lertzman, 2002, p. 5).

Indigenous education also values the preservation of ideas, experiences, and lessons to link generations in a continual and enduring link of responsibility to community, the earth, and self-determination. Stories and storytelling are critical ways for indigenous peoples to connect knowledge and cultural identity across generations—stories are told about the earth, about traditions, and about sacred ways to preserve and are often moral stories to live and learn by. Native Peoples in Canada and elsewhere treasure the life-learning and life-teaching of elders, whose lives and thoughts inform "the ethos of a community and what has driven the persistence of identity" (Ermine, 1998, p. 10). Elders "hold the stories of their family and people" (Cajete, 1994, p. 69) and tell the "sacred" and "cultural truths" through myths and the "historical accounts" of Native Peoples through *narratives* (Lanigan, 1998, p. 109). In education, through sacred circles and medicine wheels and other traditional modes of teaching and learning, knowledge and experience are deepened through a communal process of "belonging, understanding and critical reflection" (Weenie, 1998, p. 61). A sacred circle, for instance, can represent the circle of life and the stages and cycles of the human life span and growth as well as the seasons and elements—all depicted and existing in complementary and symbiotic fashion.

The educational beliefs and practices of indigenous peoples can inform multiple pathways for the construction of knowledge in international education settings. In doing so, it is critical to avoid lumping indigenous groups and peoples into one group or category, overdramatizing "indigenous" and "primitive" aspects of Native Peoples, exoticizing indigenous education as "otherworldly" and unnatural, fossilizing a culture in time and space, and misappropriating traditions without regard to cultural and historical integrity and self-determination (Romero, 2013).

International Early Childhood Educators

The current expansion of global early childhood ideas and practices has created a dizzying array of research and policy agendas and curricular frameworks. While certain ideas become favorites of the most influential policy makers, governmental authorities, private philanthropies, and nongovernmental agencies, the "here-and-now" and "soon-to-be" decisions and teaching are made by educators in local contexts.

Expanding Human Capabilities

The journey toward seeing oneself and one's colleagues as international early childhood educators involves encountering and experimenting with new ideas, philosophies, and practices. It hinges, at least initially, on one's interest in changing one's practice and working with others to change collective practices. The journey is also one of expanding and transforming human capabilities. The Nobel Laureate Amartya Sen (1985) noted two benefits for expanding human capabilities—increased productivity and growth as well as the promotion of and increase in human freedom, well-being, and quality of life. This is the great promise for educators interested in expanding their knowledge of international practices and ideas, crossing borders of practice, and dialoguing with colleagues on a regional and global scale.

One of the foundational constructs of this volume is the power of teacher reflection and inquiry for taking a discerning and even skeptical stance toward entering the global marketplace of educational ideas. It is a key disposition for educators interested in pursuing "life-wide" and "life-long" changes in their work and personal lives. It then becomes a way of thinking and living, part of educational lives and philosophies that keep teaching and learning vibrant and reflective.

The journey, especially in its early phases, is also a sifting-through process, examining which aspects of one's current teaching and practice to hold on to and keep. While it can be difficult to discern which values and practices of culture and practice actually underlie what is enacted unconsciously in daily teaching, the sifting-through process can uncover what is sacred and valuable and thus worth retaining and building on.

Another key element involves looking critically at local teaching goals, philosophies, strategies, materials, and environments to ascertain particular aspects that educators want to change and improve. This strengthening process can be set in motion by coming into contact with new ideas and practices on a global level—the international ideas are the catalyst for critical self-reflection.

Dialogue and collaboration with colleagues and other stakeholders such as children and families and administrators also involves the "testing" of possible new directions and changes to be enacted at the local level. This process might also involve making contact with international professional associations, NGOs, or individuals to find more information and seek advice on effective avenues for curricular translation and change.

Professional Growth and Development

The process of moving toward seeing oneself as an international early childhood educator has personal, political, ethical, and professional implications for teachers on a global level. Early childhood teachers in certain educational contexts are afforded a plethora of international ideas and practices, and the challenge is to sift through and find those particular gems that might prove useful for refining local practices. For other educators working in contexts with less support and fewer resources, the initial challenge is to gain access to new ideas and practices that might prove applicable to local needs and talents. This is a global equity issue for the early childhood profession that needs to be redressed. As the field expands and spreads a more equitable distribution of varied educational approaches and practices, this effort can unite international educators with a common mission and a shared interest in change and transformation. It can then become part of educators' "life-long" professional development and growth on a global level.

I now present three early childhood professionals who view themselves as international early childhood educators. Nodelyn Abayan is an infant/toddler teacher who currently teaches at a university-based children's center in the United States and has taught in her home country of the Philippines and in Thailand. Nodelyn views herself as a teacher for all children everywhere—"I know that I am always a teacher in my heart, where I go and wherever I am." Having taught early childhood in three countries and teaching in Tagalog and English, Nodelyn views her role as an international educator to "make people aware of the differences and similarities of educational systems in different parts of the world" and believes that "I am called to share my talents, gifts and teaching experiences to whomever I encounter to help them enrich their lives." To stay abreast of ideas and practices internationally, Nodelyn maintains contact with former colleagues in Thailand and travels back and forth to the Philippines to conduct informal research on new trends in early childhood education. In her current work, Nodelyn draws upon her international experience to mentor her teaching assistants and "to respect the cultural backgrounds of all children and adults wherever they come from, and share my own cultural background and traditions."

Ros Marshall, an early childhood teacher in Edinburgh, Scotland, specializes in outdoor learning for young children, either on school playgrounds or as part of a program of visits to local woodlands. She believes that early childhood educators are "always moving forward in our practice by a process of blending current influences" both locally and internationally. Ros wants "to educate children in the best way possible, and I want the children with whom I work to think internationally and globally through their own lives." Ros regularly reads Internet blogs written by teachers and keeps up with organizations such as the U.S.-based Children & Nature Network for its nature ideas and strategies and the International Play Association because of its "commitment to the United Nations Convention on the Rights of the Child." In Edinburgh, Ros seeks out conferences with international speakers and meets with visiting international teachers, and her school has invited "visitors from other countries so we can exchange ideas." Ros continues to enliven her teaching by adapting international education ideas, "drawing heavily upon Scandinavian ideas on nature kindergartens which has led to the British forest school movement, and on ideas seen in San Francisco, California in regard to greening up playground spaces, the role of garden educators and the outdoor curriculum."

Born and raised in Mumbai, India, Divya Vyas worked at Mumbai Mobile Creche, which supported children of construction workers as the mobile creche moved with the children when their parents changed job sites. In Mumbai, Divya "felt a responsibility to prepare children for a life that could be in any part of the world and with a diverse set of people—a life that will not just define children as Indian but as global citizens." Moving to the United States, Divya faced certain challenges teaching in the United States as she immersed herself "in a new culture, shifted from British to American English, and re-learned the definition of family." Moving "between different cultures, languages, race and socioeconomic status," Divya believes that a key goal in her role as an international educator is to be "adaptable." Further, as a parent of a U.S.-born child, Divya "feared that he would no longer be an Indian," and her son's birth "forced me to understand that being an international educator is also about respecting individuality of every child and not trying to detach them from their roots." To sharpen her ability to adapt international practices to her local teaching, Divya has maintained a reflective teaching journal and constantly engages in reflective practices as a binational parent and teacher.

Nodelyn, Ros, and Divya, like many other educators, take it upon themselves to investigate new ideas and practices at the global level and to initiate and maintain contact with colleagues in other countries and regions. This process enriches their lives as educators, keeps their ideas and practices fresh and engaging, and empowers them to reflect continually on ways to improve and change.

Toward an Authentic Union

A few years ago, I traveled to Chengdu, Chengdu Province, China, to give a series of presentations to early childhood administrators and to visit local schools. I gave a presentation to a large group of administrators on children's first and second language and on literacy learning. It was my first time in China and my first experience presenting to Chinese early childhood educators. I prepared my presentation based on what I knew to be most relevant from research, theory, and policy over the last 30 years in the United States and elsewhere. I was confident in my material and its value, but the presentations did not go as planned. I didn't feel a strong sense of rapport with the Chinese educators and reflected later that perhaps my material was not so relevant to the audience.

A few days later, I found a key missing link for me when we visited a local school outside Chengdu City in a rural area. The school visit allowed me to see and hear and feel particular values and beliefs in action and to discern nuanced aspects of teaching and learning in that context. The preschool had a large, open play and gardening space adjacent to large farming fields. I saw a large group of children waiting their turn to work in the garden with their teacher, and I marveled at the children's ability to wait—some chatting with each other, some playfully jostling each other, some looking at other children in the garden—and I noticed that no teacher was close to the children or even supervised or watched them from afar.

At the same time, their teacher was working with other children in a small garden plot about 30 feet away, and she had her back turned to the waiting group of children. This scene ran counter not only to the U.S. belief in the value of supervising and observing children at all times (Tobin et al., 2009) but also to my own belief that it is a pedagogically sound practice to reduce wait time and instead have children actively participating, playing, and engaged at all times. I realized, though, from this brief garden scene in Chengdu, that there is pedagogical value in waiting, in the calm expectation that the children's turns were coming, and in the communal comfort and familiarity of being with one's classmates in the garden on a fall day.

Educational change at the global and local levels relies on this kind of cycle of observation, comparison, and reflection—with an eye toward internal and external change and growth. It is essential for inquiry and reflection, at some point, to have an action component—it must lead to real and tangible educational change and transformation. As Paulo Friere (2006) noted, "Critical consciousness is brought about not through an intellectual effort alone, but through praxis—through the authentic union of action and reflection" (p. 69). For reflection to be united with action, educators must be curious about themselves and about others. And there is a political and ethical dimension to this curiosity—as Freire (1996) asked, "In favor of what do I study? In favor of whom? Against what do I study? Against whom?" These are helpful questions to keep in mind as we look in the next chapters at specific international contexts for inquiry and reflection.

References

Bhabha, H. K. (1994). *The location of culture.* New York, NY: Routledge.

Cajete, G. (1994). *Look to the mountain: An ecology of indigenous education.* Durango, CO: Kivaki Press.

Coleman, W. D. & Sajed, A. (2013). *Fifty key thinkers on globalization.* New York, NY: Routledge.

Ebrahim, H. (2012). Tensions in incorporating global childhood with early childhood programs: The case of South Africa. *Australasian Journal of Early Childhood, 37(3),* 80–86.

Ermine, W. (1998). Pedagogy from the ethos: An interview with Elder Ermine on language. In L. A. Stiffarm (Ed.), *As we see … Aboriginal pedagogy* (pp. 9–28). Saskatoon, Saskatchewan, Canada.

Freire, P. (1996). Interview with Paulo Freire: An incredible conversation. Retrieved from http://www.youtube.com/watch?v=aFWjnkFypFA&feature=related-

Freire, P. (2006). Cultural action and conscientization. In B. Piper, S. Dryden-Peterson, & Y-S. Kim (Eds.), *International education for the millennium: Toward access, equity, and quality,* Harvard Educational Review Reprint Series #42, pp. 55–74.

Harvey, D. (2011). Time-space compression and the postmodern condition. In L. Connell & N. Marsh (Eds.), *Literature and globalization: A reader* (pp. 5–17). London, England: Routledge.

Hemphill, D. & Blakely, E. (2014). *Language, nation, and identity in the classroom: Legacies of modernity and colonialism in schooling.* New York, NY: Peter Lang.

Henry, P. B. (2013). *Turnaround: Third world lessons for first world growth.* New York, NY: Basic Books.

Lanigan, M. (1998). Aboriginal pedagogy: Storytelling. In L. A. Stiffarm (Ed.), *As we see … Aboriginal pedagogy* (pp. 103–114). Saskatoon, Saskatchewan, Canada.

Lertzman, D. A. (2002). Rediscovering rites of passage: Education, transformation, and the transition to sustainability. *Conservation Ecology, 5(2),* 1–30. Retrieved from http://www.consecol.org/vol5/iss2/art30/

Lewis, W. A. (1955). *The theory of economic growth.* London, England: George Allen & Unwin Ltd.

Mabardi, S. (2000). Encounters of a hetergeneous kind: Hybridity in cultural theory. In R. DeGrandis & Z. Bernd (Eds.), *Critical Studies, Vol. 13: Unforeseeable Americas—Questioning cultural hybridity in the Americas.* Atlanta, GA: Rodopi.

Machel, G. (1996). *The impact of armed conflict on children.* New York, New York: UNICEF. *The Machel Review 1996–2000.* UNICEF.

Machel study, 10-year strategic review: Children and conflict in a changing world. (2009). New York, NY: UNICEF. Office of the Special Representative of the Secretary-General for Children and Armed Conflict in collaboration with UNICEF.

Madjidi, K. & Restoule, J-P. (2008). Comparative indigenous ways of knowing and learning. In K. Mundy, K. Bickmore, R. Hayhoe, & M. Madden (Eds.), *Comparative and international education: Issues for teachers* (pp. 78–106). New York, NY: Teachers College Press.

Mignolo, W. (2011). *The darker side of western modernity: Global futures, decolonial options.* Durham, SC: Duke University Press.

Millenium Development Goals Report, pp. 1–68. (2013). New York, NY: United Nations.

Pence, A. & Nsamenang, B. (2008). *A case for early childhood development in Sub-Saharan Africa.* Working paper #51. The Netherlands: Bernard van Leer Foundation.

Romero, P. (2013). *Understanding indigenous education: Verbs for going deeper.* Unpublished paper, San Francisco State University.

Sen, A.K. (1985). *Commodities and capabilities.* Oxford, England: Oxford University Press.

Smith, L. T. (1999). *Decolonizing methodologies: Research and indigenous peoples.* London, England: Zed Books.

The Dakar framework for action, education for all: Meeting our collective commitments. (2000). Paris, France: UNESCO.

Tobin, J., Hsueh, Y., & Karasawa, M. (2009). *Preschool in three cultures revisited: China, Japan, and the United States.* Chicago, IL: University of Chicago Press.

UNICEF Annual Report. (2012). UNICEF. Retrieved from http://www.unicef.org/publications/index_69639.html

Weenie, A. (1998). Aboriginal pedagogy: Storytelling. In L. A. Stiffarm (Ed.), *As we see ... Aboriginal pedagogy* (pp. 59–75). Saskatoon, Saskatchewan, Canada.

PART II

Power of Reflection:
The Perspectives of Teachers
in Cross-National Contexts

3

DEVELOPING TEACHER COLLABORATION ALONG A GLOBAL PERSPECTIVE: USING INQUIRY IN A KENYAN PRESCHOOL

Trevor Valentino

> We are immersed in our culture the way a fish is immersed in water. ... Fish die out of water, but humans are luckier; when we find ourselves moving within a culture different from our own, we not only survive but we even grow from the experience. From learning about other cultures, we come to understand ourselves and other people better.
>
> *Janet Gonzalez-Mena, 2000*

As the airport doors slid open, the warm air touched my cheeks, and before I had time to realize what I was doing, I was greeted by dozens of cab drivers calling out for my patronage. It was the summer of 2010, and my first experiences in Kenya were ones in which I zoomed through traffic barely missing one vehicle after another. During the first two and half hours, I looked out from the matatu's window, marveling at the countryside as one small village after another slowly crept into view only to disappear quickly. When I arrived at Nakuru, I stepped off the matatu with the hope of bridging my twelve-year early child education experience with Kenyan teachers who were dedicated to helping the children of their rural community. I was hoping to co-create a learning space that empowers the children, develop the foundations for the possibility of teacher research, and form friendships, while at the same time learning more about my own cross-cultural views on early child education practice and philosophy. Was I the idealistic dreamer gasping for my last breath as I flopped around the Western romanticized version of global travel, or would this trip have lasting impressions on my professional and personal lives?

Research and Instructional Background

To better understand my experience at Morokoshi School, it is imperative to learn about my views on early child education and practice. I have been an early childhood educator for the last 12 years and have taught under the social constructivist philosophy where knowledge is *constructed* by the learner, rather than transmitted to the learner, through the *system of relationships* that exist within various social contexts. I am particularly drawn to the work of Vygotsky, who includes the child's cultural influences within these systems. Bodrova and Leong (2007), in their examination of the Vygotskiian approach to early child education, argue the following: "The idea that culture influences cognition is crucial because the child's entire social world shapes not just what he knows but how he thinks. The kind of logic we use and the methods we use to solve problems are influenced by our cultural experiences" (p. 11). Within this framework, I see children as being capable, competent, and open to exploring their own world to make meaning of what they discover. The critical and creative thinking skills a child learns "does not follow as an automatic result from what is taught. Rather, it is in large part due to the children's own doing as a consequence of their activities and our resources" (Malaguzzi, 1998, p. 67). Within this framework, children learn by what they do and the teacher is only a guide throughout this process.

During my Masters of Arts studies in early childhood education studies at San Francisco State University, I examined more closely how early child education practices, when viewed from a cross-cultural perspective, could influence my practice. I concluded that when entering a foreign country, the best strategy for learning from cross-cultural perspectives is built on creating relationships with the teachers that mirror the systematic relationships that exist in schools. Believing that I would learn from them as much as they would learn from me, I would seek to develop a foundation of trust between all participants. Many researchers have concluded that the true value of cross-cultural educational exchanges comes about through fostering self-sustaining local communities and making them integral members of the decision process. In particular, Cannella and Swadener (2006) argue that when outside organizations and nations actively include local community members in creating education programs, they in turn create a unique cultural identity. This model follows Pence and Nsamenang's (2008) recommendation to first world countries with regard to efforts in Africa when they write, "Those powers should not be used to 'show the way' but to support Africa's efforts to hear its own voices, among others, and to seek its own way forward. It will find that way through the children who understand and appreciate multiple worlds, through young scholars that frame their own contextually sensitive research questions, and through leaders that appreciate the riches of the past, as much as the possibilities of the future" (p. 43).

When I walked through Morokoshi School's gates, I searched for ways that would highlight this reciprocal system of relationships—a reciprocal relationship where the early child development strategies I enter with will grow from the very experience and strategies I will learn from the teachers there.

Kenya's Approach to Early Child Education

To better understand the cultural situation that I was embarking on, it is important to begin with Kenya's view on education and in particular how Kenya's cultural identity helps shape its approach to early child education practices. To make sense of the context, one must take note of how a nation redefined itself after post-colonial independence in 1963, while at the same time it attempted to maintain balance among growing national and global issues such as AIDS/HIV, poverty, and the 2007–2008 post-election violence.

Kenya's Ministry of Education's task force (2012), which oversees Kenya's early child education centers, reported that in 2010, there existed 38,523 early child education centers. Of these, nearly 15,000 are private centers with the majority of schools still being public. This same report identifies that enrollment at these centers will "increase from 1.9 million in 2010 to approximately 2 million in 2012 and to 2.5 million by 2015" (Ministry of Education, 2012, p. 113). According to Adams and Swadener (2000), parents and local communities support 75% of Kenya's preschools and many of these programs are religion-sponsored preschools. In 1984, the Ministry of Education created the National Centre for Early Childhood Education (NACECE) that oversees early childcare, development, and education. Recognizing the diverse indigenous groups throughout its urban and rural areas, Kenya created the District Centre for Early Childhood Education (DICECE), which facilitates the "training of preschool teachers, supervises and inspects district ECE programs, mobilizes communities around local care, health, nutrition and education of their youth, development of local preschool curriculum and materials, assessment of programs and carrying out research on the status of preschool age children" (Adams & Swadener, 2000, p. 390).

In 2001, the government established guiding policies for early childhood education in Kenya under the Children's Act. The guidelines addressed the following areas:

1. meeting children's needs holistically to maximize the realization of their full potential;
2. safeguarding the rights of the child;
3. ensuring that programs are child-centered by recognizing that children are active participants and learners shaping the events that influence their lives;
4. appreciating and recognizing parents and families as the primary caregivers and health providers of their children and hence empowering and supporting them in their role;
5. supporting and strengthening community-based management of early childhood services for sustainable development (Nganga, 2009, p. 229).

It would appear that Kenya values preschool programs as a starting place for its children to learn and be prepared for the early elementary years. However, in the Ministry of Education's 2012 report on the quality of early child development centers, it concluded that there is a shortage of early child development centers relative to demand, a lack of trained teachers, and a lack of learning materials;

it also reported that most parents cannot afford the fees associated with such schools, resulting in most children between the ages of 3 and 6 not attending early child development centers (Ministry of Education, 2012, p. 126–127).

One of the main challenges that influence children's enrollment in early child development centers is the growing economic instability facing many Kenyan families. Despite the recent economic growth in Kenya, UNICEF reports that "it is among the world's 30 poorest countries, ranking 152 out of 177 countries on the 2006 Human Development Index" (*Kenya at a Glance*, 2011). Recent figures suggest that 50% of Kenyans are living below the poverty line, making less than one U.S. dollar a day, with unemployment rates as high as 80% nationally, particularly among young people who have dropped out of school (Andang'o & Mugo, 2007; Kabiru, Njenga, & Swadener, 2003; *Kenya at a Glance*, 2011). In both rural and urban areas, where poverty is a major concern, children between the ages of 0 and 6 are not enrolled in early child development centers. In 2005, the government in Kenya reported that there "was only 35% enrollment into ECE centers in all of Kenya, with a depressingly lower percentage (9%) in the arid and semiarid regions of the country" (Andang'o & Mugo, 2007, p. 45). Others report that the two main reasons for such low enrollment include the inability of families to provide basic needs and lack of school fees for items such as uniforms and materials (Adams & Swadener, 2000; Murungi, 2013). Furthermore, such economic restraints force many older children to stay home to take care of younger siblings while their mother, who is often alone in child rearing, must find work (Adams & Swadener, 2000). These issues alone force many of Kenya's children to miss out on the benefits of early child development centers in or around their local communities.

The second major concern of early child development programs in Kenya is the failure of government agencies and their programs to support and adequately educate preschool teachers. This results in ineffective teacher training, low wages, and high levels of turnover. Currently, Kenya requires all teachers to be registered by the Teacher Service Commission (TSC); however, preschool teachers do not fall within this requirement. Adams and Swadener (2000) write, "[T]heir exclusion (preschool teachers) from the TSC is a contentious factor in recruitment, training, terms of service, pay levels, and continuing service of teachers in early childhood programs throughout the country" (p. 394). This results in early childhood programs that have untrained teachers as well as an average teacher-to-child ratio of 1:40 (Adams & Kabiru, 1995).

Like many other developing countries, Kenya looks to its children as its future and many of the preschool settings offer an approach that is academic, setting up children to be successful in the primary school years. However, due to the post-election violence in 2007 and early 2008, where an estimated 800–1,500 people were killed and 250,000 people were displaced, there has been a greater need for national cohesion. In ECE, as in all other levels of schooling, "there is a call for an education that socializes pupils to live in Kenya and to maintain their national identity wherever they may live" (Andang'o, 2009, p, 810). However, similar to what may soon be happening in U.S. preschools, Kenya's preschools are putting more pressure on teachers to better prepare learners for their Standard 1 interview and the structured primary curriculum (Adams & Swadener, 2000, pp. 399–400). This in turn creates a learning environment that is more academic in design and practice and, some argue, fails to prepare children in all areas of their development, particularly toward social development (Kariuki et al., 2007; Nganga, 2009). Coupled with very little help from the government in developing and supporting curricula that include all types of developmental domains, much of the curricula found in Kenya's preschools reflect the communities in which the schools are found (Nganga, 2009). As a result, many families who live below the poverty line believe their child's only way to escape poverty is to achieve academic success.

Shortly after Kenya gained its independence in 1963, then-President Jomo Kenyatta, gathered his fellow countrymen around the Kiswahili term *Harambee*, meaning "to pull together." This national motto has been at the root of many government-sponsored programs, especially early child development programs, where community participation is a must to accelerate economic and social development. Using this national theme of *Harambee*, I entered Kenya with a goal of developing a system of relationships that values teacher collaboration. This short-term project was created in an effort to establish a global exchange of ideas and practices regarding early child education within a new cultural landscape that deals with issues of poverty and violence.

Data Collection and Methods

In the summer of 2010, I carried out a two-month self-study where I examined, facilitated, and participated in teacher collaboration in an early childcare center. I looked closely at how this global exchange of ideas influenced both the school's approach and philosophy and my teaching philosophy. The research for this project was conducted at Morokoshi School through the nonprofit organization spanafrica.org. Morokoshi School has approximately 75 children ranging in age from 2–5; the school is located just north of Nakuru. The owner of the school is Steve Muriithi, who funds all aspects of the program from the profits he makes from his juice stand in Nakuru and the small amount of money he receives from students' tuition. Morokoshi School has one ECD-certified head teacher and two teachers who have no early child education background. The school also welcomes several teaching interns from the nearby teacher's college who help facilitate classroom lessons. The school has three classrooms based on the children's ages. The "Baby Class" consists of 35 three- to four-year-old children and has one teacher. The "Middle Class" consists of 21 four- to five-year-old children and has one teacher. The "Top Class" consists of 21 five- to six-year-old children and also has one teacher.

The children are in class from 8 a.m. to 4 p.m., and their day consists of a health check, four lessons throughout the day, two meals (a snack and lunch), and homework. The overall educational approach of the lesson plans is academically structured and theme-based. The teaching style is teacher-directed, based on rote learning with very little emphasis on the children's interests. The language spoken in the school is primarily Kikuyu, with some of the lessons spoken in English, a legacy of Britain's earlier colonial rule in Kenya.

The data for this research consisted of notes on the daily informal conversations I had with the three teachers concerning curriculum, environment, and classroom routine. I wrote down the interactions and conversations in my teaching journal and took photographs of the children's work and learning spaces (such as writing samples, artwork, and classroom setup prior to learning experiences). After each day working at the school, I spent time writing daily reflections that consisted of questions, concerns, and goals that I could pursue in the upcoming days with the teachers.

In addition to studying the programs and interacting informally with the teachers, I also wanted to foster and study cross-cultural teacher collaboration. I created and facilitated four teacher workshops that covered early child education practice, materials for children to use in the classrooms, and classroom setup and management and that addressed specific concerns of the teachers, including conflict resolution strategies, assessment, and the creation of lesson plans based on the children's needs and interests. I also worked closely with the director/owner of the school to understand his role. Through several meetings both on- and off-site, the director shared his needs and the various goals he had for his school and explained how some of these goals could be achieved within the limited time frame that existed.

Strategies in Developing Teacher Collaboration: Development of Morokoshi Handbook

When I first entered Morokoshi School, I was overwhelmed by the warm welcome from the school's director, teachers, and children. They immediately brought me into their community with very little hesitation. One would think that this overabundance of politeness would ease my transition into the space and offer me a quick understanding of the school and its community. However, Rogoff (2003) warns the outsider of this when she writes, "In seeking to understand a community's practices, outsiders encounter difficulties due to people's reactions to their presence (fear, interest, politeness) as well as their own unfamiliarity with the local web of meaning of events. Outsiders are newcomers to the meaning systems, with limited understanding of how practices fit together and how they have developed from prior events" (p. 26). While working at Morokoshi School, it was imperative that I develop relationships with the teachers that moved away from them being polite, into a place where they could openly challenge the questions that I posed. This process of building relationships was done over the course of my two months at the school.

To get to Morokoshi School, I had to walk along a dirt road for 30 minutes. On several occasions, I had the opportunity to walk with one or two of the teachers either before school or after school. These opportunities, coupled with our tea and lunch breaks, allowed us to get to know one another. During these conversations, we discussed the following: (1) their personal interests: popular Kenyan TV shows and music; (2) their ideas on the new referendum vote that was coming up; (3) information from them regarding my weekend travels; (4) future plans the teachers had; (5) my atheist views. With regard to this last point, when I shared my atheist beliefs, one teacher was caught with her mouth open wide. Kenya is 80% Christian with the rest celebrating various forms of Islamic beliefs. Being an atheist is unheard of, especially in a school that sings religious songs and prays during meals. However, by sharing my views, it demonstrated that I trusted them and that I hoped they would trust me. In spite of our religious differences, we continued to collaborate in the classroom and during the workshops.

Getting to know them on a personal level was the first step in gaining their trust. I also had to show them that I did not judge their teaching methods. During the first part of my visit, the school's owner, Steve, asked me to leave daily written observations. In these observations, I began by pointing out the teachers' strengths. When making observations on what I thought could be changed, I used the collaborative phrase "Things *we* can work on." During one of my visits, I returned to the school to find the teachers reading the notes I had left for Steve. It provided me with an opportunity to openly discuss with them any feelings they had about what I had written. The teachers politely told me they were happy with what I had written. Later, the teachers came to me to discuss some elements of early child development on which they wanted me to work more closely with them. To my surprise, many of their ideas were in direct correlation with what I had written in my daily observations.

Finally, to create a space where the teachers and I had a collaborative working experience, I praised them at every opportunity. During and after working with the teachers, I would tell them how great a job they were doing, especially given the huge shift in their philosophical and methodological approaches to teaching young children that I was recommending. After setting up new practices, I would check in with the teachers and ask them how they felt about the process and what questions they had. In particular, while reflecting on the first walk one of the classes had taken, I asked the teacher to share how she felt about the experience. She informed me how much she loved the experience but then brought up some initial concerns she had with the process, including the children's safety and overall engagement. When I returned the next day, I noticed that she had hung on the classroom's walls some of the natural materials (flowers, leaves) the children had brought back from their walk.

Using these three different methods to develop a strong collaborative teacher relationship, I was able to work more closely with the teachers in developing new strategies that demonstrated children's respect for one another and offered the children a space to work and play within open-ended learning activities. Two of the initial concerns I had when I observed Morokoshi School were the heavy-handed teacher-directed lessons and the continual lack of respect the children had for one another as demonstrated by hitting and teasing. As noted, many of Kenya's early child education programs are designed to get the children ready for their primary schooling. In this regard, children are taught in an academic environment where teachers are instructing the children based on various lesson plans covering early literacy, mathematics, and social skills. Morokoshi School was no different. I discovered that in each of the three classrooms, the teachers would teach the children using a teacher-directed style, using rote learning (call and response), having children use workbooks to copy what the teacher had written on the board, and completing daily assigned homework.

Early in my visit, when discussing Steve's goals for the school, he mentioned how important it was for him to prepare the children along the same academic routines of primary education and how Morokoshi School, in particular, has a strong reputation for preparing their students for primary school. This goal is most evident in that the children have final exams at the end of each term. The exams are not initiated from the KIA, but are created from Morokoshi School's head teacher to mirror the type of exams the children see when they enter the primary schools. When I sat down with the teachers, they requested that some of the workshops be based on new early child development practices. I immediately saw this as an opportunity to offer the teachers a more open-ended approach to teaching young children that would include the three lessons the teachers held at the beginning of each school day.

In creating a new approach to teaching young children, it was important for me to show the teachers how these new, more child-centered activities would benefit their own understanding of what the children know and would help them develop goals for specific children. The teacher workshops that I held and the activities that were subsequently practiced in the classroom were designed with the teachers actively participating in the process. For instance, when sharing an activity with the teachers that invites the children to look around the classroom for basic geometric shapes and then asks them to represent these images graphically, I had the teachers practice this activity on their own. When they finished, we discussed what the children would learn from this activity. The teachers discussed what conversations would emerge when the children had different views, what social play would happen, and how this would further develop the children's understanding of geometry.

After this workshop, the teachers were willing to practice some of these activities in the newly designed learning centers (writing, clay, duka or shop area, block building, drawing, mathematics, and science and nature) that were co-created in each classroom following an earlier workshop. After each class's morning lessons, we set up the rooms for smaller group play and activities that would begin after lunch and continue until the end of the school day. While the children participated in the different activities, the teacher and I would walk around the room and I would model for the teachers how to engage with the children. The teachers were then encouraged to do this on their own with the goal of leading these activities with no guidance from me.

From these hands-on-experiences, the teachers learned how effective these activities could be in extending their morning lesson plans. For instance, after a morning lesson on mathematics, a group of children working with modeling clay began sculpting the same numbers they had been taught. Another child was using the modeling clay to sculpt her name. The teacher went over and pointed to each number or letter while the students repeated it aloud. From this point, an integrated approach to academic learning with child-centered, free-play activities was born in Morokoshi School.

The other concern I had with my initial visit to Morokoshi School—and one that would prove to be the most difficult as well as the most rewarding—came in the form of the children's disrespect for each other. On numerous occasions, I witnessed children hitting, kicking, and pushing each other down with few reprimands from the teachers. I also witnessed children laughing at other children who had fallen or were hit by some of the older children, again with little intervention from their teachers. I brought this to the attention of the family I was staying with, and they agreed that this often happened in schools and was a way for children to "get tough." Rogoff (2003) explains that this is not uncommon in African countries, particularly in Kenya. She argues that Kenyans believe that "teasing helps children learn from toddlerhood to discern the difference between what is real or true and what is not, and to deal with symbolic meaning" (p. 218). Although there may be some merit to this argument, I wonder what long-term repercussions develop when children are not taught empathy in the face of teasing, hitting, and disrespecting others' possessions. While I was in Kenya, the country was preparing to vote on a new referendum in response to the post-election violence that rocked the country in 2007 and early 2008. With the vote approaching, many families in Muruynu, some of whom were harmed or displaced from the 2007 post-election violence, were preparing for a possible repeat of violence. This deeply troubled me, and I brought my concerns to Steve and the teachers. I expressed to them the inherent need for children to learn empathy and suggested that an environment that condones children causing physical and emotional harm to one another sets the stage for them to be aggressive later in life.

Sheldon Berman (2003) argues this point further when he states, "Empathy may, in fact, be an innate human attribute that is either nurtured or inhibited by the child's environment. Empathy can be developed by helping children become sensitive observers of the states of feeling of others and by helping them understand the causes of these feelings" (p. 111). During the workshop on building a classroom community, the teachers and I looked at solutions to some of the problems we were seeing and the strategies we could use to support the children involved. One of the strategies I offered—having the children hug each other—was met with much concern from the teachers. They shared with me how many of the families, based on their culture, show empathy through other ways and would be upset if they learned that their child was forced to hug another child. Using this crucial information, we looked at what strategies would be mindful of the cultural practices of the families. I was only acting as a scribe while the teachers worked together to develop the strategies. The most influential moment came at the end of the workshop when the teachers told me that each of the conflict resolution strategies would come from the understanding of peace—or in Swahili, *amani*.

By considering the needs of the local community and acknowledging the teachers' evaluation of their own program, we developed a learning environment that balanced the needs of the families (preparing the children for the academic rigor of their primary schooling) with the children's individual learning needs. In addition, the teachers were empowered as they reflected on and reconstructed their own practice to better meet those needs of the children and the community. Furthermore, the teachers and I created systematic approaches to solve the children's conflicts under the new Morokoshi School value: *amani*. Carlina Rinaldi (2001), director of early child education in Reggio, Emilia, argues the following: "School is a place of culture—that is, a place where a personal and collective culture is developed that influences the social, political, and values context and, in turn, is influenced by this context in a relationship of deep and authentic reciprocity" (p. 38). This co-reflective inquiry effort resulted in the creation of the Morokoshi Handbook that highlighted the work the teachers and I did over the two months and offered the teachers a reference to support them in better understanding their classroom environment and child-centered activities and in building classroom communities. The strength of the handbook comes from the goals the teachers gave me early in my visit, their reflections from the workshops, and the hands-on experiences they had in the implementation of the learning areas in their classroom. My goal for creating this handbook was that the teachers could continually use it to support the children's educational experiences by integrating an open-ended, child-centered approach while preserving and honoring some of their traditional teaching goals and practices. It was my hope that the teachers' experience in co-creating this handbook empowered them as teachers, showing them how they are active participants in this holistic learning experience.

Influence on Early Child Development Practice

One of the major shifts in my thinking since returning from Kenya has been my growing support for teacher collaboration and the strategies that early child educators can take with their teaching teams to develop a reciprocal partnership. This is no easy task. Edwards (1998) explains this further when she writes the following: "The co-teaching organization is considered difficult, because two adults must co-adapt and accommodate constantly, but nevertheless it is powerful because it requires each adult to become used to peer collaboration, acquire a value for the social nature of intellectual growth, and become more able to help children (and parents) as they undertake joint learning and decision making" (p. 185). When this co-teaching organization extends beyond the cultural practices of one's own experience, this relationship, this "intellectual growth," expands even more. Barbara Rogoff (2003), a cultural development psychologist, writes, "Forays of researchers and theorists outside of their own cultural communities and growing communication among individuals raised with more than one community's traditions have helped the field move beyond these ethnocentric assumptions" (p. 21). These "ethnocentric assumptions" shape the very practice, techniques, and cultural norms that are found in U.S. preschools. When teachers open their experiences to include the view of others, they begin the process of looking more closely at their practice and can reflect with an open mind on ways to expand beyond their comfort zones.

Since my return, I have taken on new administrative responsibilities at my school and reflect on my experiences in Kenya as a way to develop my leadership skills. In particular, I want to continue to develop new leadership techniques that support teachers in working together more closely and in adapting to the rapid changes that may occur in the classroom. My goal is not simply to lead them, but to challenge them to rethink their own practice in a reflective inquiry process. One particular area that I continue to examine more closely is the adaptive leadership theory. Defined as the "practice of mobilizing people to tackle tough challenges and thrive," adaptive leadership encourages organizations to "build a culture that values diverse views and relies less on central planning and the genius of the few at the top" (Grashow, Heifetz, & Linsky, 2009, pp. 2, 4). When I reflect on my experience in Kenya, I did not employ a top-down system but, instead, observed what was happening in the classrooms, offered positive and constructive goals, and developed trust with the teachers. This inclusive and open process broke down the defenses the teachers had built, allowed us to step over the rubble, and invited me into their thinking and wonderings about early child development. Together, by addressing their questions and concerns, we were all empowered as learners and teachers.

At my school, we thrive on creating a space that is based on the reciprocal relationships that exist between administrators, teachers, parents, and children. Before our 2013–2014 school year began, Darcy Campbell, Cow Hollow School's Executive Director, and I got together to think about what our two-day planning retreat would focus on. Many of our staff have been with us for several years, and this particular year, teachers began working together for the first time. Darcy Campbell and I wondered how we could begin creating strong co-teaching teams that would push the teachers to take risks and exhibit flexibility in their thinking and how we could support them in tackling the daily challenges that occur in their individual classrooms when they are on their own. Darcy Campbell shared with me her values evidence worksheet, adapted from Paula Jorde Bloom's work in *Blueprint for Action: Achieving Center-Based Change Through Staff Development* (2005). At the retreat, we had the teachers independently write down three values they believe are important to their teaching. They were then asked to provide ways that interactions, curriculum choices, and environment setup can reflect their values. In the final step, and one that proved to be the most crucial, the teaching teams got together to share their values with one another. Returning from our retreat, we have witnessed many of these values posted on the classroom walls for the parents to see. This provided an opportunity for self-reflection, group reflection, and enactment of the values.

When Darcy and I sit down and meet with the teachers to discuss curriculum choices, problems that may be occurring in the classroom, and their overall work, we often pull directly from their value evidence worksheet. Because it came from them, much like it did with the teachers in Kenya, they are more willing to examine their practice. My goal for the teachers is that they become adaptive leaders in their own classrooms. When they believe their values are acknowledged and respected, they become more willing to create goals, both personal and collective, that strengthen their classroom curriculum and community.

Conclusion

Entering a new situation, whether it is in a community you are familiar with or a country that you have never visited, is a daunting task. It invites you, sometimes forces you, to look more closely at who you are and what values you take into every aspect of your life. When I worked in Kenya during the summer of 2010, I wanted to look more closely at the collaborative experience that could happen along a global perspective. I knew I was walking into a situation that would be very different from my own teaching and values and that it would be a challenge to meet the needs of the school's owner, teachers, and families. Through teacher workshops that invited active research and participation and the informal conversations that I had with the teachers, I was able to develop a friendship with them that was built on trust. From this collaborative experience, I created and drafted a handbook that the teachers could use after I left. Within the school's culture, the teachers and I established a reflective inquiry practice that best suited the children and the families' needs. By looking more closely at our own practice, we worked together in creating a learning environment where all participants feel empowered. It was an honor to work in Morokoshi School, which values children and childhood. The experience enabled me to continue this work in the United States at my own school, where teachers and administrators reflect on their practice through a value-based perspective. In both situations, teachers grew from this reflective practice and together strive for best practices in their specific classroom communities.

References

Adams, D. & Kabiru, M. (1995). *Training for early childhood care and education services in Kenya (a consulting report for the World Bank ECD Project)*. Nairobi, Kenya: National Centre of Early Childhood Education.

Adams, D. & Swadener, B. (2000). Early childhood education and teacher development in Kenya: Lessons learned. *Child & Youth Care Forum, 29(6),* 385–402.

Andang'o, E. (2009). Synchronizing pedagogy and musical experiences in early childhood: Addressing challenges in preschool music education in Kenya. *Early Child Development and Care, 179(6),* 807–821.

Andang'o, E., & Mugo, J. (2007). Early childhood music education in Kenya: Between broad national policies and local realities. *Arts Education Policy Review, 109,* 43–52.

Berman, S. (2003). The bridges to civility: Empathy, ethics, civics, and services. In M. Seymour (Ed.), *Educating for humanity: Rethinking the purposes of education* (pp. 108–121). Boulder, CO: Paradigm.

Bloom, P. J. (2005). *Blueprint for action: Achieving center-based change through staff development* (2nd ed.). Mt. Rainier, MD: New Horizons.

Bodrova, E. & Leong, D. (2007). *Tools of the mind: The Vygotskian approach to early child education.* Upper Saddle River, NJ: Pearson.

Cannella, G. & Swadener, B. (2006). Contemporary public policy influencing children and families: Compassionate social provision or the regulation of others? *International Journal of Educational Policy, Research and Practice: Reconceptualizing Childhood Studies, 7(1),* 81–93.

Edwards, C. (1998). Partner, nurturer, and guide: The role of the teacher. In C. Edwards, L. Gandini, & G. Forman (Eds.), *The hundred languages of children: The Reggio Emilia approach—advanced reflections* (2nd ed.) (pp. 179–198). Greenwich, CT: Ablex.

Gonzalez-Mena, J. (2000). *Foundations of early childhood education: Teaching children in a diverse society.* New York, NY: McGraw-Hill.

Grashow, A., Heifetz, R., & Linsky, M. (2009). *The theory behind the practice: A brief introduction to the adaptive leadership framework.* Boston, MA: Harvard Business Press.

Kabiru, M., Njenga, A., & Swadener, B. B. (2003). Early childhood development in Kenya: Empowering young mothers, mobilizing a community. *Childhood Education, 79(6),* 358–363.

Kariuki, M., Chepcheing, M., Mbugua, S., & Ngumi, O. (2007). Effectiveness of early childhood education programme in preparing pre-school children in their social-emotional competencies at the entry to primary one. *Educational Research and Review, 2(2),* 26–31.

Kenya at a glance. Retrieved from http://www.unicef.org/kenya/overview_4616.htm

Malaguzzi, L. (1998). History, ideas, and basic philosophy: An interview with Lella Gandini. In C. Edwards, L. Gandini, & G. Forman (Eds.), *The hundred languages of children: The Reggio Emilia approach—advanced reflections* (2nd ed.), (pp 49–98). Greenwich, CT: Ablex.

Ministry of Education. (2012). Ministry of Education Task Force on the Re-alignment of the Education Sector to the Constitution of Kenya 2010, *Towards a globally competitive quality education for sustainable development.* Republic of Kenya. Retrieved from http://www.vision2030.go.ke/cms/vds/Task_Force_Final_Report_Feb_20123.pdf

Murungi, C. (2013). Reasons for low enrollments in early childhood education in Kenya: The parental perspective. *International Journal of Education and Research, 1(5),* 1–10.

Nganga, L. (2009). Early childhood education programs in Kenya: Challenges and solutions. *Early Years, 29(3),* 227–236.

Pence, A. & Nsamenang, B. (2008). *A case for early childhood development in Sub-Saharan Africa.* Working paper #51. The Hague, The Netherlands: Bernard van Leer Foundation.

Rinaldi, C. (2001). Infant-toddler centers and preschools as places of culture. In *Making learning visible: Children as individual and group learners* (pp. 38–46). Reggio Emilia, Italy: Reggio Children & Project Zero.

Rogoff, B. (2003). *The cultural nature of human development.* Oxford, England: University Press.

4

CULTURAL CONSCIOUSNESS: A CHINESE IMMIGRANT TEACHER'S UNDERSTANDING OF CULTURE AND CULTURALLY RESPONSIVE TEACHING IN THE UNITED STATES

Fengyuan Sun

October 23, 2010—Reflective Teaching Journal

Today was my first day working as a teacher at a toddler classroom in San Francisco, California. At snack time, children were eating black beans and rice at the table. Each child was provided with a spoon. Eighteen-month-old Jason tried to scoop the rice, but scattered most of it on the table. Noticing this, I was about to take his spoon and feed him. Amy, my co-teacher, stopped me. "As a toddler class, one of our goals this semester is to help children learn to feed themselves." I was surprised because from my growing up in China, most children at this age had to be fed; otherwise, they would make a mess and eat only a little food. Soon, Lily pushed her bowl away and stood up. "Are you all done, Lily?" asked Amy, "If you are done, please go wash your hands." I noticed that Lily had eaten only a little of her food. "Oh, Lily, you didn't eat up the rice in your bowl. Would you like to have more?" I asked. I was concerned that she might still be hungry; also, I expected children to eat all the food in their bowls, and it was my belief that encouraging them to eat more could teach them not to be wasteful. "No! All done!" Lily shook her head. "It's OK. You don't have to eat more if you don't want to. Wash your hands, please," said Amy.

I am a Chinese-origin early childhood administrator currently working at a Head Start program in San Francisco, California. My experiences as an early childhood educator in the United States were initially inspired by my early social work education and practice experience. When I had studied social work with a concentration on children and families in New Jersey and interned as a social work case manager at a preschool, I was often confronted with situations where I was not sure how to respond to children's words and behaviors and how to approach and communicate with their families. By observing other teachers' interactions with children and their communication with parents, I always wished I could do what they did. I wanted to learn more about working with young children in the United States and learn how to support their development. After

I received my Masters of Social Work degree, I entered a master's program in Early Childhood Education (ECE) in San Francisco, and during my MA studies, I taught as an assistant teacher at the university's child development center, serving children of the university's faculty and staff.

In my first experience as an early childhood educator in the United States at this campus-based child development center, I quickly confronted issues of cultural differences. I was a Chinese-origin immigrant teacher who had received my own early education in Dalian (northeastern China), Liaoning Province, China, and my early education and upbringing at home were based on Confucian traditions and socialist ideas. Yet, I received all of my ECE professional training in the United States. Over the last several years, having worked in two settings in the United States, I often encountered uncertainty and dilemmas as I navigated between Chinese and American cultural expectations, beliefs, and practices.

For instance, my experience helping children eat at meal and snack times, as described in my journal entry above, is just one example of cultural and educational differences that I have encountered and reflected on. I have experienced a range of other differences in cultural and educational beliefs and practices between China and the United States. For instance, in a Chinese classroom, if two children want a toy, a typical Chinese teacher would encourage both children to yield to the other. In the United States, though, the toy is usually given to the child who got it first and the other child is told to wait for a turn. Teachers in different cultures have varied belief-forming experiences that are guided by different cultural norms (Wang, Elicker, McMullen, & Mao, 2008), and my original beliefs on socializing and teaching young children were guided by traditional Chinese norms and by my early family and community environment. Through a process of reflective inquiry (Stremmel, 2008), an approach I studied in the United States, I now more clearly see the influence of my upbringing and early schooling on my current beliefs and teaching. I have become more mindful, critical, and analytical in my work through melding Chinese and American early childhood beliefs and practices.

My Early Childhood Experiences in China

My early education in China was quite different from what I have learned from my U.S. early childhood courses and what I have experienced in my American classrooms. When I was in preschool and elementary school in China, the primary teaching method teachers used was teacher-centered, direct instruction. Children seldom worked independently or in small groups on self-selected or child-initiated activities. Instead, teacher-constructed and teacher-directed whole class activities were emphasized. Most of the time, my classmates and I were expected to do the same thing at the same time. In a typical art activity, for example, the teacher first explained the steps to the whole class and modeled how to do it. Then she provided guidance to particular children who did it "incorrectly" before proceeding to the next step for the whole group. In general, most art lessons consisted of children copying the artwork completed or prepared by the teachers.

Many of our activities were communal and focused on the group. A typical group activity for all children every morning at school was the "*guangbo ticao* 广播体操 (broadcast physical exercise)." All the children gathered on the playground and stood in lines facing the instructor (usually a P.E. teacher) who modeled the movements, and then everybody performed the exercises accompanied by music and instructions from a loudspeaker (Tobin, Hsueh, & Karasawa, 2009). Throughout my P-12 schooling, each preschool, elementary school, middle school, and high school had the same group exercise as part of the daily routine. Currently, most schools (except colleges and universities) in China still include this daily activity in their curricula. The emphasis on these kinds of large group activities is partially due to the high teacher-student ratio and the limitation of resources. Further, the essential purpose of group activities is to instill a sense of collectivism in children starting at a very young age (Tobin et al., 2009). In Eastern cultures such as China, group goals, interrelatedness, and harmony among groups are highly valued and emphasized more than they are in Western cultures (Chan & Rao, 2009; Freeman, 1998; Pang & Richey, 2007; Tobin et al., 2009). Currently, while more and more early childhood professionals in China have begun to see the value of small group activities, due to the high teacher-student ratio, small-group and child-centered approaches have not been widely implemented across China. The traditional teacher-directed large group model remains dominant.

My early childhood education experiences were greatly influenced by traditional Chinese culture and particularly by Confucian values. Historically, most Chinese parents, grandparents, and teachers believe that children learn through memorization. At school, children are encouraged to memorize for the acquisition of new knowledge. Typically, when a new word is introduced in a traditional Chinese classroom, such as my kindergarten class, the basic learning steps for children involve repeating the pronunciation after the teacher and practicing writing the Chinese character over and over again. This cultural belief can be illustrated by a popular Confucian proverb, "*Dushu po wanjuan, xiabi ru youshen.* 读书破万卷，下笔如有神." ("Read it one hundred times, and understanding will follow spontaneously.") (Hess & Azuma, 1991, p. 6, as cited by Chan & Rao, 2009, p. 264). It is also believed that rote learning and whole group modeling promote Chinese language teaching because there are so many Chinese characters and they are complicated for young children to recognize and write. Further, whole group instruction is also designed to "bring up" every child in the class, so that teachers' use of whole group instruction and modeling helps the children most in need of structure and support to keep up with the group (Huang, 2013).

In a whole group setting, children in China are also taught how to behave based on Confucian ideas of *li* 礼(etiquette). Chinese culture and society have historically valued etiquette and the following of group social norms. In traditional Confucian tradition, which is now seeing a resurgence in China, respect for teachers is highly honored and teachers are regarded as the authority in the classroom. From the very first day I went to school, I was taught to always listen to teachers and follow their directions. My classmates and I rarely questioned our teachers or raised opinions that opposed teachers.

Parent or family involvement in Chinese children's learning at school is not emphasized as in the United States; instead, home-based support and socialization are strongly encouraged in China (Ho, 1995). Although many Chinese parents, as mine did, care very much about their children's learning at school and contribute as much as possible to support their children's development, there remains a lack of dialogue and collaboration between parents and teachers. Many parents are not aware of the necessity and significance of school-based parent involvement or teacher-parent partnerships in children's learning and development. Most Chinese parents usually don't spend time interacting with children in the classroom at drop-off or pick-up time, let alone participate in classroom or school activities. One reason is that the large number of families and children at most Chinese preschools and elementary schools discourages opportunities for parent-teacher contact. Currently, in many Chinese cities, a typical preschool has 400 to 500 children; and as more and more Chinese parents work long hours, grandparents and others are dropping off and picking up children.

In addition, some parents believe that the main way they can contribute to their children's learning is through financial support and that when children are at school, it is the teachers' responsibility to take care of and teach the children. On the other hand, even today, Chinese schools and teachers seldom take the initiative to raise parents' awareness by inviting or encouraging their involvement in school activities. Also, due to the belief in teachers' authority in Chinese culture, many parents often hesitate to express suggestions or comments, but rather follow the teachers. In addition, although the Chinese government has recently relaxed its "one-child policy," the restriction for urban couples to have only one child had been in force since 1979. Parents and grandparents from both the maternal and paternal sides have been known to pay a great deal of attention to their only child and put a great deal of pressure on the child to excel academically, which sometimes leads to exorbitant demands on schools and teachers. Therefore, it is a real challenge to achieve an equal partnership between teachers and parents (Pang & Richey, 2007). I was born in China in the early 1980s, in the first generation to grow up under China's one-child policy. I remember that starting at a very young age, I already felt too much pressure from my parents because as the only child of my parents, I was their "only hope." They spent a lot of energy on me and were willing to provide anything to support me in competing with my peers. Their wish for me was to continuously achieve academically and have a successful life. During my childhood, I often wished that I could have received less of my parents' attention and care and more freedom to do things that interested me and to make my own choices.

Reflecting on Early Childhood Beliefs and Practices in a New Culture and Society

> … people develop as participants in cultural communities. Their development can be understood only in light of the cultural practices and circumstances of their communities—which also change …
>
> *(Rogoff, 2003, pp. 3–4)*

As I decided to undertake the responsibility of educating young children in a culture different from mine, I started my journey of pursuing a deeper understanding of cultures and cultural influences on young children's learning and development. My journey has not been "smooth sailing," but remains a rewarding experience as I've learned more about different cultures and the importance of culture in teaching and learning. In the following sections, I present my experiences and practices as a Chinese immigrant teacher in U.S. early childhood settings. These stories describe my process of constructively adapting to a new culture, discovering the influence of culture on education, and defining developmentally appropriate practices in my new American multicultural social and educational context. Throughout this journey, I have reflected on my cultural beliefs and behaviors as an early childhood educator and have broadened my responsiveness to the cultures of young children and their families. My cultural transition has not been a complete shift of values, beliefs, or practices, but more like a "holding" of the past and present together (Elbaz-Luwisch, 2004) as I continue to build my unique identity as an immigrant teacher. In this process, I adopted the teacher research methods of inquiry and reflection, which I learned during my MA studies. The process of investigating questions about my teaching empowered me to generate my own knowledge and understanding about what works and benefits my teaching and children's learning.

I officially entered the field of early childhood education as a teacher assistant in a toddler class on a campus-based child development center in San Francisco. During the first few months, I constantly had feelings of unease, embarrassment, and isolation that I never expected. Looking back, I see that my early discomfort as a cultural outsider was caused by many differences in the education environment and practices from what I had experienced in China. I sometimes hesitated to ask questions of other teachers or parents because I was afraid of asking "stupid" questions to which the answers seemed obvious for people who were more "experienced" in the culture and who took them for granted. As one of the few new immigrant teachers at my center, I struggled to find a sense of belonging in my teaching team. I thought that because I was new to the country, the culture, and the field, I was overlooked by my colleagues, which made me feel even more upset and lonely. The children's parents rarely approached me with questions or to initiate conversations about their children. All of these experiences really discouraged me, and I began asking myself, "Am I qualified to be an early childhood educator in the United States?"

Mentorship

Although discouraged, I never considered giving up my dream of becoming an effective educator in the United States. As I continued to learn from my MA early childhood courses and engaged in more communication with my co-teachers and with teachers and administrators from other schools, I discovered many immigrant teachers who were succeeding and truly enjoying their work. This helped me become more confident that cultural barriers can be overcome and to realize that rather than waiting for help, I needed to take the initiative to seek support and information.

I was very grateful to my mentor, Amy, the head teacher in my first class, who changed my professional life. Amy was an immigrant teacher from Malaysia, but educated in American schools in China, and had more experience than I living and teaching in the United States. She noticed my emotional struggles and initiated a conversation with me, and after we talked, she gave me a very special gift, a notebook. As she handed it to me, she looked into my eyes and said, "Let's use this notebook as a shared teaching journal between us. Feel free to write down any of your questions, concerns, and ideas regarding practice. Whenever I get a chance, I will read through your notes and reflections and share my thoughts with you in this journal." From then on, I never felt alone. Instead of hiding my questions and struggles, I started to open up not only to Amy but also to the other teachers to learn more about American culture and the cultures and backgrounds of my colleagues. Gradually, I overcame my early hesitation and concerns and deepened my understanding of early childhood education in the U.S. context. My pain and struggle of being a cultural outsider eventually faded away, replaced with the joy and beauty of mutual learning and collaboration among former insiders and outsiders.

Through journaling and conversation and other forms of reflection, I realized that my personal history contributes considerably to my current beliefs about children's learning. Through the personal journey of understanding adults' and children's cultural realities and recognizing and reflecting on the differences between my own cultural background and American culture, I deepened my understanding of the significant role culture plays in young children's learning and development (Ramsey, 2004). I learned to become more conscious that some of my expectations for children's behaviors may not match American children's early experiences and cultural backgrounds, even with the diversity of children's cultures in my San Francisco early care and education centers. Introduced to the American idea of developmentally appropriate practice (Copple & Bredekamp, 2010) and reflecting on its fit with my Chinese background and education, I realized that truly effective and developmentally appropriate teaching must embrace children's, parents', and teachers' cultures. I first saw the need for this cultural responsiveness with the children and adults I encountered in American classroom environments. In the following four examples, I use excerpts from my reflective teaching journal to show how I tried to make sense of differences in Chinese and U.S. ECE environments.

Classroom Environment

Where is the Nap Room?

It was my first day working as a teacher assistant in a U.S. toddler classroom. I came into the class at noon. Naptime had just started. What I saw was very different from what I had expected. I had pictured children sleeping in a nap room on their individual beds like schools in China (see Figure 4.1). However, in this center, I didn't find a nap room for toddler or preschool classes. Each child was sleeping on a cot, which was a simple, very low, and portable bed covered by a thin sheet. All cots were placed on the classroom floor at naptime. When children woke up, teachers would stack all the cots in a corner of the classroom.

The first time I saw American children sleeping on cots in the classroom, I asked myself, "How can children fall asleep in an environment like this?" In my childhood, most floors were made of hard materials, such as cement, bricks and tiles, which all feel cold. Wooden floors, let alone carpets, are rarely seen in China. Even currently, although better materials are widely used, many Chinese classroom floors still consist of hard materials. Therefore, taking sleep hygiene and quality factors into consideration, cots are not a good option for Chinese early care programs. I thought that the U.S. environment was not good enough for young children to fall sleep and that it would have been more comfortable for children to sleep in a separate nap room rather than the classroom. But as I observed more of the children napping, I was surprised to see that children could sleep quite well on their cots as long as they were used to the routine. I was also amazed by the convenience and space-saving function of the cots, which did not require another room.

Aren't Children Supposed to Sit in Chairs in the Classroom?

After working at this American school for a week, I noticed another difference between American and Chinese schools—the way children sit in the classroom. In China, children usually sit on small chairs in a classroom (see Figure 4.2). It is very rare that children sit on the floor or ground. While in the United States, I have observed that it is quite common for children to sit on the carpet or the floor in the classroom and even on the ground. Typically, at circle time, rather than sitting on chairs, children all sit very close to one another on a carpet; some children may also sit on teachers' laps. It appears to be more relaxing and interactive.

My first impression of an American classroom was that it was more like a home than a classroom. I had never thought that a classroom could be so relaxing, and I reflected on how Chinese and American classroom environments were influenced by their respective cultural beliefs, values, and goals. Chinese children are taught to sit according to one of the five virtues of Confucianism, *li* 礼 (etiquette), which refers to any of the secular social functions of daily life, usually translated into English as manners, customs, morals, or rituals (non-religious). Generally speaking, the meaning of the Confucian term is similar to the definition of the

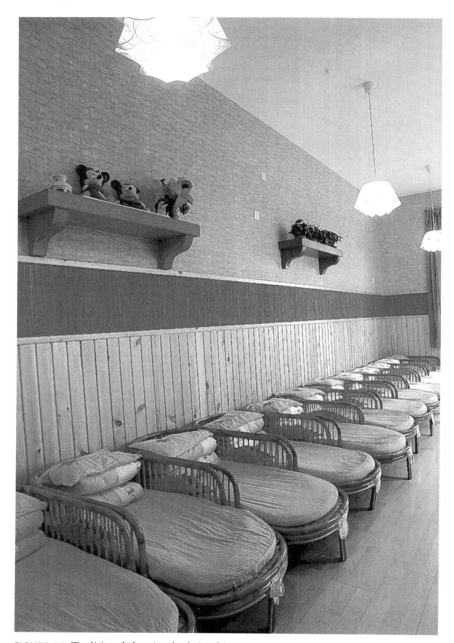

FIGURE 4.1 Traditional sleeping beds in china.

FIGURE 4.2 Typical classroom seating arrangement in China.

Western term *culture*. *Li* as a comprehensive system of norms guides the propriety or politeness, which colors everyday life. American children, though, are encouraged to make their own choices of where and how to sit, which reflects a cultural emphasis on individualism and liberty (Pang & Richey, 2007; Ramsey, 2004).

Exploring Mud Puddles — Is it OK to Get Messy?

After a break in the first rain of the season, my class went outside to get some fresh air. Lily, Jimmy, and Ruby noticed the puddles around the tree and immediately ran over to explore (see Figures 4.3 and 4.4). I was just about to stop them from touching the puddles and stomping in them, when I heard my co-teacher, Amy, encouraging the children to play with puddles by saying "Splash, splash!" She was also asking them questions about their sensory experiences with the puddles. "Is it cold?" Amy asked Lily. "It's cold, wet!" Lily said and smiled at Amy. I was very surprised to see that children were allowed and even encouraged to play freely in the puddles. In my childhood in China, playing in puddles was one of the "messy activities" that was strongly discouraged by my parents and teachers; adults usually gave children a lot of reminders about sanitary rules rather than encouraging their play. I asked Amy whether it was OK to allow children to splash with their hands and shoes and "get messy." She told me that it was totally fine, although we might need to change a child's clothes several times a day due to their exploration of puddles, water, dirt, or paints. I asked her what parents thought about it. She told me that most parents are understanding of these "messy" explorations and supportive about the clothes changing, although one grandmother did tell the teachers that she would prefer not to have her granddaughter playing in the puddles to keep her clothes clean.

FIGURE 4.3 Children playing in the puddles.

Initially, when I supervised children's sand and water play, I often confronted a dilemma. On one hand, I wanted the children to engage in free exploration as I learned its value for self-discovery and play from my U.S. early childhood classes. On the other hand, I also still had concerns about hygiene issues and about children forming good health habits, which is highly emphasized in China. I remembered that my preschool teachers and parents always gave a lot of reminders about sanitary rules and manners when I played. Further, to incorporate sanitation and safety practice into daily operation, most schools in China have school nurses to provide onsite health and medical services to children (Tobin et al., 2009).

Over time, I found that U.S. children are given more "freedom" to explore sand, water, and puddles and sanitary rules are not emphasized as strongly by teachers. As I read and learned about educational theories and perspectives on American and Western schooling, this new information helped me reflect on how I could see the value of some American open-ended play practices while retaining some Chinese values around hygiene and safety. I agreed with Lisa Delpit's (2006) idea that "we all interpret behaviors, information and situations through our own cultural lenses" (p.151), and slowly my cultural lenses were incorporating American ideas on play and exploration. I began to see that I could understand the root causes of my dilemma if I could see how and why "alternative worldviews" (Delpit, 2006) exist.

Piaget's (1945) constructivist theory also helped me understand how children have an inner drive to build an understanding of their world as they explore and

FIGURE 4.4 Children playing in the puddles.

interact with materials. I saw that children explore puddles, sand, or water because they are interested in what they can do with the materials and want to find out more. If we overemphasize rules, we can discourage children from making important discoveries about the physical world and to satisfy their sensory and cognitive needs. For instance, I noticed that when one U.S. colleague kept reminding children working at the water table not to spill water on the floor, children easily lost interest in playing. The Western cultural framework of exploration and freedom also helped me see how Lily used different body parts to fully explore the mud puddles. In addition, Amy's encouraging Lily to explore the puddles and asking her open-ended questions created opportunities for Lily to practice articulating her sensory experiences and promoted Lily's language development.

In China, more early childhood settings have begun to adopt more open-ended, child-centered activities and teaching. Since the National Education Commission of China issued the *Regulations on Kindergarten Education Practice* in 1989, early childhood education in China has made great reforms and has adopted and adapted more Western-based teaching practices. The concept of early childhood curriculum is shifting from "subject" to "experience," and play is more widely recognized by Chinese early childhood professionals as a basic component of young children's active learning, which is a developmentally appropriate teaching approach in early childhood programs (Liu & Feng, 2005).

Spoon-Feeding or Self-Feeding?

At two-and-a-half years old, Ricky was one of the children in my class. Occasionally, his parents asked me to babysit him at home. I noticed that his eating habits at home were very different from what we teach children at school, where at mealtimes, all the children sit around the table and are encouraged to use dinnerware to feed themselves. Based on my observation of Ricky at school, he was capable of eating by himself, but he often appeared to be inattentive while eating and did not eat much. While at home, at mealtime, Ricky's parents spoon-fed him while he watched his favorite TV cartoon and Ricky ate much more than he did at school. Similar in Chinese culture, many parents and grandparents spoon-feed young children and use different strategies, such as what Ricky's parents did—using TV as a distraction, to make children eat more.

The first time Ricky's parents asked me to feed him, I was reluctant to do so because I did not believe it was the right way to rear a two-and-a-half -year-old child. The early childhood trainings I had received in the United States made me believe that at this age, Ricky was supposed to learn to feed himself. After pondering this dilemma for a while, I decided to initiate a conversation with Ricky's father about Ricky's eating routines. Ricky's father explained that they used this strategy to help Ricky eat more because of their concern about his health and nutrition. As I listened to his explanation, I started to see that both the school's and the home's routine of eating had its pros and cons. The mismatch between Ricky's home and school eating routines was due to certain differences in goals. By encouraging children's self-feeding, the teachers wanted to promote children's self-help skills and help them become independent. Ricky's parents, though, were most concerned with Ricky eating more; so they played cartoons to attract Ricky's attention and spoon-fed him at the same time. The conversation with Ricky's parents reminded me of my own personal early childhood experience with eating in China, which helped me understand their perspective as my parents also had had the same concern when I was young. Historically, in Chinese culture and society, most adults believe that young children need to eat as much as possible to grow and be healthy. I respected Ricky's parents' ways of thinking and their norms, as these were part of both of our home cultures. In addition to expressing my understanding of their goals around eating, I also shared and discussed with Ricky's father the school's eating routine. Our conversation provided an opportunity for me to reflect on links between my upbringing, my center's philosophy on eating and self-care, and the varied perspectives of parents in the United States. Ricky's father and I agreed that helping Ricky eat well and become more independent were equally important. We decided to work collaboratively to find new ways to increase Ricky's self-feeding at the dining table.

The conversation with Ricky's father was an opportunity for me to reflect on the varied ways that parents raise their children and that establishing culturally sensitive and meaningful communication between teachers and parents can help avoid cultural clashes between home and school (Eberly, Joshi, & Konzal, 2007). I learned the value in the American early childhood context to recognize my own biases, put them aside, and nonjudgmentally reach out to parents to understand their ways of thinking and the norms in children's homes.

My Role as a Binational and Bicultural Early Childhoood Educator

I currently work as a Head Start Program Specialist working on program improvement and development. We serve over 250 children of mostly Chinese heritage at six preschool sites. Although I work with children and families from my home country of China, there are a number of linguistic and cultural differences between myself and the families. Many of the children were born in mainland China; they are from new immigrant families; and their home language is Cantonese, a Chinese dialect that I do not speak as my home language is Mandarin. My personal experience and background as an immigrant also differs from the families in my program, as I have lived and studied in the United States for several years and have been immersed in American cultural expectations and beliefs.

A multicultural education curriculum, an important curricular goal in many U.S. early childhood settings such as my Head Start program, is designed to incorporate children's cultures as a primary part of a program's mission and curriculum. Our program also has unique cultural goals to be culturally inclusive and responsive by supporting children's home languages and cultures and enhancing English language skills and children's cultural competency. I continue to learn about the cultures and experiences of the children and families at our sites, trying to understand their unique needs and goals and utilizing my professional knowledge of curriculum and the art of teacher reflection to help the program fulfill its mission. As a program specialist, I am responsible for raising cultural awareness among the diverse management and teaching team members and to advocate for cultural respect and understanding to promote a cohesive support system for cultural sensitivity and responsiveness.

In my continuing bicultural and binational journey, I have tried not to judge the different educational beliefs and practices from China and the United States and instead to reflect on the value of accepting and adapting particular cultural beliefs and values. This kind of reflection on particular cultural values has helped me understand how child-rearing goals, strategies, and outcomes can vary and yet still be effective (Ramsey, 2004). Through journaling and other forms of reflection (Stremmel, 2008), I have also worked to "broaden my own perspective of what's normal—to quit applying a single standard for adaptive, healthy and competent behaviors" (Gonzalez-Mena, 1993, p. 2).

Recognizing the important role of multiple cultures in shaping my educational values, beliefs, and teaching practices and seeing the influence of cultural values on how children in different social contexts are reared and educated, I now realize that teachers' cultural consciousness is critical in early childhood classrooms. As an immigrant teacher, I continue to learn about the cultural values that affect children's learning and development in the U.S. context and to remember that cultural beliefs and practices do change (Ramsey, 2004; Rogoff, 2003). However, as I continue to learn about the "mainstream" U.S. culture and dominant educational practices in my daily work, I also realize the necessity of understanding each child's home culture and that "when children caught between expectations of home and school are forced to choose one over the other, there is inevitable loss" (Trumbull, Rothstein-Fisch, & Greenfield, 2000, p. 7).

Working at a Head Start program serving mostly Chinese immigrant families and their children, I experience new challenges in my journey of understanding and embracing diversity and search for ways to support families when their child-rearing goals and strategies may not align with those of our program. My cultural consciousness journey also aids in my work with the program's teachers, who often confront the dilemma of making a choice between the "ways" of school and children's homes. The integration of reflective tools into my personal experience helps me provide these teachers with professional support and to tailor our curriculum and program to the cultures of the families we serve.

The personal teaching experiences and stories about cultures that I have shared in this chapter are meaningful because they shaped my identity in a new social context as an early education professional. Understanding and truly celebrating diversity is a continual process. Teachers need to position themselves as learners and researchers while seeking to embrace children's cultures as a critical part of the curriculum and to move toward more culturally relevant practices. A mutually beneficial relationship between an early childhood program and parents can make multicultural practices within the school truly effective (Hernandez, 2004).

In the ECE field, we all see the necessity for immigrant teachers to acquire and create a sense of belonging in their new social and educational contexts.

Nevertheless, at the same time, the cultural influences and beliefs that immigrant teachers bring should not be overlooked but taken into account. As Casey (1993) argues, "persons who live in places—who inhabit or reinhabit them—come to share features with the local landscape; but equally so, they make a difference to, perhaps indelibly mark, the land in which they dwell" (p. 305). I also agree with Elbaz-Luwisch (2004), who points out that teachers "who have made a transition from one cultural setting to another are likely to have developed an awareness of teaching and schooling in the new culture that other teachers may not have" (p. 387). I look forward to new discoveries in my journey of reflecting on my role as a bicultural and binational early childhood teacher.

References

Casey, E. (1993). *Getting back into place: Toward a renewed understanding of the place-world.* Bloomington, IN: University of Indiana Press.

Chan, C. & Rao, N. (Eds.). (2009). *Revisiting the Chinese learner: Changing contexts, changing education.* Hong Kong, China: HKU Comparative Education Research Centre.

Copple, C. & Bredekamp, S. (Eds.). (2010). *Developmentally appropriate practice in early childhood programs serving children from birth through age 8* (3rd ed.). Washington, DC: National Association for the Education of Young Children.

Delpit, L. (2006). *Other people's children: Cultural conflict in the classroom.* New York, NY: The New Press.

Eberly, J. L., Joshi, A., & Konzal, J. (2007). Communicating with families across cultures: An investigation of teacher perceptions and practices. *School Community Journal, 17(2),* 7–26.

Elbaz-Luwisch, F. (2004). Immigrant teachers: Stories of self and place. *International Journal of Qualitative Studies in Education, 17(3),* 387–414.

Freeman, N. K. (1998). Look to the east to gain a new perspective, understand cultural differences, and appreciate cultural diversity. *Early Childhood Education Journal, 26(2),* 79–82.

Gonzalez-Mena, J. (1993). *Multicultural issues in child care.* Mountain View, CA: Mayfield Publishing.

Hernandez, D. J. (2004). Children and youth in immigrant families: Demographic, social and educational issues. In J. A. Banks & C. A. McGee Banks (Eds.), *Handbook of research on multicultural education* (pp. 3–29). New York, NY: Jossey-Bass.

Ho, S. C. (1995). Parent involvement: A comparison of different definitions and explanations. *Education Journal, 23,* 39–68.

Huang, B. (2013). *Chinese preschool education and direction instruction.* (Unpublished paper). San Francisco, CA.

Liu, Y. & Feng, X. (2005). Kindergarten educational reform during the past two decades in mainland China: Achievements and problems. *International Journal of Early Years Education, 13(2),* 93–99.

Pang, Y. & Richey, D. (2007). Preschool education in China and the United States: A personal perspective. *Early Child Development and Care, 177(1),* 1–13.

Piaget, J. (1945). *Play, dreams, and imitation in childhood.* New York, NY: Norton.

Ramsey, P. G. (2004). *Teaching and learning in a diverse world* (3rd ed.). New York, NY: Teachers College Press.

Rogoff, B. (2003). *The cultural nature of human development.* New York, NY: Oxford University Press.

Stremmel, A. (2008). *The value of teacher research: Nurturing professional and personal growth through inquiry.* Retrieved from http://www.naeyc.org/files/naeyc/file/vop/Voices-Stremmel(1).pdf

Tobin, J., Hsueh, Y., & Karasawa, M. (2009). *Preschool in three cultures revisited: China, Japan, and the United States.* Chicago, IL: University of Chicago Press.

Trumbull, E., Rothstein-Fisch, C., & Greenfield, P. M. (2000). *Bridging cultures in our schools: New approaches that work.* San Francisco, CA: WestEd.

Wang, J., Elicker, J., McMullen, M., & Mao, S. (2008). Chinese and American preschool teachers' beliefs about early childhood curriculum. *Early Child Development and Care, 178(3),* 227–249.

5

LEARNING FROM REFLECTION: LESSONS LEARNED FROM A U.S. EARLY CHILDHOOD EDUCATOR TEACHING IN GUATEMALA

Molly Van Houten

My fascination with Guatemala began several years ago, sometime during my "two-month" trip to learn Spanish in 2006. I returned to Guatemala in 2010 to teach for four months and then again in 2011 to teach kindergarten and first grade for two more years. It was my initial experience in Guatemala that captured my interest and passion for teaching cross-culturally and cross-nationally. I saw the beauty in the Guatemalan culture: the traditional way of dress; the flavorful foods; the colorful buses; the "with trust in God, we'll get through it" attitude; and the over 20 Mayan languages and their indigenous ways of learning. In 2010, when my Spanish had reached near fluency from working in a Spanish immersion preschool in San Francisco, California, I decided to conduct a research project internationally as part of my MA studies. I contacted a nonprofit organization that focused on preschool development in rural Guatemala. I chose this specific organization, based in La Antigua, because it focused on not only creating preschools in rural Guatemalan towns but also educating rural teachers in early childhood development. I spoke with the schools' directors about the role I could play as an international educator.

In June 2010, I visited the organization's affiliated schools in the Antigua area and then moved north to the rural Mayan communities where I spent four months developing a relationship with affiliated schools in the Chimaltenango region. The children in these schools were from impoverished families who spoke little to no Spanish. All lived in isolated rural communities. On average, there were 15 children aged 4–6 in the preschool classrooms. The school day consisted of three hours in the morning, and due to popular demand, some schools offered afternoon classes. The teachers were educated in "learning through play" and followed a mixture of Creative Curriculum and *Curriculum Nacional Base* (CNB), Guatemala's national preschool curriculum. Many of the preschool teachers worked out of cramped classrooms located at public schools, which consisted of four rooms for the different age groupings—a preschool, a first grade, a second/third grade, and a fourth/fifth/sixth grade. The families of the villages spoke only Kaqchikel, worked primarily in agriculture, and had the most malnourished children in the area. While there, I observed constant political struggles with a cement company that wanted to put a freeway through one of the towns, and on numerous occasions, school was cancelled due to various hazards such as dangerous weather. The teachers and I communicated in Spanish, sharing ideas, challenges, and advice. My inquiry and reflection tools—written journal entries, snippets of audio-recorded conversations, photographs, and examples of children's work and play—served as data for my project and as opportunities to talk with local teachers about documentation and how to revisit aspects of children's learning.

My written journal entries quickly became both personal and professional. I carried a small notebook in my pocket and took notes wherever and whenever I could. At night, in the quiet of my damp room behind one of the schools, I reread my notes and wrote my reflections in the form of stories and poetry. I realized that I could not write only professional notes because so much of my teaching and learning involved my personal life. I lived, ate, and breathed Guatemala for five months. The photographs I took while teaching and living in the community helped document and preserve my personal memories and, in a wonderfully unexpected way, helped me share with my Guatemalan colleagues how photographs can act as a form of inquiry and reflection. At first, the teachers wondered why none of the children in my photos was smiling. They didn't understand why I avoided pictures of children posing for the camera. Explaining inquiry to the teachers was tricky at first. They had never heard of teacher research. I began printing the photos on weekend trips to Antigua and brought them back to the schools in Chimaltenango so that we could analyze them together. I modeled how to analyze a photograph, and soon we were sharing observations and reflections about student learning. By writing down their words, I believed that I was providing more visibility to their roles in Guatemala's early childhood education system as reflective practitioners.

In this chapter, I tell selected stories about my initial cross-cultural and transnational teaching in Guatemala. I describe key elements of Guatemalan early childhood education, my role as a new international ECE teacher, and the importance of community and cross-cultural understanding in international early childhood education.

This chapter chronicles my thoughts, fears, and accomplishments as I learned to navigate my new role as an international ECE educator and as a member of a new social community. My original inquiry question was: how does my status as a cultural outsider affect how I collaborate with early childhood educators in rural Guatemala? During my immersion in rural Mayan communities, the question developed into: how does an international ECE teacher, a cultural outsider, gain membership to a social and educational community to become a more effective educator? I reformulated my question by rereading and thinking about the teaching journals I had kept during my first time living in Guatemala (2006–2008).

Although I was reflecting daily, I didn't begin organizing my reflections until two months into my trip. My reflections on my teaching and learning closely followed Andy Stremmel's (2007) cycle of teacher inquiry, which emphasizes teacher questions leading to action. I used Gary Howard's (2006) achievement triangle to understand my cultural journey and looked for places where my "passion for equity" intersected with my "cultural competence" and how it led to "culturally responsive teaching" (p. 133). By first identifying myself as an individual, then looking at the Guatemalan children in the schools, and then taking a closer look at my teaching practices in rural Guatemala, I began to realize that the events happening in my day-to-day life were not only stories from my travels but also moments of professional growth in myself as an international early childhood teacher.

My teaching in Guatemala helped me work toward the goal of becoming a transformationist teacher and understanding that multiculturalism means learning continually and taking risks to become an advocate for children (Howard, 2006, p. 104). Howard's framework looks primarily at transformationist teaching in the United States. I applied his theory of what it means to be a transformationist teacher to an international context. I explored "unshared experiences," which Howard (2006) calls "knowing myself." I defined these unshared experiences as the experiences that, based on my socioeconomic, racial, and cultural upbringing, I do not share with communities in Guatemala. Next, I explored "shared experiences" as part of Howard's "knowing my students," which were the realities that the Guatemalan children, adults, and I experienced in our daily lives. Finally, I explored my practice through "shared events," such as Tropical Storm Agatha and Guatemala's Independence Day, which Howard calls "knowing my practice."

I reflected on my teaching and life in the schools' communities through a mix of teacher inquiry, narrative, and memoir. In his children's picture book *A Movie in My Pillow/Una Película en Mi Almohada*, Jorge Argueta (2001) reflects on the power of poetry as "*mis memorias, mis sueños—mis películas en mi almohada* (my memories, my dreams—the movies in my pillow)." I was also inspired to write poems and stories as a way of recording and understanding my experiences and goals as a reflective practitioner (Meier & Stremmel, 2010).

Reflective Journal:
When walking home under the moonlight, when I thought that no one would be able to hear my scream, I would put my house key facing up between my knuckles, clenching until they turned white. Those nights I would walk quickly, sweating even though it was 60° outside, stepping over a passed out *bolo* (drunk) on the street. At night I couldn't hide behind my oversized *mercado* (market) sunglasses. I was exposed.

I discovered that a critical part of transformation involves feeling "exposed" as an individual in a new cultural and social context, and the raw stories I recorded and told show how I tried to "make a place for" (Elbaz-Luwisch, 2004, p. 406) myself as an international teacher and a community member. My stories helped uncover the layers of my Guatemalan teaching experiences and how I became a member of a community of educators and of Guatemalans and expatriates in the Sacatepéquez and Chimaltenango areas. My stories and reflections relied on "small moments" (Meier, 1997) of teaching and learning and situated my learning in place and time like characters in a narrative (hooks, 2009).

These stories taught me the challenges in becoming community insiders, the pain we feel when we are community outsiders, and the beauty when insiders and outsiders collaborate and learn from each other. My stories are sacred stories, or "elusive expressions of stories that cannot be fully and directly told, because they live, so to speak, in the arms and legs and bellies of the celebrants. These stories lie too deep in the consciousness of the people to be directly told" (Crites, 1971, p. 294). They are also secret stories (Clandinin & Connelly, 1996) that I choose to share only within trusted and safe communities and that, upon meeting me, one would never guess I could tell. I tell some of them here in this chapter to share what I have learned with other early childhood teachers on a global level. Dave Huebsch (2004) argues that such personal stories relate to everyone who leaves their comfort zones to embrace new experiences as readers and listeners say, "Yes, that is me also. I have been there, too" (p. 11).

Knowing Myself

Living a Dual Identity

The story in this section is an example of Howard's (2006) "knowing myself" and its importance for the growth of my professional identity. As I tried to become part of the educational and social communities in which I lived and taught in Guatemala, I began to recognize who I was, what my biases were, and how I viewed myself as a teacher and member of the larger communities. The following story explores how I changed both personally and professionally as a multilingual, U.S.-born, White early childhood practitioner in Guatemala. This story is part of an attempt to "acknowledge the collective White reality of White complicity in dominance and oppression" both in Guatemala and my home country and to "claim a positive connection to White racial and cultural identity" (Howard, 2006, p. 110). By learning to acknowledge my past and the ways that I have ben-efited from White privilege at home and internationally, I have become more effective as an international ECE educator. My Guatemalan experiences held up a mirror, and I am more aware of how race, ethnicity, and language affect my role as a teacher and my relationships with children, families, and the communi-ties in which I live. My stories of identity change have since "remain[ed] in the background" of my evolving life story, "subtly influencing the story that is lived and told, often in ways that can only be guessed at" (Elbaz-Luwisch, 2004, p. 396).

> It wasn't until she left it all that she realized what she had to begin with.
> Room mother. PTA father.
> Every lesson a little girl could dream of:
> > gymnastics, ballet, hula, circus, ceramics, tae kwon do, judo, swimming.
> Horse shows and blue ribbons.
> Kappa Kappa Gamma & fraternity boys.
> The City.
> Home-cooked meals, organic and locally grown.
> A door always open.
> Mom, Dad, Ben, Kait, baby Isa, and Lucy Q, the little white dog.

When I first arrived in Guatemala in June 2010, I tried to keep my own childhood out of the classrooms as much as possible. It felt innappropriate to share my memories of horseback riding and ballet when these children barely had food on their plates at night. In September, a U.S. teacher sent us a box of homemade wooden Lincoln Logs, and I distributed the Lincoln Logs in our schools. I played alongside the children and teachers and remembered how my brother and I had built Lincoln Log houses for my Barbies on the living room rug (Figure 5.1).

FIGURE 5.1 Laying the foundation for una casita (a little house).

The Lincoln Logs showed me that there were objects and treasures that I could share from my childhood and that the children in Guatemala would also enjoy the same materials. I remembered Anna Golden's (2010) insight that memories for teachers "touch the core of who we are and inspire us beyond childhood, into adulthood" (p. 2). Just as Golden's teaching was influenced by childhood memories of her father, a dual identity as an international educator began to emerge for me once we shared familiar childhood toys as a community. By opening up part of my personal life to the children and teachers, I started to create new memories and new connections and I started to feel less like a social and cultural outsider.

During my first few months of teaching, I often felt pulled between two worlds, unsure where I belonged. To better understand these worlds, and my desire to belong to both, I looked at my relationships with the Guatemalan children and teachers and tried to see how we could become reflective as a community. I tried to keep in mind what Lella Gandini, in an interview with Vea Vecchi (1998), said about reflection—it is an adventure to "be shared by teachers" (p. 146). I worked to meet the nonprofit's requests of talking about early literacy and math learning while maintaining my interest in multilingualism and multiculturalism. I recognized that the teachers and I would not agree 100% on curriculum and culture. There were times of frustration and desperation, but the teachers, children, and I were able to create a mutual respect for the other's language, culture, and history. We shared challenges together. This was our adventure.

Realities of who I am and what I believe sometimes made it more difficult for me to become a part of the community in which I lived and worked. The majority of our differences were based around gender roles and equality. I understood the importance of young girls wearing *traje típico*, but encouraged teachers to allow them to change before outdoor time so that they too could run and jump and play *fútbol*. I struggled to explain to teachers and community members why it was important for little boys to play in the housekeeping corner of the classroom. And finally, while encouraging children to keep their hands on their own bodies, I was stunned by a child's response that her father didn't keep his hands on his own body. Instead of viewing these as things that I would have to overcome, I looked forward to how I could, after acknowledging my biases, still build relationships with people and become a trusted member of the teaching team. The stories, poems, and pictures presented here are part of my journey to the realization that community building and cultural understanding is an ongoing process. While I shared experiences and tried to understand the different cultural traditions and beliefs in Guatemala, I remembered Howard's (2006) words: "The unfinished work for transformationist educators is that of helping America *become* what America *says* it is. And beyond the United States, our responsibility is to join hands and share power with people everywhere who cry out for the ideals and of pluralistic democracy, not as defined by us, but as defined by them" (p. 144). As members of the educational community, we have to understand who we are to know the children in our programs so that we can make changes in education both in the United States and abroad.

Knowing the Students and Teachers

The Climb

By July 2010, I had immersed myself in the world of the students and the teachers. I lived in a spare back room of an affiliated school and ate my meals with the director's family next door. I was surprised at how quickly the teachers and I became friends, and they often invited me to town events. The town butcher knew my name, and the marketplace woman who sold *tostadas* knew that although I liked *ceviche tostadas* (fried tortillas garnished with mixed vegetables), I much preferred *remolacha* (beet salad). The children also initiated me into their community. On weekends, they spied through the window of the school to see what I was doing and if I would let them come in and play while I journaled or cleaned. They wanted to hold my hand when we saw each other on the street, telling their parents that they would accompany me to the market or the butcher or the soccer field or wherever I was headed.

Through their play, the children showed me what it meant to be a member of their communities—teaching me both inside and outside the classroom. Compared with children I had worked with in the United States, I was particularly surprised by the Mayan children's knowledge of everyday life and adult tasks. Because they are part of all community activities, "they often play[ed] at adult work and social roles" (Haight et al., Morelli et al., 2002 as cited in Rogoff, 2003, p. 299). Through observation, I used their imaginary play and knowledge of everyday life to learn how to navigate socially and culturally in my new world. My curiosity was usually well received by the children and teachers.

While the classroom was a place for the children and me to learn about one another, the walk to and from one of the affiliated schools became an opportunity for the teachers and me to get to know one another and form friendships. The teachers would often tell me that their hike was easy, although they walked up and down a steep hill, walking an average of 45 minutes each way. The alternate route involved a 30-minute walk uphill and two cramped van rides (Figure 5.2). The way back was a different route that included crossing a river while balancing oneself on a thick tree branch.

The first time I walked to the school with the teachers, I returned home and slept the entire afternoon. After the first week, my feet were so badly blistered that I had to wear sandals everywhere I went. I journaled incessantly about the hike, wondering why the teachers walked and climbed to go to work everyday. There were teaching jobs closer to their homes that probably paid more and offered tenure. As we became friends, I asked them why they walked. Guillermo, the preschool teacher, and Lalo, the first-grade teacher, commented, "We like the children," "We like the families," "It's not so bad." These answers seemed vague—wouldn't they like the children at a school closer to home? How could 45 minutes walking at a steep incline not be "that bad"? I just didn't understand why they cared so much about the community. When I started to walk with them regularly and got to know the school's children and families, their daily hike began to make more sense.

FIGURE 5.2 La subida (the climb).

UNO
The instant coffee burns my throat.
Gagging. Mixing flavors: hot dog, catsup, white bread, coffee, sugar.
Molly!! *Ya Voy!!!!!!* (I'm coming!!!!!!)
Still rubbing sunscreen onto my shoulders as I meet the teachers at the door.
7:00 am.

DOS
The van is already full.
Three men hang off the doorframe.
Their *machetes* bang.
Hunched over my backpack.
I close my eyes.
10 more minutes of sleep.
7:30

TRES
A van change in *la terminal* (the bus terminal).
Córranse pa' atrás! Háganse pa' atrás! (Move back! Move back!)
Grasping the seats, knuckles.
Con permiso, Comper, and finally *PERMISO* (Excuse me—formally, informally, and then aggressively)
With every slam of the brakes my body thrown against a fellow passenger.
He approaches. I dig around for my *quetzalitos.*
The smell of sweat.
I pay him. The van turns.
Everyone to the right side.
"*Los tres cruces, porfa*" escapes from my lips. ("The intersection, please")
Slowing down enough for the *ayudante* (helper) to grab my hand, pulling me out.
7:50 AM

CUATRO
A cloud of dust.
The hill towers in front of us.
I feel small for the first time.
I lead the way. Guillermo follows. Lalo brings up the rear.
Their *novias* (girlfriends) and the weekend's *aventuras* (adventures)
Heavy breathing tunes out their words
A sweatshirt joins a jacket around my waist.
I jump behind Guillermo.
He assures me the snake is dead.
We continue on.
I slip, steady myself, and move behind the experienced hikers.

CINCO
A wave of "*Buenos días,* Molly! (Good morning Molly!)" and "*Ya vino,* Molly! (Molly's here!)"
The children are in the middle of a serious game of kickball.
The door is still padlocked.
We arrive.
8:25 am.

The children's enthusiasm for the school day made the hike worth it—their sneaking through a hole in the fence to play before the teachers arrived, their questions about their world, their smiles. After a bloody 36-year civil war, the Guatemalan Peace Accords were signed in 1996. Since then, there has been a strong push to educate children in rural Guatemala and finally acknowledge the Mayan cultures and languages in public school classrooms. The typical challenges continue—lack of funding and physical infrastructure—but there has been a new passion from families and teachers to educate children about multilingualism and multiculturalism in Guatemala. Lalo and Guillermo didn't want a group of children to feel as though they weren't worth the teachers' long hike. They didn't want to stifle the learning of children whose people had previously been terrorized in war. As I spent more time with the teachers and students, I still dreaded the hike, but the children made the hill feel a little less steep and the path a little less dusty (or muddy, depending on the weather).

These hikes gave Guillermo and me a chance to share concerns about early childhood education in Guatemala and worldwide. We spoke about individual students and our classroom experiences. I admired Guillermo's enthusiasm and his desire to maintain the Kaqchikel language in his classroom (in my experiences, I often found that Mayan men favored Spanish over Kaqchikel in public settings). His role as a multilingual male teacher made him a confidant for many of the children and their families. It was not unusual to see Guillermo pulled aside by a mother who needed the instructions on a bottle of medicine read to her or a father who just wanted to shake Guillermo's hand and say "*Matyöx*" ("thank you" in Kaqchikel).

Knowing My Practice

Reflection in a Time of Fear

I arrived in Guatemala on May 29, 2010. Tropical Storm Agatha arrived with me. This new and unexpected experience together was a time of fear, desperation, hope, and inspiration.

> "*Hoy por ti, mañana por mí* [Today for you, tomorrow for me]"
> —*A Guatemalan Saying*

Reflective Journal
Everyone had neglected to inform *me*. Why hadn't *I* heard about Pacaya? Jennifer met me at my homestay. She had been wearing the same clothes for two days, evacuated from her home the night before. She managed a smile, telling me she was so glad I had made it to Antigua safely.
$85 for a night at the Barceló and it wasn't even safe enough for *me* to leave the hotel for a nice dinner out in *la Zona Viva* (a nickname for Guatemala City's stylish Zone 10).

I couldn't take pictures. How do you take photographs of someone who has just lost all of their worldly possessions?

I pleaded with the concierge—*I* need a taxi to Antigua, *por favorrrrrrrr*, rolling the "r" to emphasize *my* desperation.

Her fine hair was grey, piled up on top of her head in a small knot. She averted her eyes—avoiding the stares of the volunteers. Holding the beat-up wooden chair, she walked into what was left of her house.

"Why hadn't I heard about Agatha and Pacaya?" into "How can I help?"

My hand in hers, *la nena* (affectionate term for a little girl) softly outlined my blister with her fingertip. *"Qué te pasó?* (What happened to you?)" I didn't know how to answer.

I checked the weather report 10x a day, hoping for sunshine that would transform the mud to dirt and dust.

I glanced down at her artwork, a picture of her family that she was vigorously scribbling over in blue. *"Qué estás dibujando?* (What are you drawing?)" I asked innocently. "*Agua* (Water)" was the only response I got.

The airport reopened, stuck travelers caught their flights, and the volunteer efforts slowed. A fear of typhoid brought relief to a halt.

How do I help children understand and accept something that makes me shudder and look away?

I was embarrassed to reread the beginning of my reflective journal. Self-centeredness oozed from the pages, and I could barely stand to read them. The first couple of weeks were like *el gusanito* (a children's worm-shaped roller coaster) at the town fairs. When schools finally reopened on June 7, 2010, Jennifer (the nonprofit organization's coordinator) introduced me to the teachers and accompanied me to visit the nonprofit's affiliated schools. As students chatted about their experiences, their knowledge of the situation, and the news they had heard (often from television and family members), teachers tried to facilitate discussion and help the children feel safe. I didn't know how to react. My own personal distress showed in my classroom manner, and when I saw Silvia (Figure 5.3) draw a picture of her family and color over them with blue water, I knew that I would have to swallow my own discomfort to make it through June. I would have to rely on my own education in early childhood development and sociology to work with students and teachers to better understand the environmental challenge.

The horror of Agatha was homes being washed away, people disappearing beneath the mud, and families living in churches until they could return to their properties. The Guatemala relief effort began in early June, and people banded together to create short- and long-term solutions. There were children who couldn't go to school because the Guatemalan government had deemed classes cancelled until the following week. Children saw newspapers, heard stories, and watched fear in adults' faces. Embracing the image and role of the Guatemalan teacher as someone who gets involved in the social community, I joined the relief

FIGURE 5.3 Silvia colors her family over with water.

efforts. Carolyn Edwards (2011) explains how Reggio schools "see the work and development of teachers as a public activity taking place within the shared life of the school, community, and culture; they place a strong value on themselves communicating and interacting within and outside the school" (p. 198).

On the streets of San Miguel Escobar, I joined a group of local and international volunteers. I shoveled mud and came home nightly reeking of dirt and feces, sweaty and close to tears, with blisters on my hands. As a teacher researcher, I made the conscious decision not to use photographs during this time—how do you photograph suffering? How do you tell people who have just lost everything that you're sorry for their loss? Words just didn't seem to help the hurt I saw daily in their eyes. And yet, despite this time of pain, I saw groups of people, both local and international volunteers, get their hands dirty, pass out bottled water to the workers, and hold food and clothing drives. When school started again a few weeks later, I looked again to Edwards (2011), reflecting on the realness of the situation and hoping to answer her question: "What kind of teachers are needed by our children—those real individuals in the classrooms of today?" (p. 181).

To better understand the role of "place and time" in "field-based" research, Erikson and Wilson (1982) ask, "How do the ways everyday life is organized in this place compare with other ways of organizing social life in other places and times?" (p. 40, as cited in Walsh et al., 2007, p. 43). Reflecting on my involvement in the schools and communities through stories and poetry, I came to realize the importance of shared experiences, focusing more on my role as a teacher and lifelong learner and less on myself as a cultural outsider. My attitude toward the communities shifted, and the informal moments that the children, teachers, and I shared together showed me what their world looked like from their perspectives. The children and teachers supported my learning about what it meant to live in rural Guatemala, and I supported their learning by helping facilitate the beginnings of a play-based curriculum.

As I became accustomed to my new everyday lifestyle in the community, I began to share values and practices from my U.S.-based teaching experiences and teacher training to support my colleagues in the classroom. My interest in Reggio Emilia (Edwards, Gandini, & Forman, 2011) and emergent curriculum (Jones & Nimmo, 1994; Stacey, 2008) offered a creative extension to the schools' mix of Guatemala's CNB (*Curriculum Nacional Base*) and the United States' creative curriculum (Dodge, Colker, & Herman, 2002). The CNB offered a teacher-directed approach to learning and focused more on Guatemala's national standards than a multicultural and multilingual approach to learning. I continued to write in my reflective journal and "became more reflective, more critical, and more analytical" (Stremmel, 2007, p. 4) of my teaching practice in this new educational context. I looked at my journal as a tangible "thinking space" (Schwartz, Martin, & Woolf, 2002) for reflecting on the relationships I created with families, children, and teachers, and I tried to represent their voices equally.

I was aware that this kind of disciplined reflection was not a requirement for the teachers and administrators, and I was concerned that some of my curricular views might be viewed as too progressive and unconnected with their familiar routines. The teachers and I spoke about asking open-ended questions and different ways to expand their Spanish as an Additional Language program. After holding a workshop for the teachers on ways to speak with children with intentionality, I reflected in my journal about the teachers' reactions. They felt nervous about asking children questions. In response to this, we created posters for the classrooms' activity centers. The posters contained open-ended questions that teachers could ask in that specific activity center. Through reflection, I had a better idea of what teachers needed to feel comfortable with potential curriculum changes.

Crossing Borders

Safety and Trust

The affiliated classrooms were my sanctuary, areas that I understood and could maneuver within easily. Despite differences in language and culture, the events I shared with the rural Mayan communities not only taught me about Guatemala's traditions but also created learning opportunities for the children, the teachers, and me. Sara Lawrence-Lightfoot (2003) chooses to end her book *The Essential*

Conversation: What Parents and Teachers Can Learn from Each Other by quoting Gloria Anzaldúa's Borderlands/*La Frontera* (p. 246).

> In the Borderlands
> you are the battleground
> where enemies are kin to each other;
> you are at home, a stranger,
> the border disputes have been settled
> the volley of shots have shattered the truce
> you are wounded, lost in action
> dead, fighting back

In her discussion of this quote, Lawrence-Lightfoot (2003) discusses what it means to live "*sin fronteras*" (p. 247). In Guatemala, the nonprofit's affiliated schools act as "safe havens," places where multiculturalism and multilingualism are explored and recognized. The teachers and I worked together to help the children navigate their identities, take pride in their bilingualism, and realize the power of language and culture. In the above quote, Lawrence-Lightfoot shows how parent-teacher relationships can be borderlands. I viewed our schools as the crossroads, a place "*sin fronteras*" with the outside world as a borderland.

This chapter addressed a central question for my professional growth in international education: How does an international early childhood teacher, a cultural outsider, gain membership into a social and educational community and become a more effective educator? I used stories, poems, and photographs to reflect on three basic kinds of experiences from my work in Guatemala: (1) experiences that helped me to better know myself and my background, (2) experiences that I shared with the children and community members due to my everyday immersion in rural living, and (3) events that we shared together both in and out of the classroom. I learned to see how these three types of experiences/events were intertwined and to see how my initial role and identity as a cultural and educational outsider could eventually be changed to that of community insider and more effective teacher in Guatemala, the United States, and other international settings. I also learned to acknowledge my personal background and biases to understand the daily life of the community in which I lived. Only after taking these steps did I understand how my educational philosophy and that of the Guatemalan teachers could be blended to create new learning experiences for the children, the teachers, and me.

Reflecting on the meaning of my Guatemala teaching brings to light the importance of having teachers and administrators who strive to become culturally and linguistically literate. It also shows the differences that can be made in early childhood education when materials reflect the culture and traditions of the children in the classroom. Although not my original goal, my stories brought some visibility to the experiences of Guatemalan educators, students, and families.

Guatemala's peace accords were signed in 1996, but many teachers today are still afraid to speak up. This fear to voice one's opinion relates closely to what Paulo Freire (2006) calls "the culture of silence." Communities that were previously silenced by the conflict and violence still struggle to make their voices heard, and international educational exchanges can provide a way for these communities to share their struggles and victories with a broader audience. Nongovernmental organizations (NGOs) have worked with both urban and rural communities in Guatemala to provide more international recognition for the recent changes in Guatemalan public, nongovernmental, and private schools. Many other communities around the world are rebuilding after long periods of violence in their countries, and international ECE policy must support these communities and provide training for teachers and access to materials and infrastructure.

I joined the Guatemalan nonprofit organization eager to learn and immerse myself in a community so different from my own. Making people-to-people connections, I was invited into homes, classrooms, and communities that I had never imagined. After much observation and sharing, I began to ask the what-ifs (Hubbard & Power, 2003) that promoted my internal reflection and inquiry about the individual classrooms, the nonprofit organization itself, and even the role of the Ministry of Education in Guatemala's early childhood education. I also began to question the role of the worldwide early childhood community, wondering about our responsibility as educators and academics for helping our young children see themselves as global citizens. Looking toward the future, I would like to see Guatemala make reforms in its public pre-primary schools and return to the *Escuela Nueva Unitaria* (ENU) curriculum (Kline, 2002) from 1991, which encouraged family involvement and kinesthetic learning with a lower student-teacher ratio (currently there must be at least 30 children enrolled in a public pre-primary classroom to qualify for a government teacher). Originally a pilot program, the ENU was never officially adopted as the national curriculum and therefore was not applied to all public schools. Although I continue to remain an outsider to a certain degree, I have come to question the strong socioeconomic segregation of Guatemalan schools. As Guatemala's middle class grows, there is a greater need for affordable high-quality pre-primary education in urban and rural areas. Guatemala's middle class can't financially send their children to the play-based pre-primary schools in Guatemala City, but they also don't qualify for the play-based programs opened by Western and European NGOs in the rural areas and smaller towns.

My stories and poems illustrate my struggles as a bilingual international educator and how I sought to be a member in a social and professional community and to share in the effort to strengthen local schools and teaching. By making person-to-person connections, I was eventually seen as an individual in my own right and not simply as a foreign teacher. I now see that without sharing experiences within a social and professional community, I would have inhibited daily communication with students, teachers, and families and thus ignored Guatemala's multicultural and multilingual roots. As I continue to strengthen and expand my work as an international early childhood educator, these stories stay with me as memories of my early growth in cross-cultural and cross-national teaching. They provide a foundation for who I am both personally and professionally and map out how my educational philosophy continues to evolve as I become a more experienced teacher. New stories will emerge and new memories will be created as I further develop as a bilingual educator in the United States and abroad. These stories surface in my day-to-day activities as I reflect on ways to foster communities where diversity is respected and multilingual and multicultural alliances are formed across borders.

References

Argueta, J. (2001). *A movie in my pillow/Una película en mi almohada*. San Francisco, CA: Children's Book Press.

Clandinin, D. J. & Connelly, F. M. (1996). Teachers' professional knowledge landscapes: Teacher stories—stories of teachers—school stories—stories of schools. *Educational Researcher, 25(3),* 24–30.

Crites, S. (1971). The narrative quality of experience. *Journal of the American Academy of Religion, 39(3),* 291–311.

Dodge, D., Colker, L., & Herman, C. (2002). *The creative curriculum for preschool* (4th ed.). Washington, DC: Teaching Strategies Inc.

Edwards, C. (2011). Teacher and learner, partner and guide: The role of the teachers. In C. Edwards, L. Gandini, & G. Forman (Eds.). *The hundred languages of children: The Reggio Emilia experience in transformation* (3rd Ed.), (pp. 147–172). Westport, Connecticut: Ablex Publishing Corporation.

Elbaz-Luwisch, E. (2004). Immigrant teachers: Stories of self and place. *International Journal of Qualitative Studies in Education, 17(3),* 387–414.

Freire, P. (2006). Cultural action and conscientization. In B. Piper, S. Dryden-Peterson, & Y-S. Kim (Eds.), *International education for the millennium: Toward access, equity, and quality,* Harvard Educational Review, Reprint Series #42, pp. 55–74. Cambridge, MA: Harvard University.

Golden, A. (2010). Exploring the forest: Wild places in childhood. *Voices of Practitioners.* Retrieved from http://www.naeyc.org/publications/vop/articles

hooks, b. (2009). *belonging: a culture of place*. New York, NY: Routledge.

Howard, G. (2006). *We can't teach what we don't know*. New York, NY: Teachers College Press.

Hubbard, R. S. & Power, B. M. (2003). *The art of classroom inquiry: A handbook for teacher-researchers*. Portsmouth, NH: Heinemann.

Huebsch, D. (2004). *Village assignment: True stories of humor, adventure, and drama in Guatemala's highland villages*. Little Falls, MN: Highlight Publishing.

Jones, E. & Nimmo, J. (1994). *Emergent curriculum*. Washington, DC: National Association for the Education of Young Children.

Kline, R. (2002). A model for improving rural schools: Escuela Nueva in Colombia and Guatemala, *Current Issues in Comparative Education, 2(2),* 170–181.

Lawrence-Lightfoot, S. (2003). *The essential conversation: What parents and teachers can learn from each other*. New York, NY: Ballantine Books.

Meier, D. (1997). *Learning in small moments: Life in an urban classroom*. New York, NY: Teachers College Press.

Meier, D. & Stremmel, A. (2010). Narrative inquiry and stories: The value for early childhood teacher research. *Voices of Practitioners*. Retrieved from http://www.naeyc.org/publications/vop/teacherresearch

Rogoff, B. (2003). *The cultural nature of human development*. New York, NY: Oxford University Press.

Schwartz, E., Martin, A., & Woolf, K. (2002). From a descriptive stance: Prospect teachers writing. In M. Himley & P. Carini (Eds.), *From another angle* (pp. 135–146). New York, NY: Teachers College Press.

Stacey, S. (2008). *Emergent curriculum in early childhood settings: From theory to practice*. St. Paul, MN: Redleaf Press.

Stremmel, A. (2007). The value of teacher research: Nurturing professional and personal growth through inquiry. *Voices of Practitioners*. Retrieved from http://www.naeyc.org/publications/vop/teacherresearch

Vecchi, V. (1998). The role of the atelierista: An interview with Lella Gandini. In C. Edwards, L. Gandini, & G. Forman (Eds.), *The hundred languages of children* (pp. 139–147). Westport, CT: Ablex Publishing Corporation.

Walsh, D. J., Bakir, N., Lee, T. B., Chung, Y., Chung, K. (2007). Using digital video in field-based research with children: A primer. In J. A. Hatch (Ed.), *Early childhood qualitative research* (pp. 43–62). New York, NY: Routledge.

PART III

International Views on the Practice of Reflection and Inquiry

6

CRITICAL THINKING FOR AUTONOMOUS CITIZENSHIP: THE PLACE OF PHILOSOPHY FOR CHILDREN IN SOUTH AFRICAN EARLY CHILDHOOD EDUCATION

Amasa Philip Ndofirepi

> *... create citizens, and you have everything you need; without them you have nothing but debased slaves, from the rulers of the State downwards. To form citizens is not the work of a day, and in order to have men it is necessary to educate them when they are children.*
>
> *(Rousseau, 1996a, p. 247)*

> *Children will remain second class citizens until the very idea of human rights is creatively rethought in light of childhood.*
>
> *(Wall, 2008, p. 523)*

There has been a broad global push for children to be treated as active participants in society rather than as the passive recipients of adult decisions and interventions (Nichols, 2007, p. 119). The argument that children are dependent on adults and lack 'competence' has been offered as an explanation for why children lack formal recognition as a group of citizens and why they should be excluded from citizenship rights (O'Neill, 1992). John Dewey, in his hypothetical and practical efforts, positioned communal and self-corrective inquiry at the core of education and at the foundation of democratic practice (Dewey, 1915, 1916). Further, the liberal view of education maintains that education is the development of the mind through rational and reasoned means for enlightenment (Hamm, 1989; Hirst, 1974; Mill, 1859). Such an education, in Nussbaum's (1997, 2006) opinion, develops one's capacity for critical examination of oneself and one's traditions. It enhances one's ability to see oneself not only as a citizen of some local region or group but also, and above all, as a human being bound to all other human beings by ties of recognition and concern. I argue that education for critical thinking is necessary for the cultivation of democratic citizenship. To this end, critical thinking becomes *the* aim and not *an* aim of education if schools seek to cultivate independence of thought in learners (ten Dam & Volman, 2004; Paul 1992).

Pluralistic democracies such as South Africa look to education for the inculcation of the virtues of tolerance. Education for critical thinking has a role of making human beings, from an early age, aware of their potential as human beings in order to shake off the impediments of autonomy, which constrain their full physical and mental development. In this chapter, I make a case for critical thinking as an activity of developing skills and dispositions in children to produce critical autonomous citizens in the South African context. I argue in support of the view that if democracies are to be realized, then citizens must be taught to be democrats (Enslin, Pendelbury, & Tjiattas, 2001) from early childhood.

The tradition of Philosophy for Children founded in the work of Matthew Lipman in which classrooms are turned into communities of philosophical inquiry (Lipman, 2003) informs this theoretical debate. My contention is that doing philosophy with children is a critical thinking skills activity designed to contribute to the development of rational deliberation suitable for a democratic society (Lipman, 1991; Weinstein, 1991). I link critical thinking as founded in doing philosophy from an early age to education for democracy. I argue that Philosophy for Children has the instrumental value of developing a critical, autonomous adult citizenry competent to participate in democratic societies such as South Africa. To do this, I address the following focal questions:

- What constitutes critical thinking and autonomous citizenship?
- What is the status of child in the South African context?
- What are the current developments in early childhood education in South Africa?
- How do we conceptualize critical thinking in children from the perspective of critical autonomous citizenship?
- What pedagogy or pedagogies *approximate* to the enhancement of critical thinking for autonomous citizenship in early childhood education (ECE) in the South African context?

Autonomy and Critical Thinking

In its etymological context, autonomy originates from the Ancient Greek word *autonomia*. From *autonomos*, *autos* means "self" and *nomos* means "law." Hence, *auto* and *nomy* together refer to self-rule or self-government. Dearden (1972) provides a concise definition of personal autonomy. He writes that,

> A person is autonomous, then, to the degree that what he thinks and does in important areas of his life cannot be explained without reference to his own activity of mind. That is to say, the explanation of why he

thinks and acts as he does in these areas must include a reference to his own choices, deliberations, decisions, reflections, judgments, plannings or reasonings (p. 63).

While the above definition emphasizes individual activity of the mind in making choices, Callan's (1988) conception stresses that the notion involves the individuals' interests. Interests, in this sense, refer to those values and attitudes that contribute to deep meaning and a sense of personal identity. To these conceptions, Kerr (2002) adds the social dimension, whereby autonomy is "best understood as describing a particular kind of relation between individuals and their community" (p. 15) in which a justifiable notion of autonomy must be moral, that is, must involve fair treatment of others. Hence, to be autonomous is

> … to be one's own person, to be directed by considerations, desires, conditions, and characteristics that are not simply imposed externally upon one, but are part of what can somehow be considered one's authentic self.
>
> *(Christman, 2011, n.p.)*

Autonomy concerns the independence and authenticity of the desires (values, emotions, etc.) that move one to act in the first place, and its reverse—being driven by influences exterior to the self that one cannot genuinely accept—seems to infer the pinnacle of repression. What then is critical thinking?

In Dewey's ground-breaking work *How We Think* (1933), critical thinking is defined as,

> reflective thinking, a distinction from other operations to which we apply the name of thought, involves (1) a state of doubt, hesitation, perplexity, mental difficulty in which thinking originates and (2) an act of searching, hunting, inquiring to find material that will resolve the doubt, settle and dispose of perplexity. (p. 12)

To further elaborate on this definition, Paul and Elder (2009) proposed seven intellectual traits disposed by a critical thinker:

- intellectual humility (vs. intellectual arrogance)
- intellectual courage (vs. intellectual cowardice)
- intellectual empathy (vs. intellectual narrow mindedness)
- intellectual autonomy (vs. intellectual conformity)
- intellectual integrity (vs. intellectual hypocrisy)
- intellectual perseverance (vs. intellectual laziness)
- confidence in reasoning (vs. distrust of reason and evidence)

Critical thinking is thus a way of thinking about any topic, content, or problem and seeks to improve the thinker's quality of thinking by skillfully analyzing, assessing, and reconstructing it. It therefore is self-directed, self-disciplined, self-monitored, and self-corrective thinking. Hence, one can deduce that critical thinking is thinking about one's thinking. As Lipman (1991) has argued, critical thinking contributes to the development of rational deliberation relevant to a democratic society.

Unpacking Children's Citizenship

Citizenship is a contested subject (Millet & Tapper, 2011). While many scholars concur that the concept of citizenship comprises the same constituents, "knowledge, skills, values, and participation" (Marker & Mehlinger, 1992, p. 835), there is wide dissent about the role, nature, and comparative importance of each element. Marshall (1950) provides a liberal definition of citizenship as a status with equal rights and duties, whereas contemporary theory considers citizenship as encompassing both a legal status (with complementary rights and duties) and an active participatory practice that recognizes and shapes people's membership in a society (Isin & Turner, 2002). To this end, citizenship is built on four complementary elements of membership, rights, responsibility, and equality of status (Jamieson, Pendlebury, & Bray, 2011).

Membership is about belonging to a particular community and involves the acknowledgment of others as politically relevant beings; therefore, it is about being counted as a participating social actor in a community. Without recognition and respect, one's participation and hence citizenship comes to naught. The process of becoming a member of a community entails acquiring certain knowledge and skills necessary to being an active participant, in that community (especially a pluralistic society such as South Africa) demands "... care involvement and critical political awareness ..." (ten Dam & Volman, 2004, p. 372). One's political, civil, and social rights are central to one's membership of the citizenship community (Marshall, 1950), especially one's right to express an opinion and to have that opinion taken into account. Citizenship also goes with responsibilities. If members are allowed to participate in the community of other citizens, they must be accountable for their actions toward the collective (e.g., by obeying the rules and laws of that community). Citizenship amounts to treating each other with respect. To that end, citizenship entitles all to equal recognition, respect, and participation. Given this concise characterization of citizenship, what remains unanswered is whether children are citizens.

Children as Citizens

The proposal that children should be prepared to become ideal citizens has found sympathy with educators historically and currently (Jewel, 2005). Aristotle, for example, perceives children just as much "political animals" (zoon politikon) as anyone else because they too participate in and depend upon life in common with others. However, unlike adults, they are less developed and less rational (Aristotle, 1947b, p. 598). For Aristotle, children lack what he calls moral "virtues" or "excellences," such as practical wisdom or a sense of justice, and therefore have correspondingly lesser rights to social goods and participation. Nevertheless, children prove by their developing capabilities, starting at birth, that there can be an increase in social justice and rationality over time (Aristotle, 1947a, p. 361).

Autonomy and citizenship have traditionally been visualized in terms of rugged individualism and in opposition to dependency and community (Bleazby, 2006). It is axiomatic among many philosophers of education that the cultivation of autonomy in children is a pivotal aim, if not *the* aim, of liberal democratic education (Callan, 1988; Dearden, 1972; Lipman, 1998). Society is gauged by the excellence of life it provides its children. Children need to be children here and now. They cannot be the future lest they occupy the lifetimes of adults when they are children. Indeed, if children cannot be children when they are children, they will reverse the very future they are intended to be. Children require an atmosphere that provides the impetus to learn and grow up as children and good citizens. It is simply a matter of being good citizens before they can be successful leaders. Therefore, through education, children can be socialized to remain agents for change and should be prepared to contribute to the creation of a society in which they can be children here and now. An early childhood education involving them in critical thinking would assist children in the early years of their lives to develop the capacity to "... care about valuable things involved ... [to] want to achieve the relevant standards" (Peters, 1978, p. 91). Hence, there is a need for a program in early childhood education centers that enhances children's abilities to act as a collective to contribute to the improvement of thinking from an early age to build a better way of life for all.

> The United Nations Convention on the Rights of the Child acknowledges that: Children are citizens and social participants in their own right. This is a fundamental shift from the old adage 'children should be seen but not heard.' No longer are children to be thought of as the property of their parents, unwarranted of consideration until the attainment of adulthood. Children are human beings and entitled to the same degree of respect as adult human beings.
>
> *(Boshier, 2005, p. 7)*

In the South African context, the ideal of citizenship is defined in the preamble of the Constitution, which states that:

> South Africa belongs to all who live in it, united in our diversity;" it is a society "based on democratic values, social justice and fundamental human rights," in which "government is based on the will of the people," a society that strives to "improve the quality of life of all citizens, and free the potential of each person."
>
> *(Republic of South Africa, 1996, Section 108)*

Citizenship, in the above sense, embraces a set of principles that aim to incapacitate inequality and realize social justice. These include accountability, responsiveness, and openness, including participation, as fundamental constitutional principles for the ideal. In addition, Section 3 of the Constitution of South Africa further adds that "all citizens are equally entitled to the rights and privileges of citizenship and subject to duties and responsibilities" while Section 9 qualifies that "no-one may unfairly discriminate against anyone on the grounds of age" (Constitution of the Republic of South Africa, 1996, Section 9). Children have many political rights, including the right to participate in policy and law-making (Jamieson et al., 2011), and therefore are regarded as citizens under the ideal in the Constitution. However, despite the brilliantly designated ideal of citizenship in the Constitution, such a position is "not as fully imagined in the minds of many of its citizens. A long-standing tradition of gerontocracy prevails in many of South Africa's communities and households, where elders remain the key decision-makers (and younger people—especially children—have little or no say)" (Jamieson et al., 2011, p. 71). Given the conceptions of citizenship provided above, there is every reason to treat children as citizens, listening respectfully to their views and according them credit in decision making. Considering children as citizens not only admits them as "full human beings, invested with agency, integrity and decision making capacity" (Stasiulis, 2002, p. 509) but also recognizes their relationship to the political order—in everyday life and in state and global politics (Jamieson et al., 2011), hence, giving them both local and cosmopolitan citizenship.

Early Childhood Education in South Africa

The South African Constitution Section 28(3) defines a child as a person under the age of 18 years. In mid-2011, South Africa's total population was estimated at 50 million people, of whom 18.5 million were children. Children therefore constitute 37% of the total population (Statistics South Africa, 2013); hence, the South African population structure is skewed toward children. The gross deprivation and ill-treatment of children's rights, the apartheid state's war on the increasing political involvement among children, and other incidents of the 1970s led to enhanced consciousness about children's rights and the development of a robust child rights lobby. To this end, an education that provides opportunities for critical thinking can liberate the child's mind and body from an early age. Such a liberatory pedagogy of the child's education, as Mwalimu Julius Nyerere once wrote, will "… make him more of a human being … aware of his potential as a human being … in a positive, self-enhancing relationship with himself, his neighbour and his environment" (Nyerere, 1975, p. 4), thereby enabling him to "… throw off the impediments to freedom which restrict his physical and mental development" (ibid).

The Republic of South Africa's Education White Paper 5 on Early Childhood Education (2001) defines early childhood development as an umbrella term that applies to the processes by which children from birth to at least 9 years grow and thrive physically, mentally, emotionally, spiritually, morally, and socially. As a policy document, it acknowledges the following:

- There is need to an unprecedented opportunity for all children to *grow up in dignity and equality*,
- The largest part of brain development happens before a child reaches three years old and that it is during this period that children develop their *abilities to think and speak, learn and reason* and lay the foundation for their values and social behaviour as adults
- All reasonable plans for human development *begin early* with measures to *protect the rights of the child* rather than wait for 18 years later
- The care of young children should provide them with suitable educational experiences
- Young children are *capable learners* and that *suitable educational experience* during the pre-school years can have a positive impact on school learning

(Republic of South Africa, 2001)

From the above submissions, it is noticeable that early childhood education in South Africa is recognized as a crucial period in the child's development, especially in terms of the acquisition of the concepts, skills, and attitudes that lay the foundation for lifelong learning; hence, the "… early years are critical for the development of the potential of human beings" (Republic of South Africa, 2001). To fulfill this mandate, the South African government has subsidized and prioritized that all public primary schools become sites for the provision of accredited Reception Year (Grade R) programmes. The existence of independent pre-primary schools and Reception Year attached to independent schools complements an important service to early childhood education. However, overall, just 43% of children under age 5 are exposed to an early childhood program at home, at a center, or elsewhere. There are large disparities across provinces (Mokate, Cohen, Jacobs, Gregoriou, & Okon, 2011). This is despite South Africa's commitment to provide education to children to ensure the development of the child's personality, talents, and mental and physical abilities to their fullest potential as enshrined in Section 29(1) of the Constitution, which states that "*Everyone* has the right—(a) to a basic education … which the state, through reasonable measures, must make progressively available and accessible" (Republic of South Africa, 1996).

Notwithstanding the various challenges, much advancement has been made to develop the realization of children's rights in South Africa. More children are now free to express their views and perspectives about issues affecting their lives. For Tshabalala-Msimang (2009) then Minister in The Presidency, "… that on its own is a significant milestone and there is evidence on how free the children are to make their views heard" (p. iii). In South Africa, early childhood education is deemed as the first phase in children's education. Nevertheless, more attention should be given to children's meaningful participation in the decisions taken about their lives to ensure that the initiatives taken truly address their needs and have the desired impact (Mokate, 2011). It is in their daily lives during early childhood education that children can be best prepared through opportunities for critical thinking to uphold their status as critical autonomous citizens. The question is "What is the most appropriate pedagogy that offers the practice of critical thinking for children?" I argue for the classroom community of philosophical inquiry as the pivotal starting point, emphasizing children's active participation in thinking exercises, taking into account "… the social practice of thinking; both the power relations in the dialogue and children's movement, experimentation and way of being" (Bøe & Hognestad, 2010, p. 151). The next section explores how the introduction to philosophy from an early age can be the starting point for critical autonomous citizenship in South Africa.

Philosophy, Children, and Citizenship

Since the dawn of democracy in 1994, South Africa has been subject to an enduring sociopolitical change. Societal changes have been accompanied by some strides toward developing and providing an appropriate democratic education to its citizens (Ndofirepi & Shumba, 2012). If Morgan (1993) is right in asserting that "Education in today's world means becoming the architect of one's own meaning, participating fully in the great conversations of our culture, and being able to ascertain the significance of their meaning" (p. 15), then education from an early age is not just about thinking critically and creatively, but doing both well. For Jewel (2005), "… children should be educated to be ideal citizens, capable of making rational and informed decisions … [And] … societies that favour liberalism preach the primacy of the individual autonomous citizen and a concomitant tolerance for others" (p. 494). I argue that such dispositions can only be fostered and nurtured by the power of practice. Hence, the proposition of doing philosophy with children in early childhood education becomes relevant. I, therefore, now turn to the following challenging questions:

1. How can early childhood educational aims be adjusted to develop critical thinking in the child?
2. What critical skills, competencies, and attitudes does the child need to survive and contribute to a new 21st-century South Africa?

Critical thinking for autonomous citizenship occurs if individuals are actively involved in meaningful dialogical social practices. As ten Dam and Volman (2004) argue, "… the objective of critical thinking can never be realized by means of special 'programs for critical thinking' in which the relevant skills are taught as technical skill" (p. 372). It is therefore vital that links be made between the learning process and the current and future situation(s) in which learners can and want to relate the knowledge and skills they have learned. To this end, therefore, learning to think critically is a social process.

The Matthew Lipman–initiated Philosophy for Children programme is one such innovation that seeks to prepare children for citizenship in a democratic society. Lipman developed the program "… as a response to his concerns that children do not think as well as they are capable of or as is necessary for a well-functioning, truly democratic society" (Murris, 2008, p. 668). He aimed at creating a new fashion of philosophy "… redesigned and reconstructed so as to make it available and enticing to children" (Lipman, 1994, p. 262). As an art of questioning and thinking to get the meaning of the world, Philosophy for Children is driven by the community of inquiry pedagogy rooted in Dewey's conception of knowledge as a product of inquiry. For Dewey, individual autonomy as self-determining is founded in mutual adaptation, communication, cooperation, and coordination of interests, combined actions, and communal inquiry (Dewey, 1910a/1978). Schertz (2007) sums up the notion of the community of inquiry by defining it as "… a dialogical, inquiry-based pedagogy utilized within the Philosophy for Children programme to enable students to engage in philosophical discourse whereby they ask questions and deliberate concepts" (p. 192). The fundamental goal of this practice is the acquisition of individual knowledge and thinking skills and, sometimes, dispositions and not so much a matter of creating a community of others and one's becoming a participant.

A traditional (from Lipman's original view) Philosophy for Children session starts with the children sitting in a circle and being presented with a stimulus, a story, an episode, or a picture. The children, individually or in pairs, then formulate philosophical questions inspired by the stimulus. Their questions are voted on, and a dialogue on the question receiving the most votes ensues, with the teacher being both an active participant and a facilitator. At the end of the inquiry, they are asked to make a final statement about, not a conclusion to, the question. Many activities and games can be introduced to the pupils within this traditional session or outside the session to help develop skills to enable them to gain the most from the process. Lipman provides a summary of what it means for children to involve themselves as members of the community of inquiry. Lipman writes,

> When a class moves to become a community of inquiry, it accepts the discipline of logic and scientific methods; it practices listening to one another, learning from one another, building on one another's ideas, respecting one another's point of view and yet demanding that claims be warranted by evidence and reasons. Once the class as a whole operates upon these procedures, it becomes possible for each member to internalize the practices and procedures of others, so that one's own thought becomes self-correcting and moves in the direction of impartiality and objectivity. At the same time, each member internalizes the attitude of the group towards its project and procedures,

and this translates into care or the tools and instruments of inquiry as well as respect for ideas (e.g. truth) that serve to motivate the process and regulate it.

(Lipman, 1988, p. 148)

From the above, it is acknowledged that children in a community of inquiry are involved in a process of trying to understand one another. By opening up children's hearts and minds, they become open-minded, critical, and democratic citizens (Ndofirepi, 2013). If children in early childhood centers are exposed to the activities of the Philosophy for Children model as suggested above, activities that start from children's lived experiences in a democratic classroom setting, a positive sense of what it is practically to live a life of a critical, autonomous citizen would be instilled. The participatory, empowering character of the philosophical community of inquiry gives the child citizens the practice to accept corrections by peers willingly, to listen to others attentively, to revise one's views in light of reasons from others, and to open up to new ideas. By participating in a community of inquiry with others, the individual child, from an early age, develops the capacity to take control of his or her own world which, in turn, becomes a means of self-discovery and a vehicle of self-determination. As Sharp (1987) affirms, "… through speaking to other persons … one becomes a person oneself" (p. 40), and Philosophy for Children as higher-order thinking is an initiation of children into a democratic and free life (Lipman, Sharp, & Oscanyan, 1980). Early childhood education centers that adopt the principles of doing philosophy with children in South Africa will become sites where children are educated to be ideal citizens who are capable of making informed and rational decisions that affect them not only as they are in their present stations as children but also as they grow into adult citizens. While through practice in a community of philosophical inquiry with others, children will gain the traits of intellectual humility, courage, empathy, integrity, and perseverance, it is the disposition to be an autonomous critical citizen that is epitomized. Assisting children to become critical thinkers is meant to inspire them to ask questions, to seek for evidence, to pursue and examine alternatives, and to be critical of their own ideas as well as those of others. Like a critical thinking skills program, doing philosophy with children concerns treating the child as a person as well as a thinker—respecting them as persons and understanding them as "meaning making" subjects and preparing them for their adult roles (Siegel, 2003). The core enterprise of the early childhood center should therefore be "… to teach children how to think and communicate: to train them how to reflect upon knowledge on their own" (Vansieleghem & Kennedy, 2011, p. 178). Children deserve to be treated as active participants and equal subjects who do not necessarily need to be changed and prepared for something else. This view is opposed to the idea of *futurity*, which aims "to prepare students for the choices and civic responsibilities they will have in their future adult lives" (White & Wyn, 2004, pp. 2–3), thereby ignoring and devaluing children's contemporary experiences, understandings, and interests.

Current practices in early childhood education in South Africa can be criticized for making deposits of adult facts in children's heads through recitation and memorization activities at the expense of those that permit the development of independent reflective thinking. If we need critical, autonomous thinkers, then it is only pertinent to provide children from an early age with sites and opportunities that permit them to "… critically reflect on their own interests and ideas, to solve problems, to create and transform knowledge, to shape their environment and to make decisions for themselves" (Bleazby, 2006, p. 34). Philosophy for Children as pedagogy is not focused on preparation of children for future autonomy and citizenship. Instead, it is founded on the assumption that irrespective of their greater dependency, children have the capacity to think for themselves and construct their own meaning. It is acceptable to grant that although children have an undeveloped amount of autonomy, they still have a right to practice it; Philosophy for Children in early childhood education can be one such program that, if given to children, can improve their potential for autonomy.

If early childhood educators are to cultivate children as critical democratic citizens, children's daily lives must be the beginning for reflection, questioning, and gathering and assessing information that affect children's lives and are guided by an ethics of care, informed by what Siegel (2003) calls the 'critical spirit,' in which besides using reason in making a judgement, an attitude of caring is also required. Hence, Swarts (1992) came to the conclusion that "Education in the critical faculty is the only education of which it can be truly said that it makes good citizens" (p. 5). To this end, early childhood centers should take the initiative of granting children opportunities of deliberation and engagement to develop open minds necessary for the cultivation of autonomous critical citizens capable of surviving in and sustaining a democratic society that South Africa seeks to be.

Children's participation in society supports a sense of belonging and inclusion but, more importantly, teaches children how they can bring about change. Giving children early prospects for democratic participation cultivates a feeling of collective ownership and responsibility as well as problem-solving skills in collaborative ways. Maybe most critically, children acquire a belief in themselves as players empowered to impact the unfavorable conditions that shape their lives. In the process, they develop confidence and learn attitudes and practical lessons about how they can improve the quality of their lives.

With children constituting nearly 40% of South Africa's population, there is a need for a paradigm shift from seeing children as future citizens to seeing them as citizens in the here and now—from seeing them as unthinking and *becoming* beings to seeing them as critical thinking *agentic beings* that have the capacity to participate in the citizenship community. Critical thinking, through doing philosophy from an early age, favors the freedom of individuals and liberates the mind from gullibility (the unthinking acceptance of what others assert), closed-mindedness (uncritical resistance to self-correction and self-questioning), and emotive clouding (the affinity for beliefs and actions to be guided by emotions at the expense of rational considerations), all of which conflict with the spirit of free inquiry necessary for autonomous citizenship.

Conclusion

Adults and activists for children's rights have sloganeered aphorisms such as "children are now social actors, subjects in their own right, and active citizens." Evidence on the ground has proved such generalizations untrue. No substantiated programs have been put forth in support of these claims. In this chapter, I argued that critical thinking starting from an early age in the early childhood center becomes the entry point for autonomous citizenship. An education that promotes deliberative engagement among children marks a beginning of mental liberation especially given the mentality of colonialism and apartheid in South Africa. I submitted that Philosophy for Children, through the pedagogy of the community of inquiry, is one program that, if implemented in early childhood centers, makes children aware of themselves as equal members of the South African community with rights and duties of their humanity. This in turn will allow them to embrace and celebrate their democratic, autonomous citizenship. This chapter has delivered a significant foundation for policy and decision making aimed at full realization of the rights of South African children. Doing philosophy with children from an early age can become a powerhouse for the promotion of critical thinking for autonomous citizenship. South Africa's socioeconomic background demands rational citizens who can deliberate about what is in their best interest. Critical thinking skills obtained in Philosophy for Children become the root on which autonomous citizenship is founded.

References

Aristotle. (1947a). Nicomachean ethics. In R. McKeon (Ed.), *Introduction to Aristotle*. Chicago, IL: The University of Chicago Press.

Aristotle. (1947b). Politics. In R. McKeon (Ed.), *Introduction to Aristotle*. Chicago, IL: The University of Chicago Press.

Bleazby, J. (2006). Autonomy, democratic community, and citizenship in philosophy for children: Dewey and philosophy for children's rejection of the individual/community dualism. *Analytic Teaching, 26(1),* 30–52.

Bøe, M. & Hognestad, K. (2010). Critical thinking in kindergarten. *Childhood & Philosophy, 6(11),* 151–156.

Boshier, P. F. (2005). The Care of Children Act: Does it enhance children's participation and protection rights? *Children's Issues, 8(2),* 7–9.

Callan, E. (1988). *Autonomy and schooling.* Kingston and Montreal, Canada: McGill-Queen's University Press.

Christman, J. (2011). Autonomy in moral and political philosophy. Retrieved from http://plato.stanford.edu/archives/spr2011/entries/autonomy-moral/

Dearden, R. F. (1972). Autonomy and education. In P. H. Hirst & R. S. Peters (Eds.), *Education and the development of reason.* London, England: Routledge and Kegan Paul.

Dewey, J. (1910a/1978). How we think. In J. A. Boydston (Ed.), *John Dewey: The middle works* (Vol. 6, pp. 179–356). Carbondale, IL: Southern Illinois University Press.

Dewey, J. (1915). *The school and society.* Chicago, IL: University of Chicago Press.

Dewey, J. (1916). *Democracy and education.* New York, NY: Free Press.

Dewey, J. (1933). *How we think*. Buffalo, NY: Prometheus Books.

Enslin, P., Pendelbury, S., & Tjiattas, M. (2001). Deliberative democracy, diversity and the challenges of citizenship education. *Journal of Philosophy of Education, 35(1),* 115–130.

Hamm, C. M. (1989). *Philosophical issues in education: An introduction*. New York. NY: Falmer Press.

Hirst, P. H. (1974). *Knowledge and the curriculum*. London, England: Routledge.

Isin, E. F. & Turner, B. (2002). *Handbook of citizenship studies*. London, England: Sage.

Jamieson, L., Pendlebury, S., & Bray, R. (2011). Conclusion: Children as citizens. In L. Jamieson, R. Bray, A. Viviers, L. Lake, S. Pendlebury & C. Smith (Eds.), *South African Child Gauge 2010/2011* (pp. 70–73). Cape Town, South Africa: University of Cape Town.

Jewel, P. (2005). Autonomy and liberalism in a multicultural society. *International Education Journal, 6(4),* 494–500.

Kerr, D. (2002). Devoid of community: Examining conceptions of autonomy in education. *Educational Theory, 52* (1), 13–25.

Lipman, M. (1988). *Philosophy goes to school*. Philadelphia, PA: Temple University Press.

Lipman, M. (1991). *Thinking in education*. New York, NY: Cambridge University Press.

Lipman, M. (1994). *Thinking in education*. New York, NY: Cambridge University Press.

Lipman, M. (1998). Teaching students to think reasonably: Some findings of the Philosophy for Children program. *The Clearing House, 71(5),* 277–280.

Lipman, M. (2003). *Thinking in education* (2nd ed.). New York, NY: Cambridge University Press.

Lipman, M., Sharp, A., & Oscanyan, F. (1980). *Philosophy in the classroom*. Philadelphia, PA: Temple University Press.

Marker, G. & Mehlinger, H. (1992). Social studies. In P. W. Jackson (Ed.), *Handbook of research on curriculum* (pp. 830–851). New York, NY: Macmillan.

Marshall, T. H. (1950). *Citizenship and social class, and other essays*. Cambridge, MA: Cambridge University Press.

Mill, J. S. (1859). *On liberty*. Indianapolis, IN: Library of Liberal Arts.

Millet, S. & Tapper, A. (2011). Benefits of collaborative philosophical inquiry in schools. Retrieved from http://onlinelibrary.wiley.com/doi/10.1111/j.1469-5812.2010.00727.x/pdf

Mokate, L. (2011). Message by Commissioner Lindiwe Mokate, South African Human Rights Commission. In V. Barnes (Ed.), *South Africa's Children—A review of equity and child rights*. Pretoria, South Africa: South African Human Rights Commission/UNICEF.

Mokate, L., Cohen, J., Jacobs, C., Gregoriou, P., & Okon, E. I. E. (2011). South Africa's Children—A review of equity and child rights. In V. Barnes (Ed.). Pretoria, South Africa: South African Human Rights Commission/UNICEF.

Morgan, G. (1993). You say you want a revolution. *Think: The Magazine on Critical & Creative Thinking. Gr. K-8*, San Antonio, TX: ECSS Learning Systems.

Murris, K. S. (2008). Philosophy with children, the stingray and the educative value of disequilibrium. *Journal of Philosophy of Education, 42(3–4),* 667–685.

Ndofirepi, A. P. (2013). Quality education in Africa: Introducing philosophy for children to promote open-mindedness. *Africa Education Review, 9(1),* S26–S40.

Ndofirepi, A. P. & Shumba, A. (2012). Reasonable children, reasonable citizens: The contributions of philosophy for children to post-apartheid South Africa. *Journal of Social Science, 30(3)*, 251–261.

Nichols, S. (2007). Children as citizens: Literacies for social participation. *Early Years, 27(2),* 119–130.

Nussbaum, M. (1997). *Cultivating humanity: A classical defense of reform in liberal education.* Cambridge, MA: Harvard University Press.

Nussbaum, M. (2006). Education and democratic citizenship: Capabilities and quality education. *Journal of Human Development, 7(3),* 385–395.

Nyerere, J. K. (1975). Education for liberation of Africa. *Prospects: Quarterly Review of Education, 13,* 4.

O'Neill, O. (1992). Children's rights and children's lives. *International Journal of Law and the Family, 6,* 24–42.

Paul, R. (1992). *Critical thinking: What every person needs to survive in a rapidly changing world.* Santa Rosa, CA: Foundation for Critical Thinking.

Paul, R. & Elder, L. (2009). *The miniature guide to critical thinking concepts and tools.* Dillon, CA: Foundation for Critical Thinking.

Peters, R. S. (1978). Education as initiation. In R. S. Peters (Ed.), *Authority, responsibility and education* (pp. 81–107). London, England: George Allen & Unwin.

Republic of South Africa. (1996). *Constitution of the Republic of South Africa.* Pretoria: Government of South Africa.

Republic of South Africa. (2001). *White Paper 5 on Early Childhood Education.* Pretoria: Government of South Africa.

Rousseau, J. J. (1996a). A discourse on political economy. In G. D. H. Cole (Ed.), *Social contract and discourses.* London, England: Everyman.

Schertz, M. (2007). Avoiding 'passive empathy' with Philosophy for Children. *Journal of Moral Education, 36(2),* 185–189.

Sharp, A. M. (1987). What is a community of inquiry? *Journal of Moral Education, 16,* 37–45.

Siegel, H. (2003). Cultivating reason. In R. Curren (Ed.), *A companion to the philosophy of education* (pp. 305–319). Oxford, England: Blackwell.

Stasiulis, D. (2002). The active child citizen: Lessons from Canadian policy and the children's movement. *Citizenship Studies, 6(4),* 507–538.

Statistics South Africa. (2013). General household survey 2002–2011 metadata. *Statistics South Africa (2003–2012).* Retrieved from http://www.childrencount.ci.org.za/indicator.php?id=1&indicator=1

Swarts, V. (1992). *Critical thinking: Friend or foe of higher education.* Paper presented at the 78th Annual Meeting of the Speech Communication Association, Chicago, IL.

ten Dam, G. & Volman, M. (2004). Critical thinking as a citizenship competence: Teaching strategies. *Learning and Instruction, 14,* 359–379.

Tshabalala-Msimang, M. (2009). Foreword *Situation analysis of children in South Africa.* Pretoria: Republic of South Africa/UNICEF.

Vansieleghem, N. & Kennedy, D. (2011). What is philosophy *for* children, what is philosophy *with* children—After Matthew Lipman? *Journal of Philosophy of Education, 45(2),* 171–182.

Wall, J. (2008). Human rights in light of childhood. *International Journal of Children's Rights, 16,* 523–543.

Weinstein, M. (1991). Critical thinking and education for democracy. *Educational Philosophy and Theory, 23,* 9–29.

White, J. & Wyn, J. (2004). *Youth and society.* South Melbourne, Australia: Oxford University Press.

7

MY PAST IS MY PRESENT IS MY FUTURE: A BICULTURAL APPROACH TO EARLY YEARS EDUCATION IN AOTEAROA, NEW ZEALAND

Lesley Pohio, Adrienne Sansom, and Karen Anne Liley

Kia whakatōmuri te haere whakamua:
I walk backwards into the future with my eyes fixed on the past.

This chapter focuses on a specific pedagogical event situated in a local context, while concomitantly set within the milieu of national social and political debates in Aotearoa, New Zealand. We use material pertaining to the development of the New Zealand early childhood curriculum *Te Whāriki* together with current literature regarding the subsequent implementation of the curriculum as the framework for our discussion and address how the New Zealand early childhood curriculum contributes to a democratic vision for early childhood education in Aotearoa, New Zealand. First, we provide a historical overview of the reconceptualization of early years education in New Zealand and include the manner in which indigenous perspectives contributed to the shape of the New Zealand early childhood curriculum, *Te Whāriki*. Second, we look at how teachers both interpret and enact the principles, strands, and goals of *Te Whāriki* and work with the Māori assessment framework *Te Whatu Pōkeka* through the conduit of the arts from an indigenous and bicultural perspective. Incorporated in this discussion is one teacher's narrative from a Māori-medium early childhood center concerning the ways different approaches to pedagogy and assessment can contribute to a rethinking of teaching and learning in children's early years. Ultimately, we endeavor to demonstrate how a curriculum, which is seen as bicultural, holistic, and empowering, can act as a democratic and transformative agent for both children and teachers in early childhood settings for the purposes of promoting equity and social justice.

Nestled in the remnants of a historic volcanic crater, beneath the majestic mountain (ko Maungawhau te maunga), is a place called Te Puna Kōhungahunga. Te Puna

Kōhungahunga is an early childhood center founded upon the principles of kaupapa Māori. As the maunga looks over Te Puna Kōhungahunga, the mokopuna/tamariki (children) and kaiako (teachers) at Te Puna Kōhungahunga look up at the maunga, and as if connected by a large stroke of a brush, a bond is formed between the maunga and their center and between the past and the present. The connection between these two places is much more than just a view. The maunga is of historical and cultural significance to the teachers, the children, and their whānau (families and the wider community) in a way that marks a life of a people over a very long period of time. Maungawhau has become part of the center's life, just as the center has become part of the life on Maungawhau. Maungawhau bustles with mokopuna/tamariki and kaiako on a regular basis as the children and teachers visit the mountain in their fortnightly hikoi to the mountain's uppermost crater—a scar left long ago by volcanic action.

So why is this mountain important? How do regular visits to the mountain reflect the philosophical underpinnings of the early childhood center? The story about the origination of the center provides an entry point into coming to know more about the importance of the connection between the mountain and the center and what it truly means to those who inhabit both of these places. When situated within the conceptual framework of the New Zealand early childhood curriculum, *Te Whāriki*, this story, and what it stands for epitomize an indigenous and bicultural approach to early childhood education and illustrate what a democratic vision for early childhood education in Aotearoa, New Zealand, might look like.

The above scenario sets the scene and provides a context (or setting) for the content of this chapter. It is important to signify that the above description relates to one center (and, thus, community), which may or may not have correlations to other settings of a similar nature or underpinning philosophy. The center will, nevertheless, like many other early childhood centers in Aotearoa, New Zealand, have its roots firmly embedded in the foundations of the New Zealand early childhood curriculum, *Te Whāriki*. Before entering into the story of Te Puna Kōhungahunga, it is important to provide a brief overview of early years education in Aotearoa, New Zealand, and the development of the early childhood curriculum, *Te Whāriki*.

The Development of Early Years Education in Aotearoa, New Zealand

The development of the first codified early childhood curriculum in Aotearoa, New Zealand—namely *Te Whāriki: He Whāriki Matauranga mō ngā Mokopuna o Aotearoa* (Ministry of Education, 1996)—occurred concomitantly alongside other significant developments in early childhood education. These significant developments included the recognition of Māori culture, tradition, and customs (tikanga Māori) and the importance of revitalizing the Māori language (te reo Māori). With the establishment of Kōhanga Reo in 1981 (Hill & Sansom, 2010), which were full immersion Māori language early childhood centers, there was the promise for every Māori child who attended Kōhanga Reo to become conversant in both Māori and English before he or she went to school (Richardson et al., 2005). The successful growth of Kōhanga Reo, which was open to both Māori and non-Māori children, provided the impetus to create an early childhood curriculum based on Māori values and beliefs for all children in Aotearoa, New Zealand. The Ministry of Education (1996) makes this clear when noting that "all children should be given the opportunity to develop knowledge and an understanding of the cultural heritage of both partners to Te Tiriti o Waitangi" (p. 9) and that the early childhood curriculum reflects this partnership in its composition.

The basic premise for all education in New Zealand is founded on the Treaty of Waitangi (a treaty signed between the Māori people and the British Crown in 1840) (Richardson et al., 2005). *Te Whāriki*, which means "the mat" in Māori, came to fruition following ongoing reforms to New Zealand education in the late 1980s and early 1990s (Te One, 2003). According to Helen May, one of the official writers of *Te Whāriki*, the title was suggested by Tilly Reedy as a metaphor— a whāriki, which was seen "as a woven mat for all to stand on" (Te One, 2003, p. 33). What followed initially was the formation of two curricula, one in Māori and one in English. Eventually, only one overall official curriculum was written incorporating both te reo Māori and English, making it the first bilingual curriculum in Aotearoa, New Zealand.

The "whāriki" is woven with the principles and strands (Figure 7.1), which provide the warp and weft of the mat. Although the English version of *Te Whāriki* is not a direct translation of the underpinning principles found in the Māori version of the curriculum, it is fair to say that the essence of the Māori values and beliefs are adhered to as much as possible. A main focus in *Te Whāriki* is "on equity and respect for children's rights" (Lee, Carr, Soutar, & Mitchell, 2013, p. 3), with the aim to enable children to contribute to a democratic way of life as they grow up in New Zealand society. The Māori version of *Te Whāriki*, however, provides another level of insight into the foundations, and thus underlying aspiration of the curriculum especially for Māori, but also for all citizens of Aotearoa, New Zealand, pertaining to the aspirations of creating a bicultural and, ultimately, multicultural nation.

Te Puna Kōhungahunga, the center in our story, adopted a philosophy for the center based on the principles of kaupapa Māori that encourages mokopuna (the young children) to become active learners using te reo me ngā tikanga Māori me ngā akoranga o te ao whānui (holistic learning for all or, more accurately, the wider world or, in this case, the Pākehā/tauiwi world). This includes an adherence to whānaungatanga (responsibility and reciprocal obligations toward others), manaaki (respectful relationships), tuakana/teina (to look after each other), and mana tangata (to be able to stand confidently in both worlds). These principles are mirrored in the Māori version of *Te Whāriki* as evident in the following quote and support tino rangatiratanga (self-governance or self-determination) for all Māori people (Ritchie & Rau, 2010).

Te Whāriki

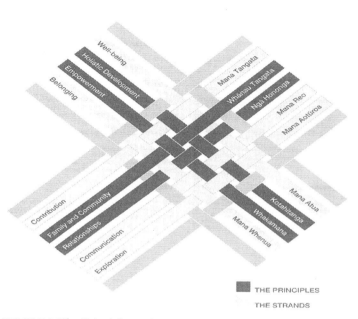

FIGURE 7.1 The Principles and Strands of Te Whāriki.

As outlined in te reo Māori (Ministry of Education, 1996, p. 35), the following is representative of mana tangata (contribution).

> Ko te whakatipuranga tānei o te kiritau tangata i roto i te mokopuna kia tā māia ai ia ki te manaaki, ki te tuku whakaaro ki te ao. E tauawhi ana tēnei wāhanga i te wairua aroha, te ngākau manaaki, me te ngākau makuru. E whakaū ana i te taura here tangata, i te mana āhua ake, me te tino rangatiratanga o te mokopuna.

Te Puna Kōhungahunga

Te Puna Kōhungahunga opened in May 2004. The center is located on the grounds of the Faculty of Education, The University of Auckland campus situated in Epsom, Auckland (Tamaki Makaurau), New Zealand (Aotearoa). It was established especially for the tamariki (children) of the Māori staff and for Māori students attached to courses held at Te Puna Wānanga (Māori Studies). The center was originally to be set up as a total immersion center, meaning that the language would be entirely in te reo Māori. Finding teachers who could provide total immersion language using te reo Māori, however, proved somewhat difficult. It was decided, therefore, to employ teachers who believed in education from a Māori perspective, even though they were not necessarily fluent in the Māori language. Following the initial instigations of some of the principle lecturing staff at Te Puna Wānanga, who were responsible for helping to establish Te Puna Kōhungahunga, Karen (whose narrative is the interweaving thread throughout this account), started as a new staff member in November 2004. She joined two others, Nan and Renee, both of whom had experience with Kōhanga Reo. Nan was fluent in te reo Māori, and Renee had some command of te reo Māori; together with Karen's passion to support all things Māori and 15 children, the life of Te Puna Kōhungahunga began.

The underlying philosophy for the center was that it would come from kaupapa Māori (as outlined above), using tikanga Māori (Māori customs, traditions, and protocols) and te reo Māori (Māori language) to underpin the curriculum. Over the years, the philosophical principles of kaupapa Māori became more established. Initially, te reo Māori was spoken at every opportunity. The use of te reo Māori was also supported by tikanga Māori, such as karakia (prayers), which were said at the beginning of each day and before meals. Other cultural protocols, such as not sitting on tables, were also adhered to. These principles became embedded in the very essence of the daily events at Te Puna Kōhungahunga.

The image of the child is of special significance at Te Puna Kōhungahunga. The child (mokopuna/tamariki) is seen as a precious taonga (treasure) (Pere, 1994). The child is honored and treated with respect—as a gift from the whānau/family. The children come to the center bringing their ancestry—their heritage—where connections are made through their whakapapa (the genealogy of a person or taonga). The teachers know who the children are and where they come from—they are related to each other (whānaungatanga). These interrelationships are intensified through the daily ritual of greeting, where a mihi mihi with the children is shared each morning. These greetings (mihi mihi), which are expressions of each child's whakapapa, engender special connections between the teachers and children. In addition, for the tamariki and kaiako at Te Puna Kōhungahunga, relationships with place are as important as relationships with people. The children share their pepehā, telling where they come from and where their mountain, their river, their waka, and their marae are.

The physical building of Te Puna Kōhungahunga and its site meant that there were places where one could stand and look at the maunga from different vantage points in Te Puna. The outdoor area of Te Puna was developed to reflect the essence, or underlying principles, of the center from a Māori perspective. This involved creating an environment that consisted of native trees and plants, such as kawakawa, titoki, and kowhai trees and harakeke (flax) and clematis to replicate the natural habitats of Aotearoa, New Zealand. The native plants, together with the sand and rocks, pool and rivers, speak about the culture of the center beyond just using te reo Māori. There is also a connection with the marae (meeting place) on the campus next door, and the children and teachers visit the marae to support the powhiri (welcome ceremony to greet people). Marae protocols, such as the karanga (a call used to invite people onto the marae), are incorporated into the children's play because the children witness these events as part of their lives and culture and replay their experiences.

Ko Maungawhau Te Maunga

Because of the physical relationship between the locality of the center and the volcanic mountain that sits next door, a different form of relationship developed that was more than just physical. Maungawhau was to become a protector and a guardian of the center. From a Māori perspective, the land (whenua), including its mountains (maunga), rivers (awa), lakes (roto), oceans (moana), forests and trees (ngahere), and native bush and flax (harakeke), is invested with a spiritual meaning (wairua) or energy (ihi) and life (ora) or life force (mauri) that cannot be disconnected from those who live on and with the land. As the following whakatauki, which is central to Te Puna Kōhungahunga's philosophy, attests, nature is critical to Māori as a source of energy—"something that can stimulate imagination and develop creativity" (Kelly & White, 2013, p. 17).

> Whangaia te manu
> o te ngahere ki te miro
> nana te ngahere
> Whangaia te tamaiti
> ki te matauranga,
> nana te Ao!
> Feed the bird
> of the forest the miro berry
> and he will own the forest.
> Feed the child
> knowledge
> and he will own the world.

It became apparent to the teachers at the center that the affiliation with Mangawhau should be strengthened. Inspired by a particular approach undertaken by another early childhood center (see Lawrence, 2005; Ministry of Education, 2007), Karen initiated a visit to Maungawhau. As Karen states: "We should really get to know Maungawhau because we've got the song for Te Puna—'Ko Maungawhau te Maunga' which is the mountain of this area. This is the mountain

FIGURE 7.2

of Ngāti Whatua who belong to this land that we're on, it's their mountain; they whakapapa to that mountain; it's not just a hill—it's got a spiritual meaning to it." Guided by someone who was knowledgeable about Maungawhau, the teachers went for a hikoi (walk) around Maungawhau to discover areas of significance, which they could then share with the children. This would also add a deeper meaning and understanding of the mountain and its importance when the children sang the song about Maungawhau.

The historical and spiritual connection with Maungawhau for those who are Ngāti Whatua is of particular importance. As expressed by Karen: "It's a place where people lived. Back in the 1600s, a huge community lived on that mountain. They bred there, they ate there, they loved there, they left there, and they are buried there. They swapped between that place and Maungakiekie. There's all that history. If you walk up there you see all the shells that were left there, so it's a place where I feel you have a real connection with the people from the past—and it is part of who we are. For me, it is particularly special for those of us who are Ngāti Whatua (local people), and the whole idea of having those atea in the cone—where they gave offerings—usually it was for a form of early civil defence such as 'don't blow up on us and keep us from harm.' Now it is about us giving something back to the maunga. When we do our walking tours we thank the mountain for protecting us."

Spurred on further by Lawrence's (Ministry of Education, 2007) excursions to O-Huiarangi (Pigeon Mountain) as referred to earlier and Maley-Shaw's (2013) forest walks in Fiordland, visits to Maungawhau became a fortnightly venture.

Karakia, to give thanks to the mountain, is a ritualistic part of every visit. The mountain rewards her visitors with fine weather almost every time the tamariki and kaiako visit, which is a sign that the mountain looks after the children and teachers from the center. There is a sense that the mountain hears the children's voices and truly appreciates these fortnightly visits. These regular trips to the mountain provide the opportunity for the children to develop a connection with the mountain over time so that they come to see it as their mountain. The children are at one with the mountain and enjoy an embodied relationship with its terrain. They like to go to the top and roll down in the grass as a way of familiarizing themselves with the mountain and all it has to offer. And while the mountain takes care of the children and teachers, they, in turn, take care of the mountain to ensure its sustainability (e.g., taking care to remove any rubbish that may be left behind after the visit so that the environment is left as nature intended). This is kaupapa Māori in action—a philosophy that has real-life consequences and can be enacted in everyday events such as this hikoi to the mountain. But what does kaupapa Māori mean to someone who grew up in Aotearoa New Zealand as both Māori and Pākehā?

Some of the reasons behind kaupapa Māori as the underpinning philosophy for the center are found in Karen's story, who, as a person who grew up in Aotearoa, New Zealand, with both Māori and Pākehā ancestry, can share something about what it means to be an indigenous person in Aotearoa as well as understand what it means to grow up "walking the space between" (Webber, 2008) both socially and politically. The early childhood center reflects this sociocultural history and acts as a place that empowers those who enter its doors, individually, collectively as a community, and as an indigenous culture.

Growing up as Maōri and Pākehā in Aotearoa, New Zealand

Karen's Story

"A lot of my whānau (family) beliefs and values came from my father (whose heritage was English and Scottish). My father's family farmed together and were very close as a family. I also received many of my beliefs and values from my mother, especially from a Māori perspective. My mum's side is where the Māori comes from via her great-grandmother. My mother's grandfather spoke te reo Māori but he never passed it on to my grandmother and in a matter of a few generations it was lost. When I first started speaking te reo, my family used to make fun of my pronunciation compared to theirs. We always knew we had Māori ancestry but we never went to the marae. My mother only talked about being Māori if one of the locals died and she went to the funeral (tangi) at the marae. Her cousins were more Māori because their mother was Māori and their father was part Māori, whereas Mum's father was Pākehā. When I go home they say I'm more Māori than the Māori—so when I'm in Te Puna I'm happy because I know everyone is supportive.

I really grew up in a Pākehā world with things Māori thrown in without realising where they came from until I went to university in Waikato and did Ki Taiao Early Childhood Education from a Māori perspective. My mother did things from a Māori perspective — like not sitting on tables. I see that not sitting on tables makes good sense, because your food goes on the table and this protocol has become important to me. Māori values were learned alongside Nan at Te Puna, and it's been integral to my life having an older woman who had grown up as a Māori and could guide me. When Nan left it broke our hearts, but she left at a time when she knew I would be all right and that my instincts were setting me in the right direction. I still check with those people who I consider have greater instincts than me on some things, but I'm strong enough in what I do. For example, if we haven't got a man to talk for us at a powhiri, we aren't going to stop having a powhiri when taking our children to school, which is what we always do when we take children to visit their school. This is our transition to school — when we take our children—our taonga—our gift—from Te Puna to that school."

These beliefs in Māori ways of being and knowing permeate throughout the curriculum. In the following section, we show how the relationship between the maunga and Te Puna is realized through the conduit of the arts in association with *Te Whāriki* and *Te Whatu Pōkeka*.

Indigenous and Bicultural Arts Pedagogy with Links to Te Whāriki and Te Whatu Pōkeka

A particular component of the visits to the maunga is an active engagement through the arts. In Aotearoa, New Zealand the bicultural early childhood education (ECE) curriculum *Te Whāriki* "emphasises the critical role of socially and culturally mediated learning and of reciprocal and responsive relationships for children with people, places and things" (Ministry of Education, 1996, p. 9). The arts hold a strong position in the ECE curriculum and act as a form of expression of one's place, culture, and identity. As Orr (2005) contends: "[T]he place itself becomes an agent in the curriculum." (p.97, cited in Kelly & White, 2013, p.15) This notion is manifest in seeing the maunga as an "atelier"—a place where children dig with their hands and minds to find meaning of their experiences at the maunga (Gandini, 2005).

An aspect of this connection between people, places, and things was giving the children sketchbooks in the hope that they would draw pictures of the maunga. What actually resulted were pictures of monsters (taniwha). This was, perhaps, because of an imaginative manifestation of the children's ability to reenvision stories they knew or had been told regarding taniwha, or monsters, that lived in the mountains. With the introduction of a visiting visual artist to the center, (see Duncan, 2011), the children became acquainted with screen printing, and following further visits to the maunga, the children began re-creating their interpretation of the maunga through screen printing or paints and taking these back to the maunga to present as gifts.

The concept of "gifting" was also part of a dance and drama performance, which grew out of the story of Mataaoho, who, as the story goes, was a giant who once lived on Maungawhau. The children and teachers created a walking performance that was enacted on the mountain. The drama performance evolved from working with a dramatist and creating a dramatic or imagined world, initially at Te Puna, before taking the penultimate performance of reenacting the story back to the mountain. It was important to give something back to the mountain because, as Karen stated, "When the mountain gives us beautiful weather and a beautiful time every time we're up there, this is our way of giving something back to the mountain." Part of the performance also involved entering the crater (which is not usually allowed because it is an archaeological site) to offer the monster food—the whole crater was the monster's food bowl. The significance of the atea (an open space in which to declare/speak) being positioned historically in the center of the crater is important, however, because it was where the people used to give offerings to the mountain as a form of early civil defense, or protection from being blown up by a volcanic eruption.

Singing on and for the mountain also occurred in conjunction with the walking performance. As the children sung the center's waiata (song) "Ko Maungawhau Te Maunga" about the mountain, they were able to understand where they were in relation to Te Puna. While they were standing on Mangawhau and looking out at Waitemata Harbour, the children knew that Te Puna was on the other side of the mountain. In addition, one of the fathers performed a stylized dance on the mountain while wielding a long spear (taiaha). The children could replicate the actions of twisting the long spear with their hands. Dance experiences also came in the form of getting in touch with the landscape and creating shapes to replicate the various landmarks that could be seen from the mountain. These embodied experiences became embedded in the children's bodies and rematerialized spontaneously on consequent ventures to the mountain. The children interpreted their surroundings through their bodies, through their voices, and through their physical and spiritual connection to the land.

This idea of connection to the land resonates with Wattchow and Brown's (2011) concept of a sense of place, which, they uphold, should be considered as "a personal, intimate and embodied encounter" (p. 72). In addition, Lines (2001) suggests that one could learn about the land from what one "could sit on, touch, taste, see, breathe, smell and move within" (p. 65, as cited in Wattchow & Brown, 2011, p. 72). In a similar vein, Davies (2000) talks about the human connection with the earth, suggesting that we are "embodied beings not separated from the earth but of it" (p. 185). She describes this state of existence as "the subterranean possibilities earthed in the human body as a result of experiencing life—*in(terre)conscious: between earth and consciousness*" (Davies, 2000, p. 185) [emphasis in the original], which is something akin to the young children's and the teachers' embodied connectedness to the earth during their excursions to the mountain. Our bodies are, in a sense, inseparable from the landscape we inhabit and all that has occupied that space over time. Correspondingly, Pelo (2013) proposes that "embodied, sensual encounters with the natural world matter" (p.123) because it not only expands how we know where we live but also engenders a sense of caring for where we live. Consequently, "body and place are inextricably linked" (Wattchow & Brown, 2011, p. 72) and our identities become connected to the place we "claim as ours" (Gentry, 2006, p. 13, as cited in Wattchow & Brown, 2011, p. 66).

FIGURE 7.3

For Karen, the bond between the people and the land was particularly important because of her spiritual relationship with the mountain and the memories
of the people who used to live there. Each of the arts experiences was a way of
assimilating what occurred in that place and space a long time ago and acted as

FIGURE 7.4

link to history and to the site. The visual arts experiences create a connection with the site, the waiata expresses the cultural identity of the people and where they are from, and the dramatization of the story and the dance experiences further generate an attachment between the people and the place.

FIGURE 7.5

In accordance, these excursions to the mountain have associations with *Te Whatu Pōkeka* (Ministry of Education, 2009), the Māori assessment framework. A whatu pōkeka is a baby blanket made of muka (fibre) from the harakeke (flax) plant. Albatross feathers are carefully woven into the inside of the blanket to provide warmth, comfort, security, and refuge from the elements. The pōkeka takes the shape of the child as he or she learns and grows. It is a metaphor for these arts experiences, where the development of what occurs is determined and shaped by the child. The principal focus of *Te Whatu Pōkeka* is the assessment from a Māori perspective of children's ways of knowing in a Māori-medium early childhood setting. This approach ensures that the children's voices are heard and their cultural capital is acknowledged. Embedded within *Te Whatu Pōkeka* are the Māori principles of *Te Whāriki* (Ministry of Education, 1996). One key principle—whānau tangata—acknowledges the relationships children have with place and their cultural and historical inheritances.

Connections to the mountain continue to be established through the gifting of natural installations using papatuanuku (items of nature from earth mother) and leaving these behind on the mountain in a variety of places—under favorite trees, behind rocks. The idea is to leave natural things on the mountain and not to desecrate the site of the tamariki and Tane (God of the Forest). Through their engagement with environmental resources on the maunga, the "children possess a natural openness to the potential of materials. When adults become aware of this process, they find different ways to watch and listen to children," providing valuable windows into children's minds (Weisman Topal & Gandini, 1999, p. 1). As Wrightson and Heta-Lensen (2013) describe, engaging with ngā toi [the arts] in the natural environment strengthens young children's affinity with the place. Here, we can make links to the Māori assessment framework *Te Whatu Pōkeka* (Ministry of Education, 2009), as the following synopsis exemplifies.

FIGURE 7.6

On one occasion, while the tamariki and kaiako were taking shelter from the rain, a chance encounter with a humanly created spider's web woven between the branches of a tree provoked the tamariki and kaiako to craft their own weaving out of small branches they found lying on the ground. The work straddles another set of tree trunks close by, creating a response to the spider web installation. The weaving connected features of the bush, just as the traditional Māori weavers wove their stories through the intricate patterns within their flax work, forging relationships between the environment and the people (Giamminuti, 2013). The collaborative work created by the tamariki and the kaiako still remains, although temporary and dependent on the elements, and serves as a reminder of the rich, yet fragile beauty and attributes the natural environment holds. Ephemeral artworks invite a closer empathy and rapport with nature and have the potential to nurture an ecologically sensitive relationship with the world (Kelly & White, 2013). These are the moments when the children and teachers can spend time studying the intimate details of nature, such as spider webs and seed pods—things that would otherwise be missed if little time was taken to appreciate the places where children stop and take notice of their world.

Curriculum as Place

Place has long been a matter of importance to the Māori people. Māori are referred to as tangata whenua (meaning people of the land) (Ritchie & Rau, 2010). The significance of place throughout the history of Māori existence is evidenced by the establishment of the marae, or meeting place, which creates a place for Māori to gather as iwi (tribes)—to stand on one's taurangawaewae (ground on which one stands). In fact, the incessant dispute over land rights in Aotearoa, New Zealand, is testimony to continuing politics regarding the ownership of terra firma between the New Zealand government and local Māori. The interplay between space and place, self and other, places and bodies (Duhn, 2010) produces knowledge that can be situated or, as sometimes referred to, that provides "a pedagogy of place" (Callejo Perez, Fain, & Slater, 2004, as cited in Duhn, 2010, p. 313). Cultural identities are validated, and people's lives and ways of being and doing become the genesis of authentic grassroots knowledge. From a cultural and/or indigenous perspective, how one sees the importance of place can differ from other understandings of attachment to place, especially those pertaining to ownership based on individualized capital gain.

As educators connected to the field of early childhood education, we are committed to the Treaty of Waitangi (Te Tiriti o Waitangi) and the principles embedded in *Te Whāriki*. This calls us to consider the ways in which principles, such as kotahitanga (holistic development)—a commitment to the collective and relationship to "people, places and things" (Ministry of Education, 1996, p. 11)—and whakamana (empowerment) are brought into play in the everyday process of teaching and learning. Wrightson and Heta-Lenson (2013) illuminate this point, claiming that "Ngā toi [the arts] provide an opportunity to deepen understandings of the implicit beliefs held by Māori, particularly in relation to the natural world, but also in relation to Māori histories, values, and their locations within the land to one another." (p. 18) Moreover, Pohio (2009) claims that "connections to New Zealand's indigenous culture and its history as a bicultural nation" (p. 29, in Fuemana-Foa'i, Pohio, & Terreni, 2009) are strengthened and enriched through the exploration of those experiences that have meaning imbued with Māori ways of being or knowing.

The arts are "not separated from the life world of Māori kaupapa (cultural customs and protocol) and Māori tikanga (cultural values and beliefs)" (Pere, 1994; Ritchie, 2008; Sansom, 2013, p. 35). The arts are integral to daily life and are shared through meaningful experiences alongside others (tamariki and kaiako) in the spirit of ako, which is the Māori concept for reciprocity between teacher and learner, history and culture, place and people (Pere, 1994). This form of reciprocity reflects "the Maori value of manaakitanga, the obligation to care for others" (Ritchie, 2008, p. 205) in all its forms.

Conclusion

The encounters between the mountain and the children and teachers through the conduit of the arts, as illustrated in this chapter, provide an example of the significance of place, history, culture, and identity and explain how this is enacted from a kaupapa Māori perspective. Both the real and spiritual ways of being connect to indigenous ways of knowing that signify an educational setting that is different—a setting that honors the capacities and strengths young children bring to the center on a daily basis. This cultural capital, which is embedded in Māori customs, traditions, and protocols using tikanga Māori and te reo Māori underpinned by the principles of ngā akoranga o te ao whanui (holistic learning for all or learning about the wider world), whanaungatanga (responsibility and reciprocal obligations towards others), manaaki (respectful relationships), tuakana/teina (to look after each other), and mana tangata (to be able to stand confidently in both worlds), supports the concept of tino rangatiratanga (self-governance or self-determination) and echoes a pedagogy of equity and social justice. This is a sanctioning of a commitment to indigenous rights within a country that is facing its colonized past and engaging in a decolonizing process, which, in its own way, is plagued by the nuances and specters of the not quite distant past (Jones, Holmes, MacRae, & MacLure, 2010).

Revisiting and historicizing the concepts of traditional understandings of teaching and learning begin to debunk entrenched perceptions of ways of knowing and foster different constructions of what constitutes knowledge, both in and outside educational settings, especially when imbued with the richness of culture. An educational setting such as Te Puna Kāhungahunga epitomizes a space and, indeed, "a living, breathing curriculum of humanity" (Sansom, 2011, p. 111) or *currere* (Pinar, 1975, 1994, 2004) that is both democratic and transformational for all who enter its doors—the tamariki, kaiako, and whānau. It is a place where everyone can stand—a space that is democratic and acts as a transformative agent for children and teachers, where the curriculum is not only place but also the children and the teachers (Pinar, 1994, 2004; Sellers, 2013). As Wattchow and Brown (2011) explain: "Our experience of place is always a combination of a specific physical location, our embodied encounter, and cultural ideas that influence the interpretations that we make of the experience" (pp. ix–x).

The final words are Karen's: "The Pākehā come to our center too, and I think—'what can they get from it?' But then, they are learning about te reo Māori, and if you feed them knowledge, Pākehā are also finding a place—a relationship with which to stand strong in who they are. We all have stories—heritages—you whakapapa to where your roots are. We honor the Māori whakapapa—but we could also honor the Samoan, Tongan, Niuean and Pākehā, but I suppose we are selective and just use the Māori whakapapa. But people choose to come to the center because, even if they're not Māori, they see some connection. Although I ask the question, 'are we practising reverse apartheid?' in actuality, I think we need an environment like this until such time as Māori are completely sure of who they are, or are acknowledged in that way by everybody in New Zealand. Until that time, you might always have to have places like this—this is a place where we declare."

Glossary of Māori Terms

ako	learning through reciprocity
Aotearoa	Maori name for New Zealand
ātea	free space to speak/declare
awa	river/stream
hikoi	walk/excursion
ihi	energy
iwi	tribe
kaiako	teacher
karakia	prayer
karanga	call of welcome
kaupapa Māori	Maori principles
Kōhanga Māori	early childhood language nest
kotahitanga	holistic development
manaaki	respect
Māori	Indigenous person of New Zealand
marae	meeting place
maunga	mountain
mauri	life force
mihi	greeting
moana	sea
mokopuna	children/grandchildren

ngā toi	the arts
ngahere	bush/forest
ora	life
Pākehā	white European
pepehā	short statement
powhiri	welcome ceremony
reo	language
roto	lake
taiaha	wooden spear
tamariki	children
tangata whenua	people who were first on the land
tangi	mourn
taniwha	fabulous monster
taonga	valuable/treasure
tauiwi	foreigner
taurangawaewae	ground on which one stands
Te Tiriti o Waitangi	The Treaty of Waitangi
tikanga	cultural practices/customs
Tino rangatiratanga	self-governance/self-determination
tuakana / teina	siblings/peers
waiata	song
wairua	spirit
waka	canoe
whakamana	empowerment
whakapapa	genealogy
whakatauki	saying/proverb
whānau	extended family
whāriki	mat

References

Davies, B. (2000). Eclipsing the constitutive power of discourse: The writing of Janette Turner Hospital. In E. A. St. Pierre & W. S. Pillow (Eds.), *Working the ruins: Feminist poststructural theory and methods in education* (pp. 179–198). New York, NY: Routledge.

Duhn, I. (2010). Mapping globalization and childhood: Possibilities for curriculum and pedagogy. In G. S. Cannella & L. D. Soto (Eds.), *Childhoods: A handbook* (pp. 309–318). New York, NY: Peter Lang.

Duncan, J. (2011). *Visual arts inspirations: People, places, things.* [DVD]. Auckland, New Zealand: The University of Auckland.

Fuemana-Foa'i, L., Pohio, L., & Terreni, L. (2009). Narratives from Aotearoa New Zealand: Building communities in early childhood through the visual arts. *Teaching Artist Journal, 7(1),* 23–33.

Gandini, L. (2005). From the beginning of the atelier to materials as languages: Conversations from Reggio Emilia. In L. Gandini, L. Hill, L. Caldwell, & C. Schwall (Eds.), *In the spirit of the studio: Learning from the atelier of Reggio Emilia* (pp. 6–15). New York, NY: Teachers College Press.

Giamminuti, S. (2013). *Dancing with Reggio Emilia: Metaphors for quality*. Mount Victoria, Australia: Pademelon Press.

Hill, D. & Sansom, A. (2010). Indigenous knowledges and pedagogy: A bicultural approach to curriculum. In D. E. Chapman (Ed.), *Examining social theory: Crossing borders/reflecting back* (pp. 259–270). New York, NY: Peter Lang.

Jones, L., Holmes, R., MacRae, C., & MacLure, M. (2010). The critical politics of play. In G. S. Cannella & L. D. Soto (Eds.), *Childhoods: A handbook* (pp. 291–305). New York, NY: Peter Lang.

Kelly, J. & White, E. J. (2013). *The ngahere project: Teaching and learning possibilities in nature settings*. Hamilton, New Zealand: The University of Waikato.

Lawrence, R. (2005). Stories beyond the gate. *The First Years Ngā Tau Tuatahi: New Zealand Journal of Infant and Toddler Education, 7(2)*, 15–17.

Lee, W., Carr, M., Soutar, B., & Mitchell, L. (2013). *Understanding the te whāriki approach: Early years education in practice*. New York, NY: Routledge.

Maley-Shaw, C. (2013). *Nature discovery: A research project on the effects on the holistic development and wellbeing of children being in nature on a regular basis in a New Zealand context*. Invercargill, New Zealand: Southland Kindergarten.

Ministry of Education. (1996). *Te whāriki: He whāriki mātauranga mō ngā mokopuna o Aotearoa: Early childhood curriculum*. Wellington, New Zealand: Learning Media.

Ministry of Education. (2007). *Kei tua o te pae assessment for learning: Early childhood exemplars*. Wellington, New Zealand: Learning Media.

Ministry of Education. (2009). *Te whatu pōkeka: Kaupapa Māori assessment for learning*. Wellington, New Zealand: Learning Media.

Pelo, A. (2013). *The goodness of rain: Developing an ecological identity in young children*. Redmond, WA: Exchange Press.

Pere, R. (1994). *Ako: Concepts and learning in the Māori tradition*. Wellington, New Zealand: Te Kōhanga Reo National Trust Board.

Pinar, W. (1975). *Currere*: Toward reconceptualization. In W. Pinar (Ed.), *Curriculum theorizing: The reconceptualists* (pp. 396–414). Berkeley, CA: McCutchan.

Pinar, W. (1994). *Autobiography, politics, and sexuality: Essays in curriculum theory, 1972–1992*. New York, NY: Peter Lang.

Pinar, W. (2004). *What is curriculum theory?* Mahwah, NJ: Lawrence Erlbaum.

Richardson, L. et al. (2005). *Bateman New Zealand encyclopedia* (6th ed.). Auckland, New Zealand: David Bateman.

Ritchie, J. (2008). Honouring Māori subjectivities within early childhood education in Aotearoa. *Contemporary Issues in Early Childhood, 9(3)*, 202–210.

Ritchie, J. & Rau, C. (2010). Kia mau kit e wairuatanga: Countercolonial narratives of early childhood education in Aotearoa. In G. S. Cannella & L. D. Soto (Eds.), *Childhoods: A handbook* (pp. 355–373). New York, NY: Peter Lang.

Sansom, A. (2011). *Movement and dance in young children's lives: Crossing the divide*. New York, NY: Peter Lang.

Sansom, A. (2013). Daring to dance: Making a case for the place of dance in children's and teachers' lives within early childhood settings. In F. McArdle & G. Boldt (Eds.), *Young children, pedagogy and the arts: Ways of seeing* (pp. 34–49). New York, NY: Routledge.

Sellers, M. (2013). *Young children becoming curriculum: Deleuze, te whāriki, and curricular understandings*. New York, NY: Routledge.

Te One, S. (2003). The context for te whāriki: Contemporary issues of influence. In J. Nuttall (Ed.), *Weaving te whāriki: Aotearoa New Zealand's early childhood curriculum document in theory and practice* (pp. 17–49). Wellington, New Zealand: NZCER Press.

Wattchow, B. & Brown, M. (2011). *A pedagogy of place: Outdoor education for a changing world.* Victoria, Australia: Monash University.

Webber, M. (2008). *Walking the space between: Identity and Māori/Pākehā.* Wellington, New Zealand. NZCER Press.

Weisman Topal, C. & Gandini, L. (1999). *Beautiful stuff! Learning with found materials.* Worcester, MA: Davis.

Wrightson, H. & Heta-Lensen, Y. (2013). Ngā taonga tuku iho—Māori visual arts and cultural fusion: Studying authentic engagement. In B. Clark, A. Grey, & L. Terreni (Eds.), *Kia tipu te wairua toi—fostering the creative spirit: Arts in early childhood education* (pp. 13–25). Auckland, New Zealand: Pearson.

Māori Whakatauki. Retrieved from http://natswb.wikispaces.com/Whakatauki

8

DISCOURSE ON A PEDAGOGY OF LISTENING: THE ROLE OF DOCUMENTATION IN PROMOTING REFLECTION AND ANALYSIS OF LEARNING IN ITALY AND THE UNITED STATES

Brenda Fyfe in consultation with Carlina Rinaldi

Introduction

This chapter was written by Brenda Fyfe, Dean of the School of Education at Webster University in St. Louis, Missouri, in collaboration with longtime colleague and friend, Carlina Rinaldi, President of Reggio Children. Our purpose is to present the core concepts and values of the Reggio Emilia approach to early education that resonate with the focus of this book, the role of teacher reflection in educational change and transformation in international early childhood contexts.

Our aim is also to point out signature elements and systemic characteristics of the Reggio Emilia approach that are challenging for any teacher, but perhaps even more so for U.S. educators who are operating in the contexts of school systems that are not grounded in this approach or the values underlying it. But first we share some of the history of this impressive school system, a history that illustrates the strong collective movements that led to this transformative educational approach. Then we examine the process of collaborative action research and collective reflection that are at the heart of the pedagogy of listening in Reggio Emilia schools and schools in the United States that have been inspired by the RE approach.

History of the Reggio Municipal Preschool and Infant-Toddler Centers

The story of the current municipal system of preschools and infant-toddler centers that has inspired the world began in the early 1960s when women's organizations convinced the municipality of Reggio Emilia to develop a network of educational services for children from 3–6 years old. In 1963, the municipality opened its first preschool. And in 1971, a year before national legislation mandated services for infants and toddlers, the first municipal infant-toddler center opened in Reggio Emilia. "These schools were inspired by and gave continuity to the experiences of a number of self-managed schools for young children established by women's organizations, opened just after the end of World War II, particularly in the country villages and outlying areas of Reggio Emilia" (Historical and Cultural Notes on the Reggio Emilia Experience, 2010).

The women and men of Reggio Emilia were determined that their children and future generations of children would never again submit to a dictator such as Mussolini. They were determined to uphold the rights of all citizens to a free and democratic society, where children's rights and voices were recognized and embedded in early childhood educational experiences. They were not aiming for minimal quality to meet the "needs" of young children; rather, they sought to create public schools that continuously strove to achieve the maximum level and quality of educational services that are the "rights" of all young children and their families.

In a publication from the Preschools and Infant-Toddler Centres Instituzione of the Municipality of Reggio Emilia, a fundamental declaration of rights is articulated. It reflects what the early promoters of this school system believed in the sixties and what the city of Reggio Emilia continues to support.

> Education is the right of all, of all children, and as such is a responsibility of the community. Education is an opportunity for the growth and emancipation of the individual and the collective; it is a resource for gaining knowledge and for learning to live together; it is a meeting place where freedom, democracy, and solidarity are practiced and where the value of peace is promoted. Within the plurality of cultural, ideological, political, and religious conceptions, education lives by listening, dialogue, and participation; it is based on mutual respect, valuing the diversity of identities, competencies, and knowledge held by each individual and is therefore qualified as secular and open to exchange and cooperation.
>
> *(Indications: Preschools and Infant-Toddler Centres of the Municipality of Reggio Emilia, p. 7, 2010)*

The distinction that Reggio educators make between needs and rights is all-important when considering ways toward a socially just and humane world where dialogue and reflection are highly valued. As Loris Malaguzzi, the founder and guiding genius of the Reggio Emilia pedagogical approach, once said, "If the children had legitimate rights, then they also should have opportunities to develop their intelligence and to be made ready for the success that would not, and should not escape them." He explained that if we believe that children have rights, we must treat their ideas seriously, learn with them side by side, and provide rich opportunities to develop their intelligence, not just offer safe and secure custodial services to meet their basic needs. Malaguzzi and his colleagues operated on the premise that children possess extraordinary potential, strengths, ideas, opinions, and theories and that this should lead educators to the role of colearners with children—learning from them as well as with them (Gandini, 1993).

The women's organizations that fought for this kind of quality public service convinced the municipality of Reggio Emilia that this was the right of all children, not just the children of families who could afford expensive schools. Today 89% of children aged 3–6 years attend the municipal, state, private, or co-op schools that have a special agreement for professional development support from the municipal school system. Forty-one percent of children aged 3 months to 3 years attend a municipal or co-op school. This is in a city of 170,000 inhabitants that has increased by 30,000 residents in the last ten years. Most of these new residents are immigrants from 120 different countries and cultures. So the city has experienced new families, new languages, and new expectations.

The municipal schools have always given first-priority acceptance to families with low incomes or other challenging family contexts. They fully include and support children with disabilities, who they refer to as children with "special rights." These children are fully included and dispersed across the school system rather than segregated or clustered in a few schools. The criteria for acceptance are established by the Community-Early Childhood Councils and made public to all residents. "The contribution of families to the operating costs of the educational services are determined by criteria that inform "a sliding scale for the fees according to family income; equity and solidarity, with particular attention to the most socially and economically disadvantage families" (*Indications*, 2010, p. 19).

At this point in history, as at many other moments in time over the past 50 years of the school system's existence, the city is experiencing difficult financial challenges due to economic crises in Italy and the world. But this city and school system continue to persist, working collaboratively with its citizens to find creative solutions without diminishing quality. Howard Gardner, a longtime admirer of the Reggio approach, states the following in his preface to *The Hundred Languages of Children* (1993, 1998, 2012):

> It is tempting to romanticize Reggio Emilia. It looks so beautiful, it works so well. That would be a mistake. It is clear … that Reggio has struggled much in the past and that, indeed, conflict can never be absent from the achievements of any dynamic entity. The relationships to the Catholic Church have not been easy; the political struggles at the municipal, provincial, and national levels never cease, and even the wonderful start achieved by the youngsters is threatened and perhaps undermined by a secondary and tertiary educational system that is far less innovative. Reggio is distinguished less by the fact that it has found permanent solutions to these problems—because, of course, it has not—than by the fact that it recognizes such dilemmas unblinkingly and continues to attempt to deal with them seriously and imaginatively.
>
> (*Edwards, Gandini, & Forman, 1993, 1998, 2012, p. xv*)

Jerome Bruner, who has been visiting, studying, and supporting the municipal preschools and infant-toddler centers over the last 20 years, commented that upon first visiting the world-famous preschools of Reggio, he was not prepared for what he found. "It was not just that they were better than anything I'd ever seen. What struck me about the Reggio preschools was how they cultivated imagination and, in the process, how they empowered the children's sense of what is possible" (Commentary in *The Hundred Languages of Children* catalog, 1996). Bruner recognized that these schools, this community, and this pedagogical approach were promoting a truly humane way of being. "We were involved collectively in what is probably the most human thing about human beings—what psychologists and primatologists nowadays like to call 'intersubjectivity,' which means figuring out mutually what others have in mind. It is probably the final flowering of our hominid evolution, without which human culture could never have developed, and without which all deliberate efforts at teaching would fail" (p. 117).

Becoming an International Force in Early Education

American educators started to become aware of the Reggio Emilia schools and their pedagogy of listening in the late 1980s. Teachers in the St. Louis, Missouri, area were introduced to the approach in 1991 when The Hundred Languages of Children Exhibition was sponsored by Webster University with support of the St. Louis Association for the Education of Young Children and local educators. Today the Reggio approach, as it is commonly called, is a force in early education around the world. It is a movement that is always seeking new understandings of young children's thinking through ongoing research embedded in the daily life of its schools.

At the heart of this approach is a pedagogy of listening (Rinaldi, 2006). This pedagogy requires daily reflection and analysis of children's learning processes and paths, which teachers document through photos, video, audio recordings, and collections of children's work. Group reflection with colleagues, children, and families is supported by documentation, which serves as a common platform for discourse about children's learning. This discourse informs the design of new learning experiences that will have continuity with children's thinking.

Peter Moss, Emeritus Professor at the Institute of Education, University of London, is one of the foremost experts on comparative early childhood education, especially in the realm of public policy and educational quality. In a personal communication solicited for and quoted in another article (Fyfe, 2012), he wrote: "Reggio Emilia is part of a vibrant and creative international movement contesting a hegemonic Anglo-American narrative on early childhood education that is highly instrumental in rationality, positivistic and economistic in its thinking, and supremely technical in its practice. Reggio helps resist this 'dictatorship of no alternative' by showing there are alternatives, alternatives that welcome and desire complexity and diversity, politics and ethics, dialogue and democracy" (personal communication from Peter Moss, 2012).

Educators from around the world visit Reggio Emilia, many repeatedly, because they know that each time, they will learn of creative new research, new discoveries, and new hypotheses about teaching and learning that the Reggio Emilia educators have observed, documented, and analyzed. The ongoing collaborative action research that is part of daily life for Reggio educators, children, and families drives continuous educational change and transformation.

In a speech to educators in St. Louis (2001), Carlina Rinaldi explained, "The aim of this path and this educational experience is to form individuals who are autonomous and capable of participating in a community that they will be able to transform without necessarily denying themselves. Individuals who are interested in humanity in all its strengths and weaknesses. People who are convinced that the main good to pursue is that of a shared humanity, shared universality, people who know how to look at the universe beyond the tribes and privileges with which we so often identify ourselves, who know how to look toward the future with optimism, with the courage of optimism that children know so well and know how to give to us."

Reggio has given educators across the world a common set of principles to explore and enact in many different cultural contexts. The Reggio principles of collaboration, interdependence, and colearning demand a cultural shift for U.S. educators in their everyday life with children and adults. It demands that teachers move from individual study and reflection on learning to collective reflection on children's learning processes and pathways. It requires educators to shift from a focus on children as individual learners to an additional focus on the learning of the group and of children as group learners (Krechevsky, 2001).

The essential elements for the operation of the infant-toddler centers and preschools include organizational strategies for participation and coresponsibility that ensure community-based management; democratic decision making at the classroom, the school, and the system levels through vehicles such as regular class meetings with children; a community early childhood council for each school; a system-wide council (the interconsiglio) that serves as a liaison with the city administrators in relation to school policy and qualitative development; and pedagogical coordination to ensure professional development and ongoing research and innovation to constantly reexamine and update quality of experiences and learning (Fyfe, 2012).

When she spent a semester as a visiting professor at Webster University in 2001, Carlina Rinaldi helped those of us in St. Louis to recognize culture as something we produce, not just exist within. Culture is not stagnant. It is created through patterns of human activity that are based on shared values and become visible through symbolic structures that give activities significance and importance. The Reggio Emilia approach promotes a culture of reflection. It promotes a shared commitment to the pedagogy of listening that involves collective reflection on documented traces of learning. Educators, parents, and children value participation, democracy, interdependence, difference, and dialogue. The Reggio Emilia approach to early childhood education is by no means culture-bound. Rinaldi emphasizes that each Reggio program is an "original." While the pedagogy of listening, dialogue, and parental involvement form Reggio's backbone, she says, "There are many Reggio approaches because … every place has to be different" (Schwartz, 2002).

In many of her publications and speeches, Carlina Rinaldi emphasizes that the Reggio way of listening means to be open to doubts and uncertainty. She goes further to state that this listening means to be open to being in crisis.

> When I was in the United States, many, many teachers were worried because a child was in crisis or they themselves were in crisis. It is not always bad to be in crisis, because it means that you are changing. The problem is when you are not in crisis, because maybe you are not really listening to the life around you. To be open to the others means to have the courage to come into this room and say, "I hope to be different when I leave, not necessarily because I agree with you but because your thoughts caused me to think differently." That is why documentation is so fascinating and so difficult to share. Documentation as visible listening can help you to understand and to change your identity, and can invite you to reflect on your values. Listening also means to welcome uncertainty, to live in the zone of proximal development. Only if I have doubts, can I welcome the others and have the courage to think what I believe is not the truth but only my point of view. I need the point of view of the others in order to confirm or change my own point of view.
>
> (*Rinaldi, personal communication, 2010*)

The full set of core principles of this educational project and the essential elements for the operation of these schools are documented in the publication *Indications: Preschools and Infant-Toddler Centres of the Municipality of Reggio Emilia.* A summary of those principles with some elaboration follows. Reggio educators will always remind us that all of these elements are connected and cannot be separated from each other. They form a system of relations and operations.

Principles of the Educational Project [bold-faced statements below are from *Indications: Preschools and Infant-Toddler Centres of the Municipality of Reggio Emilia,* April 2010]

1. **Children are active protagonists in their growth and educational processes.** Each child has potential, capabilities and spontaneous curiosity that adults must help to sustain at a high level. Therefore, it is the role of the teacher to support children in expressing their ideas, opinions, theories—to develop their own voice and sense of agency in problem solving, researching and finding meaning in the world, and doing all of this in relationship with others.

2. **The Hundred Languages: Children possess a hundred ways of thinking, of expressing themselves, of understanding, and of encountering**

others, with a way of thinking that creates connections between the various dimensions of experience rather than separating them (e.g. through gestures, words, dance, sculpture, painting, drawing, etc.).

3. **The right to participation: children, educators and parents are active stakeholders, collaborating in learning together, researching together, and making decisions together about their learning.** This means teachers cannot operate in isolation from each other or from children and families as they plan and process learning experiences. Children and parents have the right to be involved, not just informed.

4. **Listening: Listening is an ongoing process that nurtures reflection, welcoming, and openness towards oneself and others; it is an indispensable condition for dialogue and change.** Children's ideas, opinions, observations, and work must be valued, studied with colleagues and parents, and probed in order to engage in true dialogue about the meaning they are making of their experiences and in order to know how to support their motivation and pursuit of learning. This principle applies to the learning of adults as well. It is only through active listening that true dialogue and deep understanding of each other's perspectives can be achieved.

5. **Learning as a process of individual and group construction.** While individuals make sense of their world through all their interactions with it, individual learning is enhanced through interactions and sharing of perspectives with others. Such interaction and relationships are cultivated with peers, adults, and the environment. A disposition to be responsible for each other's learning is cultivated through collaborative research and comparison of ideas.

6. **Educational research** through a process of negotiated learning through documentation, discourse and design (Forman & Fyfe, 1998, 2012).

7. **Educational documentation**—a process that supports educational research and makes learning visible and assessable. It enables children and adults alike to reflect, revisit an experience, reconstruct the meaning of that experience, assess and interpret it from multiple perspectives.

8. **Progettazione**—a process of projecting possible directions for long- and short-term experiences that support continuity for children's thinking and are responsive to their ideas, passions, and curiosities.

9. **Organization**—of time, work, and spaces to support collaboration, administrative and political activity, and working conditions.

10. **Environments, spaces, and relations**—every feature of internal and external spaces are designed to foster interaction, autonomy, explorations, curiosity, and communication.

11. **Professional development**—an ongoing right and duty of educators.

12. **Assessment**—through continuous reflection on individual and group learning processes, operational systems of support for the schools and participation of all stakeholders.

These essential elements and the organizational strategies that support them create a very strong system and an environment that enables and cultivates reflection and transformative learning of children, educators, and families. A major challenge for teachers in the United States who want to apply the principles and practices of the Reggio approach is that U.S. educational systems are not generally organized to support this level of participation, collective reflection, and ongoing study of children's learning processes.

Challenges for U.S. Educators

In preparation for writing this chapter, Carlina Rinaldi and I agreed that I would interview a number of teachers from the St. Louis area to probe what they perceive to be the most challenging features of the Reggio approach, especially in regard to the practice of collective reflection and analysis of documentation. We decided that it would be useful to talk with teachers who are new to the Reggio approach, just beginning to implement the concepts of observation and documentation that are critical to a negotiated learning process that subscribes to the pedagogy of listening. The second group to be interviewed was a group of teachers who had been studying the Reggio approach for five to six years and were working together in a diverse, urban public school district, Maplewood Richmond Heights (MRH), at the Early Childhood Center, which serves pre-K through first-grade children and their families. Webster University's School of Education has partnered with this district for six years to support the development of preservice and inservice teachers in regard to the Reggio approach to early learning. One feature of the partnership is shared funding of a pedagogista, who works side by side with teachers to mentor, coach, model, and support the pedagogy of listening and the ongoing processes of observation, documentation, and collective reflection. Jennifer Strange, an adjunct faculty member at Webster University, serves in this role of pedagogista and supervises interns who are completing a graduate certificate codesigned with colleagues from Reggio Emilia to prepare teachers for the role of pedagogista.

Summary of reflections from nine teachers who were just beginning their study of the Reggio approach through graduate coursework at Webster University
The biggest challenges they reported:

- They had difficulty finding time to observe, document, and dialogue with colleagues.
- It was hard to identify what to observe and document and why.
- They had difficulty being well-organized and prepared to document critical moments, especially those that were unanticipated.
- Some school systems do not support teachers coming together regularly to study documentation of children's learning. No time or structure is built into the workweek for such reflection with colleagues.

- Colleagues in their schools lack understanding and commitment to study documentation with them.
- Although many school systems purport to value and offer time for teacher collaboration, some interpret this to mean time for planning next week's lessons, not time for reflection on last week's learning.
- Some thought that as school systems got larger, it was more difficult to have meaningful dialogue with colleagues.

Teachers in the preschools and infant-toddler centers of Reggio Emilia have shared similar concerns in regard to the first three of the challenges identified in the list above. They discussed these concerns and reflections in an interview with Amelia Gambetti, a veteran teacher with the Reggio school system for 25 years and now an international liaison for consultancy to schools for Reggio Children. The interview was published as part of a research study conducted by Reggio Children and Harvard's Project Zero in the book *Making Learning Visible: Children as Individual and Group Learners* (Gambetti, 2001). Even in a system where support for reflection is built into the workweek, new teachers who are just beginning to understand their role as researcher think they need more time each day for reflection with colleagues. They also are concerned that they have not yet learned what to observe and document. One teacher, Teresa, states, "I had a tendency to observe everything. It was difficult to choose and therefore I felt more and more the need to exchange views with others. I think it's only by exchanging views with others that you can gain a better understanding of what you should be observing" (p. 125).

Summary reflections from five more experienced teachers from the Maplewood Richmond Heights (MRH) School District

Experienced teachers still find it challenging to organize time for documentation and collective reflection, although their weekly and monthly meeting schedules for professional development days have been reorganized many times to allow for this. School district professional development initiatives, which are required reporting for Head Start, and other testing mandates and data analysis often compete for the time set aside for collective reflection on documentation.

Teachers who work in close proximity and have been participating in group reflection on documented learning processes for many years now crave these opportunities to reflect, but all of them expressed major reservations about engaging in this kind of process when they first began studying the Reggio approach. All expressed concern at the beginning about giving and receiving feedback from colleagues—concern that they were going to hurt the other person's feelings. But they also felt deflated when colleagues would question or critique their documentation. And most of these were teachers who had taken coursework or completed graduate degree programs where they learned and practiced this kind of collective reflection and analysis of documented learning experiences; where they worked in small groups to study, question, and interpret documentation collected and presented by each of them; where they were required to put their own inter-pretations into relationship with those of others; and where they were encouraged to engage in discourse and debate as they worked together to give the strongest interpretation of learning that comes from considering multiple perspectives.

Some of the new Reggio teachers interviewed by Amelia Gambetti (2001) expressed similar concerns about the process of reflection with colleagues during the first year of teaching. One teacher, Simona, stated, "I didn't feel up to it and wasn't able to interpret my unease. I couldn't feel the solidarity of the group. I think this was because I was worried about being judged, and maybe I felt I was bothering people." Another, Paola, commented, "If I think back to my first expe-riences here, one very important thing to me was to have questions to ask. I used to find it difficult to ask questions and to find questions to ask. Then, with time, it became much easier for me to think of questions."

As noted, over time, the experienced MRH School District teachers reported that they grew to welcome feedback from peers and were eager to gather per-spectives that differed from their own. They thrive on having opportunities to dis-cuss children's learning with colleagues. They said, however, that the old feelings of being at risk come back when new colleagues join the group. They may think that a new colleague is too fragile or not open to hearing a different perspective or interpretation. They seem to fear being perceived as critical or antagonistic. They don't want to "stir the pot" as one of them said.

Many agreed that it is easier to give feedback with strangers who don't work with you than with colleagues you work with every day. Perhaps that's why it may feel less threatening in a structured college class where most teachers are not working colleagues, although sometimes college students express similar concerns.

We have learned that the use of a protocol for examining documentation can sometimes alleviate the concerns about criticism. For example, in our Webster University graduate classes, we use a protocol for looking at student work that was developed by educators at Harvard's Project Zero. This protocol asks the group to look at the documentation to (1) identify exactly what they notice, (2) determine what they question, (3) share what they interpret and (4) discuss what the implications might be for future learning experiences. The sequence of gathering multiple perspectives based on each of these questions in order provides a scaffold that seems to alleviate the anxiety that teachers might feel about a more informal study of documentation. As stated, the protocol insists that everyone begin by simply stating what he or she sees or hears in the docu-mentation and then question or wonder about what is not evident. All this is done before moving on to interpretation or speculation, which is usually the point when teachers are more sensitive to what they may perceive as critique, judgment, or evaluation by others. Once everyone, including the presenting teacher, sees that the documented learning of children, not the teacher, is the focus, everyone can relax into a common frame of mind that moves them to search for meaning, not evaluation.

In her book *Art and Creativity in Reggio Emilia* (2010), Vea Vecchi reflects that in the early years of the Reggio school system, Loris Malaguzzi was always challenging teachers and atelieristi like herself to become 'professional marvellers' of children rather than instructors. She states, "[T]he largest changes in mental framework and point of view were caused by observing and documenting children's strategies" (p. 108). Amelia Gambetti reflected that an important occasion that contributes significantly to professional development is "when we organize a visual show or a video. Indeed, I think that making a slide show, a video, or a publication means having the opportunity to construct a sort of "reflective space" that stands between ourselves and our action. A space where, to an extent we can 'invite' other people's contributions and comments." (Gambetti, 2001, p. 123).

Every one of the St. Louis experienced teachers indicated that the practice of observing and documenting children's strategies reveals incredible potential and intelligence of children that might otherwise have been overlooked. Careful study and group reflection on documentation enables them to marvel at the thinking of young children and helps them to identify new strategies for bringing forth children's imagination, creativity, and higher-level thinking. Teachers reported that the opportunity to regularly consult and reflect with the pedagogista was invaluable and essential to the experienced teachers' ability to observe, document, and analyze children's learning processes and paths in a way that supports a form of progettazione, which teachers defined as short- and long-term projects or investigations based on children's research.

Both sets of interviewed teachers from St. Louis shared their observations that when reflection becomes a part of the daily life of teachers and children, the children develop the habit of questioning, voicing opinions, sharing their thoughts, and listening with an open mind to others.

Systemic Differences

The isolationism that is built into school systems like most in the United States where the typical K-12 teacher is the sole adult in the classroom, contributes to the habit of thinking, planning, working, and reflecting independently from colleagues in the school rather than collaboratively. In Reggio schools, there are two teachers for each classroom, and they collaborate on every aspect of their daily lives with children. "Co-teaching, and, in a more general sense, collegial work, represents for us a deliberate break from the traditional professional and cultural solitude and isolation of teachers" (Gandini, 1998, 2012). Teaching teams throughout the school meet weekly to share, discuss, and analyze observations of children's learning. The schools generally include no more than four classrooms of 25 children each. This small size school is considered critical to maintaining a strong community of learners, yet the number of children in each classroom is a little larger than typical preschool classes in the United States.

As noted earlier, several teachers interviewed for this article indicated that in their experience, the larger the school is, the harder it is to build learning communities that engage in reflection on learning processes. They reported that conversations and agendas in meetings and gatherings in such large school systems frequently move to logistics, administration, procedures, and event planning. Little time is left for intense study and reflection on documented learning of children.

In U.S. schools, the Reggio concept of the pedagogista is not widely understood, nor is it a funded position. The roles of pedagogista and atelierista in Reggio Emilia municipal preschools and toddler centers are fundamental to the school system. Each school has an atelierista, who collaborates with teachers and children to support expressive language of children through the arts, especially in regard to long-term projects. The Municipal School System of the Reggio Emilia Preschools and Infant Toddlers employs one pedagogista for approximately every three or four schools. The pedagogista shares his or her extensive knowledge of child development, skills of observation and documentation, and the pedagogy of listening while serving as a coach, mentor, and coresearcher with teachers and atelieristi. Each pedagogista also works in collaboration with parents, the city government, and the School Advisory Councils. The pedagogista "collaborates closely with the work groups (teachers, atelieristi, cultural mediators, cooks, and auxiliaries) at their assigned schools or centers on all sorts of educational issues and problems concerning children in which the ultimate goal is to promote teachers' autonomy rather than take over and solve their problems. Observation, interpretation, and documentation are the processes that invite regular 'reconnaissance' among these work groups" (Cagliari, Filippini, Giacopini, Bonilauri, & Margini, 2012, p. 139).

In the U.S. Reggio–inspired schools that I have observed, the principal, the director, or a teacher leader may have some responsibility for supporting teachers' understanding of the Reggio approach, but seldom is there a designated position of pedagogista. More often there exists a position identified as an atelierista, who, depending on his or her background, may also mentor teachers in the manner of a pedagogista. In public and many private school systems, the position of art teacher is an established part of the school system and funding formula, and therefore, it may be easier from a financial point of view to transform the role of art teacher to that of atelierista. On the other hand, the position of pedagogista is not prevalent in the United States and would require new funding.

Because those of us in the United States are adapting the Reggio Emilia approach to fit our unique cultural contexts, these structural features of the staffing and administration of schools will vary. But in consideration of the focus of this book, it could be important to make further comparisons of the typical structure and administrative organization of U.S. schools with those of the Reggio school system to recognize how these systems enable different levels of reflection.

As noted earlier in this chapter, the municipal system of preschools and infant-toddler centers of Reggio Emilia build a system of relations where everything and everyone are connected (children, teachers, other school staff, parents, citizens, administrators, public officials, and outside audiences). "The pedagogista cannot interact with just one part of the system and leave the rest aside." The Pedagogical Coordinating Team is "responsible for guaranteeing the quality of early child-hood services in the municipal system and ensuring that they are consistent and unitary. The municipal infant-toddler centers and preschools of Reggio Emilia do not have on-site directors. Instead, administrative and supervisory functions are distributed across the system" (Cagliari et al., 2012, p. 136).

Community-based participation permeates the entire Reggio system. At the school level, this means community-based management through an Advisory Council made up of elected members who include parents, teachers, and other community members. The Advisory Council of each school attends to adminis-trative concerns, but more often focuses on addressing the needs of families and educators. A representative from each school's Advisory Council serves on the Advisory Council Coordinating Board, which reflects on system-wide issues and negotiates decisions, which are reported to the municipality of Reggio Emilia. At every level, the philosophy of collective reflection and community decision making is valued and enacted. Every individual is responsible for sharing his or her perspective and then listening with an open mind to those of others. The group members reflect together to come to negotiated decisions that represent agreement—or at least shared understanding—across the group.

In contrast, American schools typically have a principal or director who holds administrative, supervisory, and professional development responsibilities for his or her school. This school leader usually works within a larger school system. In public school systems, the principals report ultimately to a superintendent who reports to an elected school board. The entire system is more hierarchical than the system in Reggio Emilia, and most often daily decision making is delegated to a few individuals rather than to a collective of representatives from every constitu-ency and seldom through a negotiated consensus with teachers. At the school level, parents may participate in a parent teacher organization, but seldom is this kind of group involved in high-level school decision making.

This is not to say that there are no schools that operate from a more collabora-tive frame of reference. It is just that most U.S. school systems are not organized to require collaboration and group reflection at every level, as is the case in Reggio Emilia. The core values of participation and democracy impact every aspect of the Reggio school system.

In an article on the role of reflection in the pedagogical moment, Max Van Manen, a noted Canadian professor of curriculum and qualitative research meth-odology, explained:

> *It is usually impressed on novice teachers that good teachers are reflective teachers; beginning teachers are taught how to adopt a reflective orientation to their practice. However, beginning teachers are not usually taught that the daily life of dealing with*

children is such that there seems little opportunity for reflection—and that this is not the fault of teachers or anyone else. Rather, it is a feature of living together in constant interaction which prevents teachers from critically reflecting on what they are doing while teaching. Even more problematic is the lack of opportunity to reflect thoughtfully with colleagues about the practice and meaning of pedagogical experiences. One of the challenges of the teaching profession is to try to create those spaces and opportunities. This is partly a professional political issue.

(Van Manen, 1991)

It is clear that the municipal preschools and infant-toddler centers of Reggio Emilia have created and continue to create the spaces and opportunities for reflection as part of a continuous search for meaning with children. Educational leaders of the municipal preschools and infant-toddler centers and Reggio Children understand that the creation and sustainability of spaces and opportunities for reflection is a professional political issue that cannot be taken for granted. They work diligently to establish continuous communication and partnership with the community to develop shared understanding and support for this reflective approach to early education.

We end this chapter with an excerpt from a speech given by Carlina Rinaldi to faculty at Webster University in 2004. She spoke of the primary aim of schools that use reflection to inform change and transformation.

We feel and we know that the primary aim of schools, including schools for young children, is no longer to educate citizens of a city and of a nation with a well-defined identity, but to educate "citizens of the world" who are conscious of their roots but open to cultural and geographical horizons with no boundaries.

We were strongly convinced that individuality and intersubjectivity are not in opposition but are complementary. However, we were not able to document that conviction with sufficient sensitivity, visibility, and clarity of exposition.

We felt that we had a strategy in hand, the one known as documentation that could help to confirm our declarations and deepen our understandings. The documentation itself could become part of new ways of learning. We knew that this question of learning with others is an important issue not only in terms of pedagogical, psychological, and epistemological research, but also, and most importantly, for its cultural and political significance.

Knowing how to work in a group—appreciating its inherent qualities and value, and understanding the dynamics, the complexity, and the benefits involved—constitutes a level of awareness that is indispensable for those who want to participate, at both the personal and professional levels, in effecting change and building the future.

(Rinaldi, 2004)

Acknowledgments

I would like to thank the students and teachers who agreed to be interviewed for this chapter:

Webster University Graduate Students:
* Zahrah Abdulhamed Al Saad
* Ghadah Saleh Alhammdan
* Donna Catsavis
* Jennifer Marie Goff
* Kara Grice
* Wendy Huddleston
* Joyce Lawson
* Dawn C. Pulsipher
* Robyn E. White

Maplewood Richmond Heights Early Childhood Teachers:
* Heather Bailey
* Scott Hankley
* Ann McLaughlin
* Katie Nauman
* Nancy Wolters

Adjunct Professor of Education, Webster University and Pedagogista, Maplewood Richmond Heights School District:
* Jennifer Strange

References

Bruner, J. (1996). A little city miracle. In *The hundred languages of children* exhibit catalog. Reggio Emilia, Italy: Reggio Children.

Cagliari, P., Filippini, T., Giacopini, E., Bonilauri, S., & Margini, D. (2012). The pedagogical coordinating team and professional development. In C. Edwards, L. Gandini, & G. Forman (Eds.), *The hundred languages of children: The Reggio Emilia experience in transformation* (pp. 136, 139). Santa Barbara, CA: Praeger.

Edwards, C., Gandini, L., & Forman, G. (1993) *The hundred languages of children: The Reggio Emilia approach to early childhood education.* Greenwich, CT: Ablex.

Edwards, C., Gandini, L., & Forman, G. (1998) *The hundred languages of children: The Reggio Emilia approach—Advanced reflections. (2nd edition).* Greenwich, CT: Ablex.

Edwards, C., Gandini, L., & Forman, G. (2012) *The hundred languages of children: The Reggio Emilia experience in transformation. (3rd edition).* Santa Barbara, CA: Praeger.

Forman, G. & Fyfe, B. (2012). Negotiated learning through design, documentation, and discourse. In C. Edwards, L. Gandini, & G. Forman (Eds.), *The hundred languages of children: The Reggio Emilia experience in transformation.* Santa Barbara, CA: Praeger.

Fyfe, B. (2012). Internationality and new paradigms in early education: Is the Reggio Emilia philosophy having an impact? *Innovations in early education: The international Reggio Emilia exchange* (tenth anniversary ed.). North American Reggio Emilia Alliance.

Fyfe, B. (2012). Ways forward to a social just and human world: The Reggio movement. *Social Change 41(1),* Thousand Oaks, CA: Sage Publications.

Gambetti, A. (2001). Conversation with a group of teachers. In C. Giudici, C. Rinaldi, & M. Krechevsky (Eds.), *Making learning visible: Children as individual and group learners.* Reggio Emilia, Italy: Project Zero and Reggio Children.

Gandini, L. (1993, 1998, 2012). History, ideas, and basic philosophy: An interview with Lella Gandini. In C. Edwards, L. Gandini, & G. Forman (Eds.), *The hundred languages of children: The Reggio Emilia approach to early childhood education* (1st, 2nd, and 3rd eds.) (p. xv). Santa Barbara, CA: Praeger.

Gardner, H. (2012). Forward: Complementary perspectives on Reggio Emilia. In C. Edwards, L. Gandini, & G. Forman (Eds.), *The hundred languages of children: The Reggio Emilia approach to early childhood education* (3rd ed.) (p. xv). Santa Barbara, CA: Praeger.

Historical and Cultural Notes on the Reggio Emilia Experience. (2010). Reggio Emilia, Italy: Reggio Children.

Indications: Preschools and Infant-Toddler Centres of the Municipality of Reggio Emilia. (2010). Reggio Emilia, Italy: Reggio Children.

Krechevsky, M. (2001). Form, function, and understanding in learning groups: Propositions from the Reggio classrooms. In C. Giudici, C. Rinaldi, & M. Krechevsky (Eds.), *Making learning visible: Children as individual and group learners.* Reggio Emilia, Italy: Project Zero and Reggio Children.

Moss, P. (2012). Personal communication.

Rinaldi, C. (2001). The issue of educating today: School is a place of culture, values, and vision. Speech given to educators at Webster University, St. Louis, MO.

Rinaldi, C. (2004). The aim of education. Speech given to educators at Webster University's Celebration of 40 years of the MAT program. St. Louis, MO.

Rinaldi, C. (2006). *In dialogue with Reggio Emilia: Listening, researching and learning.* New York: Routledge.

Rinaldi, C. (2010). Personal communication.

Schwartz, D. (2002). Carlina Rinaldi: Researcher in early childhood education is the university's first Des Lee Visiting International Scholar. *Webster World, 7(4),* 14–17, Webster University.

Van Manen, M. (1991). Reflectivity and the pedagogical moment: The normativity of pedagogical thinking and acting. *Journal of curriculum studies, 23(6),* 507–536.

Vecchi, V. (2010). *Art and creativity in Reggio Emilia: Exploring the role and potential of ateliers in early childhood education.* New York, NY: Routledge.

PART IV

Reflection and Professional Learning and Growth

9

TRANSFORMATIONS AND TENSIONS IN FINNISH EARLY CHILDHOOD EDUCATION AND CARE

Kaisa Kopisto, Laura Salo, Lasse Lipponen, and Leena Krokfors

Introduction

Finnish early childhood education has been preparing for and undergoing large-scale reforms in recent years. Previously, the emphasis of early childhood education and care (ECEC) has been to enable parents to work and to support families in raising their children. Only in the 21st century have we started to talk about early childhood education (as opposed to day care) (Onnismaa & Kalliala, 2010; Karila et al., 2013). Moreover, until recently, the administration of ECEC has been divided between two central administrative sectors. From the beginning of 2013, after public and political debate, the administrating and steering responsibilities for ECEC in Finland have moved from the Ministry of Social Affairs and Health to the Ministry of Education and Culture. The idea behind the transformation was to develop and guide early childhood education as one operation. Transformations in administration sought to tie early childhood education (aged 0–6) more firmly to the overall Finnish basic education system (aged 7–16) (Karila et al., 2013).

Furthermore, a new Children's Day Care Act and decree are in preparation and are expected to come into effect in 2015. The changes they will introduce are long overdue, as the previous Day Care Act dates back to 1973. There are assumptions that the current Day Care Act (1973) could be shaped into an act on early childhood education to better reflect the main mission of Finnish ECEC (Onnismaa & Kalliala, 2010). The aim is a service that is genuinely built around promoting children's well-being and development. Furthermore, the National Core Curriculum for pre-primary and basic education is being renewed. These transformations highlight a trend toward an integrated education and schooling system in which early childhood and school education form a continuum in terms of steering as well as children's development and learning.

Transformations on different levels require the continual reassessment of professional practices for the purposes of guaranteeing high-quality early childhood education (Mäkitalo, 2009). In Finnish educational culture, which is characterized by trust and teacher autonomy, this transformation process can take the form of reflection by both the individual educators and the professional community (Ojala, 2009). Finnish teachers are considered to be autonomous professionals who are committed to continual personal development and are assumed to have an inquiry-oriented approach for upholding the quality of their work. In ECEC, this takes the form of reflection through discussion, observation, and documentation within the professional community, within families, and among children.

In this article, we highlight the recent transformations and reflect on the tensions that are present in Finnish ECEC. We first present the guidelines and special characteristics of Finnish ECEC. Then we discuss the challenges and possibilities of working within a multiprofessional work environment. After that, we describe and consider elements of Finnish research-based teacher education with regard to professional development. Finally, we conclude our discussion by envisioning the role of the development of agency and reflection in meeting the needs of the changing educational landscape and by reflecting on the implications that the discussed transformations of ECEC have for early childhood education and kindergarten teachers in Finnish universities.

Early Childhood Education and Care in Finland

Early childhood education in Finland is based on the Act on Children's Day Care (1973), which is currently being renewed. The Act's focus is twofold: social services for families and early educational activities for children. Since 1996, every child under school age (7) is granted a "subjective right" to day care services. Finnish day care services and centers (at the time, kindergartens) developed primarily to support the underprivileged and later to meet the needs of working parents and have been administered as a social welfare service. In other parts of Europe, the focus of day care has been more educational. Finnish ECEC is heavily influenced by the Fröbelian tradition and is a part of the Nordic idea of the welfare state (Välimäki, 1999; Onnismaa & Kalliala, 2010).

The term *ECEC* is used to describe the comprehensive character of Finnish early childhood education and day care. In Finnish, the term *ECEC* translates to *varhaiskasvatus*, where the prefix *varhais* refers to early and the word *kasvatus* to the combination of education and care. This "Educare" model describes the way Finnish early childhood pedagogy combines care, education, and teaching into a unified whole. In this way, the social services as well as the educational aspects of day care are realized in families' and children's everyday lives. Care, education, and teaching are combined in the daily activities as a whole, with the promotion of children's balanced growth, development, and learning as the goal. These three elements are emphasized differently with respect to children's different age groups. In practice, in addition to the educator-initiated activities (such as teaching a song or reading to children), all everyday activities such as eating, dressing, and taking naps are situations where educators' active role, pedagogical planning, and skills are needed and considered educationally valuable (Venninen, Leinonen, Ojala, & Lipponen, 2012).

Since 2006, municipalities have been able to decide whether to place day care under the auspices of social welfare or education. Even though the relationship between day care and social welfare services for families is traditionally tight, 67% of the municipalities have already moved child day care from the welfare sector to education (Association of Finnish Local and Regional Authorities, 2012). Consequently, from the beginning of 2013, the (national-level) administration and steering of ECE in Finland has moved from the Ministry of Social Affairs and Health to the Ministry of Education and Culture.

Finnish ECEC is guided by two national-level documents prepared by multiprofessional expert groups consisting of administrators, researchers, and trade union representatives. These documents serve as the basis for the curricula, devised at the municipality and day care unit levels. The early childhood education staff is responsible for drafting unit-specific curricula. The National Curriculum Guidelines on Early Childhood and Care (STAKES 2004/2005 in Finnish) gives a broad description of the implementation of ECEC and defines the educational goals and core content orientations (ages 0–5). The Core Curriculum for Pre-School Education (Finnish National Board of Education, 2000—revised in 2010 as the Core Curriculum for Pre-Primary Education) outlines the objectives and contents of pre-primary education for the final year before compulsory basic education (aged 6). This one-year pre-primary education is voluntary, and its purpose is to ensure a continuum from day care to basic education. The local authority has the statutory duty to provide pre-primary education for children living in its area (Ministry of Education and Culture, 2012).

Reflections

The administrative transformation of Finnish ECEC from a social welfare service to an education service (and discussions about what functions it should emphasize) is ongoing and has created some tension. The reformation of the legislation has taken a long time and has raised controversy among policy makers as well as practitioners in the field. This transformation mirrors a shift in thinking from a social-service-based system focusing on the family, to a system that stems from children's needs and supports a continuum of learning for the early childhood education of children. According to the Trade Union of Education in Finland, the term *early childhood education* should only be used for services that fulfill the requirements that the new act imposes on early childhood education. ECEC is a service that should be organized with the same content and quality criteria (Trade Union of Education in Finland, 2013).

Moving from a social service orientation to an educational orientation for ECEC has several perspectives and also raised critical doubts concerning not only the administration and legislation but also the Educare model. In the Starting Strong report (OECD, 2001), a comparison was made between countries with integrated ECEC models: "Countries with a strong tradition of integrated care and education—Denmark, Finland, Norway, and Sweden—take a wider view of early childhood and do not wish to assimilate the early childhood institution to a school-like model. A central understanding is that the early childhood institution should contribute, alongside the parents, to the child's development and well-being."

According to Karila (2008), our national regulations are, for the most part, of high quality, but their implementation is problematic. Onnismaa and Kalliala (2010) took a critical viewpoint of the Finnish ECEC model, its system, and its interpretations and implications. They argued that key documents seem to reflect a less-than-clear understanding of the tasks of ECEC and the role of the staff working in this field. They also questioned whether enlarging the scope of ECEC has led to an adult-centered approach, with ever greater social work goals. The authors concluded that "It seems that since the 1990s the Finnish ECEC system has striven to distance itself from genuine early childhood education approaches and in doing this it has failed to establish pedagogic practices that would be true to the principles of child-centered early childhood education" (p. 272).

Insights into the Multiprofessional Work Environment

Finnish day care centers are characterized by multiprofessional work communities with a varying combination of professional qualification levels and job descriptions, as well as their cooperation with professionals in other sectors (social and health care, schools, etc.) (Karila & Kinos, 2012). The professional staff who work with children include kindergarten teachers and practical nurses (Ministry of Social Affairs and Health, 2004). Kindergarten teachers (teaching children ages 0–6) hold either a bachelor's degree in education specializing in early childhood education (180 credits) or a bachelor's degree in social services that include studies that focus on early childhood education and social pedagogy (60 credits). Practical nurses are required to have practical nurse or nursery nurse training (Act on Qualification Requirement for Social Welfare Professionals 272/2009). According to the regulations, at least every third member of the personnel should have a kindergarten teacher's qualification or the equivalent. Kindergarten teachers providing pre-primary education (children aged 6) are required to have either a bachelor's or master's degree in education or a bachelor's degree in social sciences with an additional pedagogical course.

Finnish ECEC has received attention (OECD, 2006) for its adult-child ratio (i.e., the number of educators in proportion to children in day care). On the one hand, this ratio is higher in Finland than in other OECD countries; in the most common structure, a team of three educators is responsible for a group of approximately 21 children. On the other hand, if we look at the UNICEF ratings (2008) connected with early childhood education, we see that Finland fulfills only the minimum staff-to-children ratio criteria. According to ratings presented by the UNICEF Innocenti Research Center (2008), 50% of personnel in accredited early education services should have tertiary education and relevant qualifications. Today, staff who have a bachelor's degree in education—persons specifically trained in early childhood education—make up the smallest occupational group in day care centers, with the majority being social work or health care professionals (Onnismaa & Kalliala, 2010).

Reflections

It is widely acknowledged that Finnish early childhood educators work in a culture of trust because there is no centralized monitoring (Karila & Kinos, 2012). Decision-making powers are assigned at the local level, and teachers are responsible for designing local curricula and assessments. In the national curriculum guidelines, teacher reflection is addressed through references to the continual evaluation of the professionals' own work, objectives for the teaching and learning processes, and overall activities. For instance, the guidelines for ECEC state that "Analyzing and assessing their own work helps them (staff) act consciously in accordance with ethically and professionally sound principles. Professional and vocational knowledge and experience provide a solid foundation for competence. The educator community documents, evaluates and makes efforts to continuously develop their work" (STAKES 2004, p. 16).

There are no general nationally applied and implemented reflection tools for kindergarten teachers. Assessment of professional practice is carried out through discussions on many levels: between day care center directors and staff (individuals and teams), within multiprofessional teams, and between directors and district managers of day care areas. Moreover, children and families are involved in this process through a partnership by, for example, soliciting their feedback and inviting them to take part in regular discussions. In addition to these reflections *on* action, in everyday practices, teachers can be thought to reflect *in* action, that is, "think about doing something while doing it" (Schön, 1995).

The decentralization at the beginning of the 1990s brought changes to the funding structure that gave municipalities increased decision power, leading to a situation where decisions concerning the division of labor among different professional groups are made in the day care centers. Moreover, during this time, the discussion of the tasks of ECEC became even more complicated with the reemergence of the family work aspect; expectations concerning the educational partnership with parents and ideas of multiprofessional cooperation diverged (see, for example, Hujala, Karila, Nivala, & Puroila, 1998; Kinos, 2008; Ministry of Social Affairs and Health, 2007; Onnismaa & Kalliala, 2010).

Today there is still confusion about the work practices of early childhood education and the responsibilities and strengths of professionals with various educational backgrounds. Thus, working in a multiprofessional environment can create tension as early childhood educators seek to define their own area of expertise as well as learn from other professionals (cf. Venninen et al., 2012). Karila and Kinos (2012) pointed out that there are several interpretations of multiprofessionalism in ECEC working practices. Moreover, according to Onnismaa and Kalliala (2010), multiprofessionalism in the working environment of Finnish day care centers seems to have developed in a curious direction. Instead of clarifying the special expertise of professionals working in day care centers and developing a new kind of shared expertise based on this, we face the alarming situation where pedagogical professional expertise is not always recognized and implemented by the professionals themselves. This situation has been seen to reflect on professionals' everyday work in the field and, in particular, influence kindergarten teachers' willingness to stay in their profession (Karila et al., 2013). Onnismaa and Kalliala (2010) argued that in Finland, the current situation can in many ways be seen as the result of a series of misinterpretations of the adult role in general, as well as of early childhood education and pedagogy.

From the child's perspective, quality is achieved when every child has the opportunity to participate in pedagogical activities planned by a kindergarten teacher. Furthermore, the Trade Union of Education in Finland (2013) demands that the proportion of kindergarten teachers in early childhood education staff be increased to ensure the high quality of ECEC as well as to invest in pedagogy. Providing good quality ECEC requires professional staff who are highly educated and committed to the continuous development of their work. Working as a professional requires appropriate professional training, and thus, Finnish teachers need to be highly educated (cf. Karila & Kinos, 2012; Mäkitalo, 2009).

Teacher Education, Professional Development, and Reflective Teaching

Finland's high-quality teachers and educational system have received a great deal of attention from all over the world (e.g., Jakku-Sihvonen & Niemi, 2007; Sahlberg, 2011; Välijärvi, 2004). This quality stems from the well-trained staff with access to professional development opportunities (Karila & Kinos, 2012). Political decisions have defined class teacher and subject teacher education programs as five-year master's programs; however, the kindergarten teacher education program, which qualifies teachers to work with children under the age of 7, comprises a three-year bachelor's degree (e.g., Niemi, 2012; Jakku-Sihvonen & Niemi, 2006).

Academic (university-based) teacher education is founded on scientific research and professional pedagogical practices. The curriculum and study programs provide students with the knowledge and skills to operate as experts and developers in their fields. The aim is that professionals at all levels are not only implementers of decisions but also active partners in collective decision making (Oikkonen et al., 2007). However, it has been reported that, at least in the United Kingdom and Finland, preservice teachers learn to plan lessons and deliver curricula, but they do not learn how to respond to increasingly complex classroom situations (Edwards & D'Arcy, 2004; Edwards & Protheroe, 2003; Opetusministeriö, 2007).

The idea of a reflective teacher in Finland was introduced in the 1960s—a time when there were political reasons to raise the academic status of teacher education. The number and quality of theoretical educational courses as well as the number of methodological courses increased. Conducting a research-based approach became both possible and convenient when educating all teachers. Since the teacher reform of 1979, all teachers—except kindergarten teachers, who at the time were educated mainly in colleges—have needed to obtain a higher academic degree (MA), with class teachers (primary grades) majoring in education and subject teachers in their chosen subject. Since 1995, kindergarten teachers could obtain a university bachelor's degree, as the study program was moved from colleges to universities (Krokfors, 2007). Furthermore, since 1997, it has been possible to obtain a master's degree in early childhood education. At the moment, this degree does not provide additional qualifications in the field, but it does deepen the ECEC professionals' knowledge base.

The research-based approach has been the organizing theme for all Finnish teacher education since the 1980s. Behind the research-based approach is a holistic view of a pedagogically thoughtful teacher. The aim of research-based teacher education is to educate inquiry-oriented teachers who can make and justify educational decisions based on pedagogical argumentation (Kansanen et al., 2000). Pedagogical and content studies reciprocally interact with each other to ensure that pedagogical content knowledge is of high quality and broad enough to enable teachers to promote the development of children at various stages of the educational continuum (Kynäslahti et al., 2006; Krokfors, 2007). The idea is to integrate the theoretical aspects with practice during the studies. Research-based thinking is seen as the unifying factor in this process.

Krokfors (2007) presented three basic ideas on which the core elements in the curricula are shared and filtered to all teaching, learning, and interaction. They are based on:

- An idea of the developing student teachers' professional expertise based on an approach that emphasizes pedagogical thinking, reflective teaching, and practitioner research. Pedagogical decision making is based on the active and wide formation of students' educational knowledge base.
- An idea of interaction that is based on a collegial working culture and a variation of suitable working methods that aim to develop the student teachers' argumentative thinking skills and their personal concept of themselves as teachers.

- An idea of the orientation toward society that is based on understanding the ethical basis of a teacher's work, as well as the importance of activity as an autonomous member of the school, community, and whole society.

The curricula and study programs provide preservice students with knowledge and skills for operating as autonomous actors and developers in their fields, with the ability to make theory-based decisions by consuming as well as producing research (Toom et al., 2010). The ability to see pedagogical elements and ask pedagogically meaningful questions in educational situations is one of the most important skills future teachers require (Krokfors, 2007).

Reflections

In Finland, teacher education takes place at universities, and—particularly class and subject teacher education—has a long academic tradition. The kindergarten teacher education tradition (at universities from 1995) also has long-standing roots and recently celebrated its 120th anniversary. Although the education program has been developed in close connection with the class teacher education program, the content of the kindergarten teacher education curriculum places a unique emphasis on early childhood, which should be nurtured. At the moment, one distinctive characteristic of the program that distinguishes it from other teacher education is that it is a bachelor-level program.

The debate and tension around teacher qualifications, and thus expertise, relates to historically developed educational policies as well as to societal and economic demands being met for an adequate workforce. However, ECEC can, in fact, be viewed as the best economical investment in preventing the risk of social exclusion and marginalization (Heckman, 2007; Heckman & Masterov, 2004). Moreover, high-quality ECEC has long-term effects: it predicts later academic competence (Vandell, Belsky, Burkhinal, Steinberg, & Vandergrift, 2010). Providing high-quality ECEC requires highly educated professionals. Teacher influence persists in the early grades; starting in early childhood education, teachers can significantly affect, for example, students' reading and math scores in later grades (Konstantopoulos, 2011; Konstantopoulos & Chung, 2011). It can be argued that the best teachers should be assigned to the smallest children. It is worth considering whether a bachelor-level degree is sufficient for developing reflective professionals and whether it is right that the youngest children have less-educated teachers.

Teachers—including kindergarten teachers—use complex practical theories and personal beliefs as a framework to plan, interact, and reflect on learning and instruction (Marland & Osborne, 1990; Mitchell & Marland, 1989; Pitkäniemi, 2009). The challenge of teacher learning is to connect formal and practical teacher knowledge. A close relationship between theory and practice is the basis for developing future teachers' personal practical theories and for creating an inquiry orientation in teachers' daily work to help them teach well and solve pedagogical problems. Finnish teacher education emphasizes the importance of learning research methods to increase future teachers' autonomy and active agency in educational decision making (Krokfors, 2007).

Finnish ECEC received recognition in a report by the OECD (2006) because it supports educators' opportunities to develop their professional competence through long-term continuing education throughout their careers. Continual development of educational practices requires a reflective orientation toward work. Inservice teacher education is an important element of lifelong learning and is arranged to support teachers' professional development. Creating an intensive and concrete preservice to inservice continuum for teacher education is a future challenge for academic teacher education (cf. Karila, 2013).

Discussion: Toward Agentic Teachers as Reflective Practitioners

We have thus far established that the current transformations in Finnish ECEC have highlighted various tensions with regard to the education and work of ECEC professionals on the systemic and individual levels. Although the administrational transformation has provided the opportunity to bring forth the "heart" of ECEC, the challenge remains to have this change realized in the everyday practices of the multiprofessional community. It is relevant to ask what kind of new professional demands are set for the future and what kind of reflective and shared working approaches as well as educational structures are needed to produce and advance ECEC professionalism (Karila et al., 2013). As one perspective, we introduce the idea of teacher agency as a way of responding to the future needs of the educational landscape.

Studies on the development of working practices in early childhood education related to deepening reflective skills (e.g., Fenichel, 1991; Gettinger, Stoiber, & Lange, 1999; Karila, 2001; Ojala & Venninen, 2011; Venninen et al., 2012) show that reflection is an important tool in recognizing changing pedagogical practices. Venninen (2009) discussed essential factors in the development of working practices and structures that support a reflective work method. The leading principle is to create conditions for reflective and collegial development and to develop working practices and pedagogy arising from the field of early childhood education. The new practices must be created for the multiprofessional development of working practices by utilizing the professional skills of educators with different areas of competence (cf. Kopisto, Brotherus, Paavola, Hytönen, & Lipponen, 2011; Paavola, Kopisto, Brotherus, & Derwin, 2014). For example, in the Helsinki metropolitan area in Finland, efforts have been made to create conditions for the reflective and collegial development of working practices and pedagogy. This action research and development work is being done in cooperation with researchers and practitioners in the field through reflective, critical, and open dialogue and uses various approaches, such as pedagogical documentation and mentoring (Mäkitalo, 2009; Venninen et al., 2012).

In a multiprofessional work environment, collaboration is actualized by having experts from different professional fields work together and share their expertise (Kumpulainen et al., 2010). Shared expertise is based on the idea that every member of a work community has his or her own area of expertise that complements others and that no individual is an expert on everything (Brown & Campione, 1994). This multiprofessional approach has been seen as a solution where shared expertise is used to tackle problems. In the current situation in ECEC, there is a need to develop collaborative practices where educational expertise is not lost in the multiprofessional and holistic Educare model. Moreover, it is crucial that the idea of shared expertise does not blur the lines between the different roles, competencies, and responsibilities of professionals.

Utilizing and exploring the concept of agency can open new paths in the education and development of professional and reflective practitioners who take ownership of their expertise. Agency can be defined as the capacity to initiate purposeful action that implies will, autonomy, freedom, and choice (Edwards & D'Arcy, 2004; Lipponen & Kumpulainen, 2011). Agency is important for both the professional development of teachers and teacher identity (Beijaard, Meijer, & Verloop, 2004), and lately, the importance of understanding the social and cultural processes mediating preservice teachers' agency development is being increasingly recognized (Davydov, Slobodchikov, & Tsukerman, 2003; Edwards, 2005; Edwards & D'Arcy, 2004; Engle & Faux, 2006; Lipponen & Kumpulainen, 2011; Zuckerman, 2007). Agency can be seen as important for several reasons: for instance, if those who train preservice teachers want to educate agentic teachers who not only deliver the curricula but also have the skills and will to strengthen their own and their children's capabilities for lifelong learning and sustained professional growth, they must deeply understand the process of becoming an agentic teacher and learn how they can support this development (Edwards & D'Arcy, 2004; Edwards & Protheroe, 2003). In the future, teachers should be alerted to the possibilities of harnessing the practices of the present to promote agency in their learning communities.

The transformations and tensions depicted in our discussion center around the very core of early childhood education. Various topics remain that could provide further depth when looking at Finnish ECEC comprehensively. In an increasingly diverse society, teacher education is faced with the challenge and opportunity of educating agentic professionals who can cross cultural, regional, and global boundaries. The question of pedagogical leadership also cannot be overlooked. High-level, research-based teacher education that values collective discussion and meaning-making can provide powerful tools to support the education of active future teachers who are equipped to meet and resolve the current transformations and tensions as well as respond to future directions in Finnish ECEC.

References

Act on Children's Day Care. (1973). Retrieved from http://www.finlex.fi/fi/laki/alkup/1973/19730036

Act on Qualification Requirement for Social Welfare Professionals. (2005). Retrieved from http://www.finlex.fi/en/laki/kaannokset/2005/en20050272?search[type]=pika&search[pika]=Act%20on%20Qualification%20Requirement%20for%20Social%20Welfare%20Professionals%20272%2F2005

Association of Finnish Local and Regional Authorities. (2012). *Päivähoidon hallinto kunnissa 2012*. Retrieved from http://www.kunnat.net/fi/asiantuntijapalvelut/opeku/vasu/lph-hallinto/Documents/paivahoidon_hallinto_2012.pdf

Beijaard, D., Meijer, P. C., & Verloop, N. (2004). Reconsidering research on teachers' professional identity. *Teaching and Teacher Education, 20(2),* 107–128.

Brown, A. L. & Campione, J. C. (1994). Guided discovery in a community of learners. In K. McGilly (Ed.), *Classroom lessons: Integrating cognitive theory & classroom practice* (pp. 229–287). Cambridge, MA: MIT.

Davydov, V. V., Slobodchikov, V. I., & Tsukerman, G. A. (2003). The elementary school student as an agent of learning activity. *Journal of Russian and East European Psychology, 41(5),* 63–76.

Edwards, A. (2005). Relational agency: Learning to be a resourceful practitioner. *International Journal of Educational Research, 43(3),* 168–182.

Edwards, A. & D'Arcy, C. (2004). Relational agency and disposition in sociocultural accounts of learning to teach. *Educational Review, 56,* 147–155.

Edwards, A. & Protheroe, L. (2003). Learning to see in classrooms: What are student teachers learning about teaching and learning while learning to teach in schools? *British Educational Research Journal, 29(2),* 227–242.

Engle, R. A. & Faux, R. B. (2006). Towards productive disciplinary engagement of prospective teachers in educational psychology: Comparing two methods of case-based instruction. *Teaching Educational Psychology, 1(2),* 1–22.

Fenichel, E. (1991). Learning through supervision and mentorship to support the development of infants, toddlers and families. *Zero to Three, 12(2),* 1–8.

Finnish National Board of Education. (2000). *Core curriculum for preschool education in Finland*. Retrieved from http://www.oph.fi/download/123162_core_curriculum_for_pre_school_education_2000.pdf

Gettinger, M., Stoiber, K. C., & Lange, J. (1999). Collaborative investigation of inclusive early practices: A blueprint for teacher-researcher partnership. *Journal of Early Intervention, 22(3),* 257–265.

Heckman, J. J. (2007). Invest in the very young (2nd ed.). In R. E. Tremblay, M. Boivin, & R. D.V. Peters, (Eds.), *Encyclopedia on early childhood development*. Montreal, Quebec, Canada: Centre of Excellence for Early Childhood Development and Strategic Knowledge Cluster on Early Child Development. Retrieved from http://www.child-encyclopedia.com/documents/HeckmanANGxp.pdf

Heckman, J. J. & Masterov, D.V. (2004). *The productivity argument for investing in young children*. Working Paper 5, Invest in Kids Working Group. Committee for Economic Development.

Hujala, E., Karila, K., Nivala, V., & Puroila, A. M. (1998). Towards understanding leadership in the context of Finnish early childhood. In E. Hujala & A. M. Puroila (Eds.), *Towards understanding leadership in early childhood context—Cross-cultural perspectives* (pp. 147–170). Acta Universitatis Ouluensis. Series E 35. Oulu, Finland: University Press.

Jakku-Sihvonen, R. & Niemi, H. (Eds.). (2006). *Research-based teacher education in Finland—Reflections by Finnish teacher educators*. Research in Educational Sciences 25. Finnish Educational Research Association.

Jakku-Sihvonen, R. & Niemi, H. (Eds.). (2007). *Education as a societal contributor*. Frankfurt am Main, Finland: Peter Lang.

Kansanen, P., Tirri, K., Meri, M., Krokfors, L., Husu, J., & Jyrhämä, R. (2000). *Teachers' pedagogical thinking: Theoretical landscapes, practical challenges*. New York, NY: Peter Lang.

Karila, K. (2001). Moniammatillisuus ja päiväkotitoiminnan suunnittelun perusteita. [Multi-professionalism and planning of pedagogical activities in early childhood education]. In A. Helenius, K. Karila, H. Munter, P. Mäntynen, & H. Siren-Tiusanen (Eds.), *Pienet päivähoidossa. Alle kolmevuotiaiden lasten varhaiskasvatuksen perusteita [Toddlers in daycare. Curriculum guidelines for children under 3 years old]* (pp. 271–286). Helsinki, Finland: WSOY.

Karila, K. (2008). A Finnish viewpoint on professionalism in early childhood education. *European Early Childhood Education Research Journal, 16(2)*, 210–223.

Karila, K., Harju-Luukkainen, H., Juntunen, A., Kainulainen, S., Kaulio-Kuikka, K., Mattila,V., . . . Smeds-Nylund, A-S. (2013). *Varhaiskasvatuksen koulutus Suomessa. Arviointi koulutuksen tilasta ja kehittämistarpeista [Education and training in early childhood education in Finland—evaluation of current situation and development needs]*. Korkeakoulujen arviointineuvoston julkaisuja [The Finnish Higher Education Evaluation Council.], 7, 2013.

Karila, K. & Kinos, J. (2012). Acting as a professional in a Finnish early childhood education context. In L. Miller, C. Dalli, & M. Urban (Eds.), *Early childhood grows up: Towards a critical ecology of the profession* (pp. 55–69). New York, NY: Springer.

Kinos, J. (2008). Professionalism - a breeding ground for struggle. The example of the Finnish day-care centre. *European Early Childhood Education Research Journal, 16(2)*, 224-241.

Konstantopoulos, S. (2011). Teacher effects in early grades? Evidence from a randomized experiment. *Teachers College Record, 113(7)*, 1541–1565.

Konstantopoulos, S. & Chung,V. (2011). The persistence of teacher effects in elementary grades. *American Educational Research Journal, 48(2)*, 361–386.

Kopisto, K., Brotherus, A., Paavola, H., Hytönen, J., & Lipponen, L. (2011). *Kohti joustavaa esi- ja alkuopetusta. Joustavan esi- ja alkuopetuksen tutkimus- ja kehittämishankkeen raportti.* Helsingin opetusvirasto, julkaisusarja B1:2011. Helsinki, Finland: Yliopistopaino.

Krokfors, L. (2007). Two-fold role of reflective pedagogical practice in research-based teacher education. In R. Jakku-Sihvonen & H. Niemi (Eds.), *Education as a societal contributor* (pp. 147–159). Frankfurt am Main, Finland: Peter Lang.

Kumpulainen, K., Krokfors, L., Lipponen, L., Tissari, V., Hilppö, J., & Rajala, A. (2010). *Learning bridges: Toward participatory learning environments.* Helsinki, Finland: CICERO Learning, University of Helsinki.

Kynäslahti, H., Kansanen, P., Jyrhämä, R., Krokfors, L., Maaranen K., & Toom, A. (2006). The multimode programme as a variation of research-based teacher education. *Teaching and Teacher Education, 22*, 246–256.

Lipponen, L. & Kumpulainen, K. (2011). Acting as accountable authors: Creating interactional spaces for agency work in teacher education. *Teaching and Teacher Education, 27(5)*, 812–819.

Marland, P. & Osborne, B. (1990). Classroom theory, thinking, and action. *Teaching & Teacher Education, 7(1)*, 93–109.

Ministry of Education and Culture. (2012). *Education and research 2011–2016. A development plan.* Reports of Ministry of Education and Culture 2012, 3.

Ministry of Social Affairs and Health. (2004). *Early childhood education and care in Finland.* Retrieved from http://pre20090115.stm.fi/cd1106216815326/passthru.pdf

Ministry of Social Affairs and Health. (2007). *Education and skills of early childhood education and care staff—the present state and development needs.* Report of the sub-committee on the Advisory Board for Early Childhood Education and Care, 2007, 7. Helsinki, Finland: Ministry of Social Affairs and Health.

Mitchell, J. & Marland, P. (1989). Research on teacher thinking: The next phase. *Teaching and Teacher Education, 5(2)*, 115–128.

Mäkitalo, A. R. (2009). Pääkaupunkiseudun varhaiskasvatuksen kehittämisyksikkö, VKK-Metro-hanke. In A. R. Mäkitalo, M. Ojala, T. Venninen, & B. Vilpas (Eds.), *Löytöretkellä omaan työhön. Kehittämistä ja tutkimista päiväkodin arjessa [Discovery trip to day care work. Developing and researching in early childhood education]* (pp. 21–26). Soccan ja Heikki Waris -instituutin julkaisusarja nro 22. Helsinki, Finland: Yliopistopaino.

Niemi, H. (2012). Relationships of teachers' professional competences, active learning and research studies in teacher education in Finland. *Reflecting Education, 8(2),* 23–44.

OECD. (2001). *Starting strong: Early childhood education and care.* Paris, France: OECD Publications.

OECD. (2006). *Starting strong II: Early childhood education and care.* Paris, France: OECD Publications.

Oikkonen, J., Lavonen, J., Krzywacki-Vainio, H., Aksela, M., Krokfors, L. & Saarikko, H. (2007). Pre-service teacher education in chemistry, mathematics and physics. In E. Pehkonen, M. Ahtee, & J. Lavonen (Eds.), *How Finns learn mathematics and science* (pp. 49–68). Rotterdam/Taipei: Sense Publishers.

Ojala, M. (2009). Varhaiskasvatuksen kehittäminen reflektion avulla. In A. R. Mäkitalo, M. Ojala, T. Venninen, & B. Vilpas (Eds.), *Löytöretkellä omaan työhön. Kehittämistä ja tutkimista päiväkodin arjessa [Discovery trip to day care work. Developing and researching in early childhood education]* (pp. 27–36). Soccan ja Heikki Waris -instituutin julkaisusarja nro 22. Helsinki, Finland: Yliopistopaino.

Ojala, M. & Venninen, T. (2011). Developing reflective practices for day-care centres in Helsinki Metropolitan Area, *Reflective Practice: International and Multidisciplinary Perspectives, 12(3),* 335–346.

Onnismaa, E. L. & Kalliala, M. (2010). Finnish ECEC policy: Interpretations, implementations and implications. *Early Years, 30(3),* 267–277.

Opetusministeriö. (2007). Opettajankoulutus 2020. *Opetusministeriön työryhmämuistioita ja selvityksiä 2007, 44.* Helsinki, Finland: Yliopistopaino.

Paavola, H., Kopisto, K., Brotherus, A., & Derwin, F. (2014). Towards flexible pre- and primary education in multicultural contexts? An example of collaborative action research in Finland. In H. Ragnarsdóttir & C. Schmidt (Eds.), *Learning spaces for social justice: International perspectives on exemplary practices from preschool to secondary school.* Stoke-on-Trent, Finland: Trentham Books.

Pitkäniemi, H. (2009). The essence of teaching-learning conceptual relation: How does teaching work? *Scandinavian Journal of Educational Research, 53(3),* 263–276.

Sahlberg, P. (2011). *Finnish lessons: What can the world learn from educational change in Finland?* New York, NY: Teachers College Press.

Schön, D. A. (1995). *The reflective practitioner: How professionals think in action.* Surrey, Finland: Arena Ashgate Publishing Limited.

Simola, H. (2005). The Finnish miracle of PISA: Historical and sociological remarks on teaching and teacher education. *Comparative Education, 41(4),* 455–470.

STAKES (National Research and Development Centre for Welfare and Health). (2004/2005 in Finnish). *National curriculum guidelines on early childhood education and care in Finland.* Retrieved from http://www.thl.fi/thl-client/pdfs/267671cb-0ec0-4039-b97b-7ac6ce6b9c10

Toom, A., Kynäslahti, H., Krokfors, L., Jyrhämä, R., Byman, R., Stenberg, K., … Kansanen, P. (2010). The experiences of research-based approach of teacher education: Suggestions for the future policies. *European Journal of Education, 45(2),* 339–352.

Trade Union of Education in Finland. (2013). *Tiedotteet 31.10.2013.* Retrieved from http://www.oaj.fi/cs/Satellite?c=Page&childpagename=OAJ%2FPage%2Fsisalto&cid=1363787850943&pagename=OAJWrapper

UNICEF. (2008). *The child care transitions. A league table of early childhood education and care in economically advanced countries.* Innocenti Research Centre Report Card 8.

Vandell, D. L., Belsky, J., Burkhinal, M., Steinberg, L., & Vandergrift, N. (2010). Do effects of early child care extend to age 15 years? Results from the NICHD study of early child care and youth development. *Child Development, 81(3),* 737–756.

Venninen, T. (2009). Reflektiivinen lähestymistapa päiväkotien kehittämistyössä. In A. R. Mäkitalo, M. Ojala, T. Venninen, & B. Vilpas (Eds.), *Löytöretkellä omaan työhön. Kehittämistä ja tutkimista päiväkodin arjessa [Discovery trip to day care work. Developing and researching in early childhood education]* (pp. 37–44). Soccan ja Heikki Waris -instituutin julkaisusarja nro 22. Helsinki, Finland: Yliopistopaino.

Venninen, T., Leinonen, J., Ojala, M., & Lipponen, L. (2012). Creating conditions for reflective practice in early childhood education. *International Journal of Child Care and Education Policy, 6(1),* 1–15.

Välijärvi, J. (2004). Implications of the modular curriculum in the secondary school in Finland. In J. Van den Akker, W. Kuiper, & U. Hameyer (Eds.), *Curriculum landscapes and trends* (pp. 101–116). Dordrecht, The Netherlands: Kluwer.

Välimäki, A. L. (1999). *Lasten hoitopuu. Lasten päivähoitojärjestelmä Suomessa 1800- ja 1900-luvuilla.* Helsinki, Finland: Suomen Kuntaliitto.

Zuckerman, G. (2007). On supporting children's initiatives. *Journal of Russian and East European Psychology, 45(3),* 9–42.

10

EDUCATION AND PROFESSIONAL DEVELOPMENT OF JAPANESE PRESCHOOL TEACHERS

Kyoko Iwatate and Mikiko Tabu

In this chapter, we discuss the education and professional development of Japanese preschool teachers, focusing on the development of an inquiry and reflective stance and how that is supported in both preservice and professional education. We begin with a brief description of the preschool system in Japan and the requirements for and a description of teacher education. We then discuss how inquiry and reflection have been incorporated and are essential to teacher learning and development throughout the professional life of the teacher.

The Preschool System in Japan

In Japan, preschool is understood as "Early Childhood Education and Care (ECEC)" for children from zero to compulsory school age. A child must be 6 by the 1st of April, the first day of an academic year, to commence compulsory education. The basic philosophy of ECEC is "ECEC as a universal right of children." It is prescribed in the two fundamental Acts "the School Education Act" and "the Child Welfare Act" in 1947 that laid the foundation of the postwar educational and social welfare reforms. Efforts have been made to realize the philosophy.

Today a well-subsidized and affordable system is in operation. Of just around 1.05 million born every year in the past five years, over 95% of 4- and 5-year-olds and about 80% of 3-year-olds attend kindergarten, a day care center, or *nintei-kodomo-en* (a certified children's place/garden). About one-third of 2-year-olds, one-fourth of 1-year-olds, and one-tenth of those under 1 year attend either a day care center or *nintei-kodomo-en*. Recently the proportion of children under 3 at these centers has risen due to the increasing number of mothers who continue their careers or return to work while the children are young.

Kindergarten is defined as school by the School Education Act. It is a school for children between 3 and compulsory school age (6), and "the Course of Study for Kindergartens" has a national curriculum standard encompassing five areas of learning and development: Health, Human relations, Environment, Language, and Expression. The minimum requirement for teaching is four hours a day (most kindergartens are open longer, from around 8:30 a.m. to 4:00 p.m. or later, to meet parental needs), five days a week and no less than 39 weeks a year. The Ministry of Education, Culture, Sports, Science and Technology (MEXT) is in charge of regulating the delivery of standardized services, with a wide range of parental choices with regard to program. Parents may choose a private or state kindergarten with or without extended hours, secular or religious. The educational approach also varies greatly. There are kindergartens of "free-flow play" curriculum or of highly structured lessons with time for unstructured play between lessons. The parental costs differ widely as each kindergarten provider sets the school fee; the state kindergartens, in general, are less costly. But the central and local governments fund a large part of the basic expenditure of all kindergartens to keep them affordable. It is estimated that an average 35% of a private kindergarten's total income is from public funding nationally. Parents get direct funding as well, but the rate varies locally.

A day care center is defined as a welfare institution by the Child Welfare Act, and it is for children from under 1 to the compulsory school age; the Guidelines for Day Care Center Practices is its national standard. It sets the same five areas of learning and development as the kindergarten for its educational sphere of the program. Regular opening hours are at least 8 hours a day (normally 11 hours) throughout the year except Sundays and national holidays.

Nintei-kodomo-en is a new integrated ECEC center with both kindergarten curriculum and day care availability, established in 2006 by what is commonly known as "the *Nintei-kodomo-en* Act." It provides unified education and care based on the Course of Study for Kindergartens and the Guidelines for Day Care Center Practice.

Any child is entitled to a place in care if parents/guardians, by reason of illness or work, are unable to look after the child during the day. The local government must provide the child with ECEC by offering a place at a day care center or an alternative form of care. The Ministry of Health, Labor and Welfare (MHLW) funds and regulates the provisions with the local government. Parents who need child care apply to the local government for a place, and it is offered according to their assessed needs. When both parents are working full-time, they are placed highest on the priority list. Parental costs vary according to family income, but they are subsidized heavily.

Currently, a large ECEC structural reform is under way, as there has been an acute increase in unmet demand for day care places despite the fact that the childbirth rate is declining steadily. To cope with this issue and to ensure a stable workforce in an era of low birth rate, the Child and Child Rearing Support Act was passed in August 2012. It compels a restructuring of the current dual ECEC system of two basic acts and the two ministerial powers to make it function in a more unified way to serve all parents with preschool children. The details of its final picture are now in the stage of being announced officially step by step.

The Qualification Requirements for ECEC Practitioners

The qualifications of ECEC practitioners are also under the dual system; a teacher's license is required for kindergarten, and "Hoikushi" (Educarer) certificate is required for day care centers.

The kindergarten teacher's license allows the holders to teach children in kindergarten only. It is a graded license and is awarded at three levels depending on the academic degree held and the Designated Teacher Education Program (DTEP) completed. The special class license is awarded to those who finished a postgraduate DTEP program and obtained a master's degree; the first-class license, to those who finished a four-year DTEP and a bachelor's degree course; and the second-class license, to those who finished a two-year DTEP and received an associated bachelor's degree. The second-class teacher's license is also awarded to those who completed a two-year DTEP course at vocational schools without the associated bachelor's degree program.

Only 0.5% of all the kindergarten teachers, including the principals and vice principals, hold the special license; 22.5% hold the first-class license, and 71.8% hold the second-class license (as of 2010, MEXT data; a few work without a kindergarten teacher license). Thus, the majority of the workforce is comprised of second-class license holders, although there is a tendency for more first-class license holders to be hired. Two facts are behind this tendency: (1) More applicants are the graduates of the four-year degree course as a result of expansion of higher education in general and (2) more kindergartens employ graduate applicants to meet the increasing parental expectations as more mothers are university graduates. Teachers are required to renew their license every ten years to keep it valid.

Educarer certificate holders are able to work as fully qualified staff not only in day care centers but also in other kinds of child-welfare institutions. This is a single, permanent qualification, and the requirement is to graduate from a Designated Educarer Education Program (DEEP) or to pass the National Educarer Examination administered once a year. Students in DEEP need at least two academic years to cover all the subjects and internships. Some do it at a university with a bachelor's degree, but the majority finish the course at a junior college or vocational school.

The practitioners of the current *nintei-kodomo-en* need to hold either a kindergarten teacher's license or an Educarer certificate, but when the new ECEC system is in full operation, they will be required to hold both qualifications.

The curriculum of DTEP is specified by MEXT; the DEEP, by MHLW. There were more than 600 DTEP programs nationwide in 2013. The number of newly awarded kindergarten teacher licenses fluctuated between 35,000 and 40,000 a year for the last five years, the trend being a steady increase of four-year DTEP program graduates (37.5% in 2011). Of those, about 11,000 a year come into the profession as newly qualified teachers, but the majority of them are still graduates of the two-year program (73.9% in 2010).

There were over 600 DEEP programs in 2013, with roughly 55,000 places offered at universities, junior colleges, or vocational schools. Currently, more people get the Educarer certificate by way of passing the examination, and the number reached nearly 10,000 in 2012—3,000 more than in the previous year.

The majority of the programs are DTEP and DEEP combined that lead to both qualifications, as DTEP and DEEP have many subjects in common and future requirements of ECEC practitioners will be to hold both qualifications.

Japanese ECEC Teacher Education through Inquiry and Reflection

Shousatsu and *Furikaeri* are key words that mean "reflection" in Japanese and can represent for an international audience the essential quality of Japanese ECEC preservice and inservice teacher education. *Shousatsu* and *Furikaeri* are the core of pre- and inservice teachers' "inquiry" for improving the quality of ECEC practice. Teachers do *Shousatsu* and *Furikaeri* by themselves, or they do it collaboratively with colleagues and other teachers through the lesson study. *Shousatsu* and *Furikaeri* have been competencies cultivated among students and inservice teachers in Japan, and now, we make much of them in a cyclical process between theory and practice in teacher education.

How are *Shousatsu* and *Furikaeri* established in Japanese teacher education? Three clues illuminate the reasons and methods. First, the Japanese ECEC community has been influenced by the idea of *Seisatsu* (the same as *Shousatsu*) described by Sozo Kurahashi, the father of Japanese kindergarten education. Furthermore, since the 1980s, the image of the teacher as reflective practitioner (Schon, 1983) has spread widely. Second, the implementation of *Kyoushok Jissen Enshu*, a new subject for inquiry and reflection, to the national teaching profession curriculum enforced this image. The introduction of the subject was announced in 2009 and applied from the 2010 enrollment. Because the regulation requires this subject to be placed in the last term of the program, it was only in 2013 that the first *Kyoushok Jissen Enshu* class was given to students in the four-year course. Each school board or ECEC foundation has been offering opportunities for professional development with an emphasis on *Shousatsu* and *Furikaeri* as important learning and teaching skills. Finally, the last clue is the original curriculum and practice that promote "inquiry" and "reflection" of the students in each junior college or university for teacher preparation.

The Development of *Shousatsu* in Japanese Teacher Education

The curriculum of teacher education in each university or other teaching institute directly influences teacher education practice. Underlying the established frameworks for the curriculum for the teaching profession are the principles or content of the Educational Personnel Certification Law or Course of Study for Kindergarten that prescribes the subjects and content. These principles for the profession of ECEC teaching traditionally influence the curriculum and practices explicitly and implicitly (See Figure 10.1).

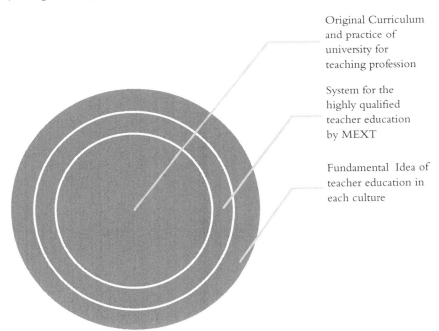

Original Curriculum and practice of university for teaching profession

System for the highly qualified teacher education by MEXT

Fundamental Idea of teacher education in each culture

FIGURE 10.1 Hierarchy to show the importance of Shousatsu.

Sozo Kurahashi (1882–1955) is said to be the father of the kindergarten education of Japan. He studied educational psychology at Tokyo University and was influenced by theorists such as Froebel and Pestalozzi. He became a professor at Tokyo Women's Higher Normal School and was designated as an overseas researcher from the Minister of Education. Between 1919 and 1922, he visited and observed at Columbia University and affiliated kindergartens (United States), McMillan Open-Air Nursery School (United Kingdom), the Pestalozzi-Froebel House (Germany), and the Montessori Child's House (Italy), thus learning about the "New ECEC" facilities.

He learned practices based on the theories of Dewey and other researchers and developed his own "Theory of New ECEC" based on their work and ideas (Otokuni, 2012). Kurahashi wrote many books that have had much influence on preschool education in Japan. He said, in writing, with regard to the specialty of the kindergarten teacher, "You should respect the personality of a child and improve it in deference to the personality ... you should learn from a child as a teacher" (Kurahashi, 1965). "Psychology describes the mind of the child analytically, so you can understand the nature of the mind. But it's important that you should *"ajiwau"* (this Japanese word means "feel and enjoy") touch the hearts and mind of the child. ... If you don't touch the hearts and mind of a child, you can't authentically educate them" (Kurahashi, 1965). He also said that you must not compare the child's mind to the adult mind, but you need deep and sharp reflection with rich experiences (Kurahashi, 1965b).

After the 1980s, the teacher image (Schon, 1983) as a reflective practitioner spread widely, and in Japanese teacher education, the concept and the importance of *Shousatsu* was recognized and emphasized in teacher education.

Inquiry and Reflection in the System that Guarantees the Quality of the Teacher Education

MEXT performs an important function in guaranteeing the quality of school education and teacher preparation in Japan. The subject contents in teacher training and the units of the required subjects are prescribed by MEXT. Professional development is required of inservice teachers by the Special Act for Education Personnel. MEXT requires the cities and districts to support further education for teachers. Such an administrative framework guarantees continuity of learning and the development of teachers and enables research and reflection at each career level. At first, we will look at the training stage.

Kyoushoku Jissen Enshu *for Self- or Collaborative Inquiry and Reflection*

The content standards for the education program are prescribed by MEXT to structure student learning for two years (for second-class qualification), four years (for first-class qualification), and postgraduate program (for special qualification). In addition, MEXT authorizes the Teacher Education Program of each university, conducts the inspection survey after authorization of the candidates by the Teacher Education Program Certifying Council, and guarantees the quality of the teacher education. However, in recent years, questions with regard to teacher knowledge about child development and parent communication have been raised, and the need to improve the quality of the teacher in those regards is currently of concern.

Because of this situation, in 2010, MEXT established a new required professional subject, *Kyoushoku Jissen Enshu.* The content of *Kyoushoku Jissen Enshu* is for students to reflect on their own learning over the years spent at the junior college or university, to reflect on their self-growth, and to recognize what they still need to learn to supplement their learning.

In earlier teacher education, students graduated without much learning being integrated, meaning they might not have been competent enough when beginning to teach children. *Kyoushoku Jissen Enshu* encourages the students to integrate their learning at the university and to find their strengths and weaknesses.

There are five underlying components to *Kyoushoku Jissen Enshu*: (1) a sense of duty and responsibility for the teaching profession; (2) development of their own socioemotional competence, particularly with regard to their role and behavior as a teacher; (3) a deep understanding of child development; (4) an understanding of class management; (5) and pedagogical content knowledge. These five components are recommended for the development and implementation of a reflective stance (MEXT, 2013).

In *Kyoushoku Jissen Enshu*, how do students learn to reflect on their own practice? The students receive orientation and instruction for making a portfolio of *Kyoushoku Jissen Enshu* as freshmen and are told to keep designated documents from the teaching profession subjects for four years. In the process of making the portfolio, students reflect on their learning. When the portfolio is completed at the end of the spring term of their junior year, they reflect on their learning over the three-and-a-half years, using the completed portfolio as documentation and evidence in the *Kyoshoku Jissen Enshu* class of the autumn semester of the fourth year. They reflect on the history of their four years of learning through the use of a portfolio or through discussion with other students under the supervision of their professors. Students identify their individual strengths and challenges more concretely through this process. They are required to supplement the learning of a domain that was identified as a weakness. Finally, just before this program is completed, an inservice teacher is invited to the university to talk about their daily practice and teacher's life; students begin to form their identity as teachers through the lecture right before the beginning of their teaching profession.

"Inquiry" and "Reflection" Inservice Training Through Lesson Study

Figure 10.2 shows the embedded and hierarchical training system for inservice kindergarten teachers. NTCC in Figure 10.2 means "National Teacher Training Center," PSB means "Prefectual School Board," and MSB means "Municipal School Board."

Kindergarten teachers are required to participate in professional development and to renew their license every ten years. The teacher pays tuition for training

	1st year	5th year	10th year	15th year	20th year	25th year	30th year
N T T C					●Principal/Vice-Principal training		
			●Mid-level Teacher training				
			○Administrative staff (Except ECCE Teacher) training				
P S B	*Legal Training*						
	●Training that mixed an veteran from a novice teacher						
	Training corresponding to experience of teaching						
		● Teacher in fifth year in the profession					
					● Teacher in twentieth year		
	Training according to each teaching profession						
			●Curriculum coordinator training				
					●Principal / Vice-Principal training		
	Dispatch training for a long term						
			●Dispatch training to government office or other institutions				
	Training for professional knowledge and skills						
	●Course instruction, pupil guidance, Motivating and prompting children's play, Studying teaching and play materials, Evaluation in ECCE, School Evaluation e.g.						
M S B	*Municipal school board, School, Teacher self training*						
	●Municipal training, in-house training at each school, Training planned by each association, Personal training						

FIGURE 10.2 MEXT: Early childhood teacher training system in Japan.

planned by the ECEC societies and various groups unless that training is established by law. The professional development can be a lecture, supervised practice, a workshop, or a variety of methods including role playing.

One form of professional development that draws heavily on inquiry and reflection is "lesson study." Teachers voluntarily gather at a kindergarten, where a teacher plans and teaches an ECEC lesson. In "lesson study," after the lesson is taught, the teacher looks back on his or her practice based on the aim and intention written in the teaching plan and publically performs a self-evaluation. After this self-evaluation process, participants who observed the lesson ask questions and discuss with the teacher and each other their observations and their note-taking records. Often lesson study is conducted using video conferencing and video pictures. A teacher visits another kindergarten teacher to observe the practice and to take notes and make a photographic or video recording. Using these as evidence, teachers gather for a lesson study session. By opening their classroom doors to others, teachers ask themselves about their own intentions and practice and learn from the opinions of others. In this way, they gain new insights and develop new meanings about their practice. The process of lesson study supports the formation of a community of open learning.

In the public and private kindergartens, the boards of education of city and district municipalities and associations of private kindergarten invite an expert in psychology, special educational needs education, preschool education, or another field as a lecturer, and the meeting for the lesson study in the kindergarten is held. Kindergarten teachers as well as elementary school teachers and educarers learn new interpretations and understanding through lesson study on child development, teaching materials, teaching methods, and the meaning of the activity. The kindergarten is a learning community for improving their teaching profession. Teachers and experts can learn together by applying the lecture content to consider their own teaching.

Original Curriculum and Practice in Junior College or University

The Use of Reflection in a Two-Year Program—A Case Study

S Women's Junior College is one of the largest preservice education institutions in Japan for preparing the ECEC workforce that offers the combined DTEP/DEEP course. As the majority of the workforce consists of two-year program graduates and as its course work is quite standardized, it is worth looking at preservice education at S Junior College to see how students are educated to be fully equipped for the profession and how reflection is involved in the process of preservice education.

The enrollment in the S Junior College DTEP/ DEEP combined program has been around 350 per year for the last five years. Applicants must pass an entrance examination, but it is not academically selective. Candidates who did well in the interview and showed good communication skills and who demonstrated a high aptitude toward the ECEC work in the interview are admitted. Academic and health records from high school are also considered.

Course Work

The students are evenly grouped in classes of 40 to 45 students, and this becomes the home base for students' college life. A whole class approach is the basic learning style, and in this familiar learning style, students learn from each other and help each other to complete assignments that require teamwork. The two-year DTEP/DEEP program consists of four terms, and students take 14 to 18 subjects per term (17 weeks) to meet the requirements of both DTEP/DEEP and the associate bachelor's degree. To complete the program, students commute to the campus six days a week and attend two to four subjects a day. Subject matter is delivered to the class as an exercise-style lesson or as a 90-minute lecture.

A short list of the subjects will show the scope of the curriculum as well as the time allocated to the subjects on academic knowledge and practical skills. Subjects given over two to four terms are counted separately, and the grouping is done by the author. Therefore, it does not follow the categories of the DTEP/DEEP curriculum regulations set by MEXT.

There are 17 subjects on general education and learning skills—for example, Japanese, English, Information and Communication Technology, and Physical Education.

Twenty-three subjects cover professional knowledge—for example, Foundation of ECEC, Foundations of social welfare, History of education, ECEC for under threes, ECEC of special needs, Methods of education, and Curriculum study on five areas of development and learning in ECE (Health, Human Relations, Environment, Language and Expression, and Methods of Education).

Eleven subjects deal with how to understand and support children and their families—for example, Developmental psychology, Understanding of children, Counseling and consultation, Health and first aid, and Food and nutrition.

Sixteen subjects deal with the practical skills in expressive arts—for example, Arts and crafts, Origami paperwork, Puppet theater, Piano lessons, Music, Movement and dancing, and Physical education for preschools.

Internship

To complete the internship requirements of the DTEP/DEEP course, students must attend all of the "Pre- and after-internship guidance" and work at least 50 days at three different types of internship sites. The internship is administered as a two-week block of fieldwork and takes place during the terms or during the breaks between the terms. Students go to kindergarten internship twice—to an affiliated kindergarten in the second term and to a local one in the fourth term. Educarer internships are divided into three parts, and students must experience both a day care center and a child-welfare institution, such as a center for special needs children, a foster home, or facilities for the mentally retarded. Students may choose one of these as the third part of Educarer internship.

Pre- and after-internship guidance is given intensively on each block of fieldwork. It consists of 90 minutes of 15 exercise-style lessons. In the pre-internship guidance, students learn in detail what they need to do and how they need to do it, using the Internship Handbook produced by the college teaching staff. It contains all the information and various forms of documentation necessary to carry out the internship. It is made clear that the main assessor of the internship is the principal/director of the site and that the Assessment Form will be sent out from the college. If the internship is reported as inadequate or interrupted, the student must repeat it.

Sample sheets of the Assessment Form are included in the Handbook and are used for various exercises and checking. Therefore, students know the goals, criteria, and standard of the assessment before they begin the internship. In the after-internship guidance, students work in groups to exchange their experiences, to learn the variations among the settings, and to conduct self-evaluation using the sample Assessment Form. Then at a later lesson, the Assessment Report from each student's internship site is disclosed and he or she is given time to compare it with the self-evaluation.

For example, the Assessment Form of the first kindergarten internship has four criteria: Work behavior and meet timelines, Understanding of children, Skills for working with children, and Aptitude towards profession. The second internship Assessment Form shows 18 goals written in rubrics and grouped into five categories: Professional responsibilities, Interpersonal skills, Understanding of children, Competence in supporting children's activities and teaching, Diary keeping. In the category "Understanding of children," four goals are set: listen to children in an accepting atmosphere and be receptive to children; keep a fair attitude toward children and communicate with them in an open manner; understand the features of children's life, play and friendships; and build up a good relationship with children. The goals grouped into "Competence in supporting children's activities and teaching" are basic professional skills to talk to children; choose effective words, control voice tones and facial expressions; know about a child's developmental stages, understand his/her interests and previous experiences, and make a good research of appropriate activities and teaching materials; be able to make an adequate lesson plan following the basic format to achieve objectives set by the intern-student herself; be able to guide/assist/support/teach children in keeping with the plan; and be able to assess her own teaching against the objectives and reflect them on the next plan and teaching.

In pre-internship guidance, diary keeping is one of the major exercises. The Kindergarten-internship Diary consists of A4 size note files. It contains several worksheets on general information about the site and the log format. During the first half of the internship, intern-students must write two formatted pages per day; in the second half, three or more pages per day, following the site's advice. Students learn the wording and the style of the log writing, and their work is edited.

The log format for the second kindergarten internship and the expected contents of the journal are shown below. The journal example is written by the teaching staff and is given in the Handbook, and the explanation for each Column has been added by the author in italics.

Log Format (in boldface) with the Journal Example in the Handbook

Month, Date (Day), Year:	Weather:	Name of the Class		Boy	Girl
	Fine	**Children's Age:**	**Enrollment**	*19*	*15*
June X, 2013		*Violet, 4 years old*	**Present**	*18*	*13*

Time	**Learning Space Arrangement(★) and Children's Activities (○)**	**Teacher's (#)/Intern-student's (☆) Interaction with Children**
	Column A: general picture of the classroom settings and routines and activities along the timeline (may differ widely between the internship sites and on the seasonal events).	*Column B: the class teacher's interaction with children (teaching, guiding, and supporting to the whole class or individuals), intern-student's interaction with children and the class teacher.*
8:00	★Various pipes and buckets filled with water near sandpit, junk materials and tools near the craft table, water tray filled with water.	☆ Arrive for work. Talk with the class teacher about the setting for the activities of the day.
8:30~	○Arrive by school bus or on foot. ○Greet the teacher, put belongings in their personal lockers, and set for play. ○Child-initiated free-flow play: Sandpit, Art and craft, Drawing, Water, Exploring the garden nature, Playground equipments, Play tag, Play house, etc. ○Several children make shower with milk carton.	# Greets each child, observing the child's health conditions and spirits. # Talks to the child who is slow to get ready for the child-initiated play. ☆ Play tag with children in the playground. Help children to settle the quarrel on the rough stuff. # Shows children how to make a shower with a milk carton, how to use the tool to make small holes in it. Makes sure they use it only when adults are around.

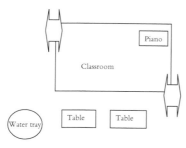

		# Tells where the materials are kept. Helps children when they find it hard to do themselves. # Puts out a big water tray in the garden for the play with handmade showers and tells children the space is ready. # Admires the boys' construction in the sandpit.
	○3 boys make a tunnel in the sandpit, set pipes and carry a bottle of water to pour into the pipe, watch the water flow to the sand tunnel. ★Put out large baskets for toys and tool hanging frames.	☆ Help teacher in the logistics and children in making shower. Respond to the children's requests. # Gives notice to the class to finish the activities and tidy up for the whole class activity.

(Continued)

| 10:40 | ○Tidy up: put things in original places, clean up the classroom to make space for group activity.

 ★Whole class time setting | ☆ Tidy up with children and move around where extra hands are needed.

 # Checks the progress and encourages children to finish chores. Reminds them to go to toilet before they congregate.

 ☆ Follow teacher's suggestions, help children get ready for the next activity. |

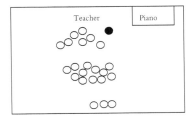

| 11:00 | ○Whole class time: each child puts out a chair in the space and sits on it; all get together.

 ○Sing songs of season with the teacher's piano accompaniment.

 ○Watch and listen to the picture book "Washing Loving Mother" read by the teacher.

 ○Make comments on the pictures of the page; respond to the story. Some ask to open the pages they want to see again. | # Talks to the class and plays the piano to introduce a new song, singing phrase by phrase.

 # Uses the piano to play familiar songs of rain and water.

 ☆ Sing with children, observing how they are doing.

 # Sits on a chair and opens a picture book, making sure the whole class is able to see it well; reads and talks to children so that they become interested in the story; responds to children's utterances.

 ☆ Listen to the story with children and observe how they respond to the teacher's book reading.

 ☆ Put out and wipe the tables kept in the corner. |

| 11:30 | ○Get ready for lunch: wash hands, gargle with water, bring out packed lunch and chopsticks, spoon and fork; arrange table.

 ○Say "Bon appetit" and start.

 ○Show the lunch box to the teacher and get her consent, then put it back in the school bag.

 ○Play quietly until after meal greeting.

 ○Play child-initiated play. | # Tells children to wash hands and gargle. Serves herbal tea to the table where the member is ready.

 # Praises children waiting quietly.

 # When everyone is ready, leads the greeting saying.

 # Sees to the relaxed atmosphere and social conversation to take place.

 # Conducts "Thank you for the meal" greeting when most children are finished. |

(Continued)

Month, Date (Day), Year:	Weather:	Name of the Class		Boy	Girl
	Fine	**Children's Age:**	**Enrollment**	*19*	*15*
June X, 2013		*Violet, 4 years old*	**Present**	*18*	*13*

Time	Learning Space Arrangement(★) and Children's Activities (○)	Teacher's (#)/Intern-student's (☆) Interaction with Children
13:40	○Get ready for home and whole class time: wash hands and listen to the teacher.	☆ Stand in front of children, take the teacher's position, and play finger rhymes with the whole class.
14:00	○Farewell greeting: sing good-bye song and greet each other. ○Picking up: go out together to meet parents.	# Tells children who did what, encourages them to look back at the day in a calm way, and fosters the expectation for tomorrow.
15:00	○Bus commuters play in the playground or hall while waiting for the bus. ★The last bus leaves the kindergarten.	# Talks to the parents about the day and provides necessary information. # Makes sure the bus commuters are safe and get on right bus.

Page 1 & 2

Column C: the focus of the day must be chosen by the intern-student herself.

<Focus of the day> On Teacher's Support to the Children's Learning in the Craft Work of Carton-shower Making

Column D: observation notes about the theme and reflection on the written artifacts.

<Observation and Reflection>

Observation: Yesterday X made a shower and played with it cheerfully for a long time. This morning, Y and several others went to the box where empty milk cartons are in stock as soon as they put away their belongings in their lockers. Y said, "I'd like to make a shower of my own" and invited others to make one together. Having picked a carton each, they searched for the tool to make holes in it, saying, "Where is it?" Then X said, "You can only use it when teacher is around." Hearing this, some children came to me saying, "Let's make it together, shall we?" The teacher showed where the tools were kept and reminded children, "There are three in the tool box, OK? Remember to return them when you have finished with them." The teacher started making a shower alongside the children and showed how to use the tool, telling them, "It is called prick punch. You need to hold the carton tight and press the punch onto the surface and push it in slowly." Y said, "I got it!" Teacher said, "Slowly, slowly, do not hurry." I helped Y hold the carton, and when she made a hole, she looked at me. When I said "You made it," she tried to make another hole.

(Continued)

Reflection: X's shower making yesterday clearly motivated the others to make their own, and I understood that play is passed on in this way. The teacher had expected this to happen and got materials and prick punches ready. Told the name of the new tool and the danger of using it without supervision. Counted the number of tools and made sure to return them to the box. I have learned the importance of letting children know the use of a tool and have them try when it was most useful. It is not wise to keep the dangerous tools away from young children and assume they cannot be cautious enough. 4-year-olds showed great care in handling them safely and shared the importance of following the safety rules. Predicting the children's interests and arranging the space to meet them are very important.

<Class teacher's feedback on the journal>

Page 3

Discussion—Reflection as an Acquired "Kata" (Pattern/Form/Mold/Type)

In the preservice education at S Junior College, and perhaps in most two-year ECEC courses in Japan, reflection maybe described as an acquired "Kata," similar to that of traditional Japanese arts. It is gained through three spheres of the student's learning in the pre- and after-internship guidance exercises and in the actual internships.

The first sphere is working on the Assessment Forms; before commencing and upon returning from an internship, every student makes a self-assessment using the sample sheet of the Assessment Form, then faces the disclosed Assessment Form reported by the site principal/director. These tasks let the student have an index of reflection; as discussed before, the goals and criteria are given in the Assessment Forms, and they clearly tell the student where to refer, what to look at, and when and how.

The second sphere is exercises on and actual tasks of diary keeping. At college, students learn that in Column B of the Log Format, they record their own interaction as well as the teacher's. In Column D, they write a journal on the focus of the day. In an actual diary, the result is clear; the students fill out the Log Format as they are taught and write journals like the journal example. It is repeated day after day during the internship, 50 days altogether. This experience shapes the frame of reflection. Over time, the students reflect upon their observational artifacts, such as children's development on using tools, relationships with other children in various scenes, and the class teacher's communication skills with children.

But students seldom refer to the theory of great educators such as Schon, Dewey, Montessori, Pestalozzi, and Froebel or psychologists such as Erickson, Piaget, Bowlby, Vygotsky, and Freud. It is not because they did not learn about these great theories, but the sample journals do not refer to them and the college staff or the site staff do not encourage the students to do so. What is considered important in diary journals is to express the writer's compassion and understanding for the children's feelings in various scenes to show that he or she reads the children's intentions in activities on the basis that children learn through child-initiated activities.

The third sphere is the internship experience. The journal example indicates the expected position the intern-student should take in the whole class time. He or she sits next to or more likely behind the children. The author's (Tabu) supervising visits to more than 100 internship sites in the last five years can attest to this, and a rough survey of all DTEP/DEEP students on their internship experiences over the past ten years also underpins this. To the question about where they stayed when the teacher led the whole class activities, more than 80% said "behind children." This means that the intern-student watches the teacher's interaction with the children from behind the children. He or she observes how to work with children effectively as an apprentice to the teacher, while often taking and acting the part of a child and perceiving the teacher's action from the children's point of view. This positioning trains the intern-student's observant eyes and supports the style of reflection.

Thus, reflection as an acquired "Kata" has a preset index, a strong frame, and a double-focus style. "Kata" can form a strong basis for continued reflection as students become professional teachers.

The Case of the Curriculum and the Teaching Practice in the Four-Year University

Another path to certification in early care and education is the four-year university. Tokyo Gakugei University (TGU) was established to perform preservice teacher education for all school levels from kindergarten to high school. The characteristic of the curriculum is to train the teacher who has the nature and the ability to bring out the children's "zest for living." The basic structure of the curriculum takes a semester system consisting of art, the teaching profession subject, and special subjects. We make much of the study that is a graduation thesis based on psychology, pedagogy, or other specialties science. In the preschool education course of TGU, the teacher preparation program allows students to earn three qualifications: an elementary school teacher first class, a kindergarten teacher first class, and the educarer qualification. Almost all students in the preschool education program earn all three licenses.

There are many features of this program. One of the most important is student teaching curriculum and practice (Figure 10.3). Intensive four-week student teaching practice is required to take the first-class license by the Teachers License Law, and in this course, a six-week practice (three-week program in the affiliated kindergarten and a three-week program in the public kindergarten) is the requirement for graduation. In addition, there are many other practical subjects and activities in the kindergarten preparation program.

High-Quality Teaching Practice Program—Using the Student Teaching Notebook and Self-Evaluation Sheet

Learning content in the program is structured so that a student can learn about each process. Each subject is considered separately and in integration with the

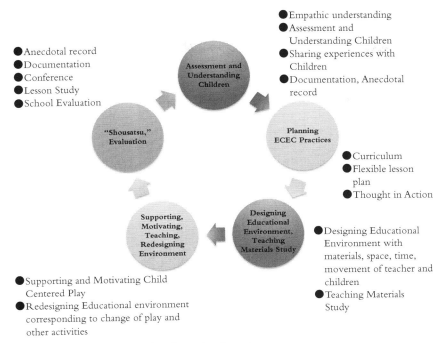

● Anecdotal record
● Documentation
● Conference
● Lesson Study
● School Evaluation

● Empathic understanding
● Assessment and
  Understanding Children
● Sharing experiences with
  Children
● Documentation, Anecdotal
  record

● Curriculum
● Flexible lesson
  plan
● Thought in Action

● Designing Educational
  Environment with
  materials, space, time,
  movement of teacher and
  children
● Teaching Materials
  Study

● Supporting and Motivating Child
  Centered Play
● Redesigning Educational environment
  corresponding to change of play and
  other activities

FIGURE 10.3 Reflective cycle of preschool teachers.

other subjects. In addition, using a training notebook and a self-evaluation sheet, we offer the opportunity for inquiry and reflection about the practice of each student. Students write their intention of designing the educational environment, flexible lesson plan, strategy and intention of interaction with children, points of assessment and evaluation, and reflection after practice. The supervising teacher meets with the student for reflection and writes comments in the notebook of each student. Students improve the quality of reflection by producing a lesson plan to implement their practice, making the teaching plan, and writing a record after practice. Based on the student teaching notebook, each student evaluates himself or herself using a self-evaluation sheet and discusses it with the head teacher and the professor as a supervisor.

Kyoushoku Jissen Enshu in Tokyo Gakugei University

Tokyo Gakugei University, located in Tokyo, is one of the leading universities for teacher education. In Tokyo Gakugei University (TGU), the ECEC program has an enrollment of 20 students each year. It utilizes the unique practice of *"Kyoushoku Jissen Enshu."* The professor monitors the learning of each student by checking the database in the university website and giving advice for students' learning, study, and career development.

In *Kyoushoku Jissen Enshu*, the supervisor and students make several documents for reflection. The documents include "Kyoushoku Jissen Portfolio" which means "the teaching profession practice portfolio" consisting of the results or deliverables of learning for four years; "Rishu Chart" (which means course record) that consists of the database of the academic record and the interview data on learning supervision, career counseling and guidance, prepared every term, written by the professor; the reports for the teaching profession subjects; a guidance; and diaries of the teaching practice. The supervisor discusses with students their learning in the teaching profession by using these documents to lead students to reflect on and inquire about their teaching practice.

In addition, cooperative inquiry and reflection is encouraged through small group discussion and role playing because our aim is cooperative inquiry and reflection in this subject. In the subsequent reports, a student wrote "I can understand and share the experience of others by the discussion with others; this becomes my own learning." Each student goes to a different kindergarten or a different class for teaching practice, so they cannot share their experience directly. Students felt the significance of personal reflection, but they also benefited from reconstituting their learning from the experience of others through these opportunities for discussion and sharing of the portfolio.

Summary: "Inquiry" and "Reflection" for Teachers to Continue Learning

In teacher education in Japan, *Shousatsu* and *Furikaeri* have been made much of for a long time. In this chapter, we identified the three clues to understand the background of *Shousatsu* and *Furikaeri*: (1) the ECEC principles that are at the root of the ECEC system in Japan, (2) the administrative quality control system (MEXT), (3) the curriculum and practice examples in the junior college and the university for teacher training.

The most characteristic point in Japanese teacher education may be collaborative *Shousatsu*. *Shousatsu* can be highlighted as an essential characteristic of the ECEC practice of Japan. We design and set the whole kindergarten environment as a place of rich life for children. We embed educational values and meanings in many things and locations and activities in the environment. Teachers can give effective support to a child so that the child can choose what kind of play and activity in which to participate in the environment. A child may choose to carry out any activity, as long as it is not dangerous and does not interfere with the rights of others. All teachers must be aware of all of the children and where each child goes throughout the kindergarten, and it is required that every teacher watch and understand each child's activity and development. Therefore, the exchange of information and the sharing of experiences between teachers are indispensable. Thus, the preschool education culture is raising the quality of ECEC by collaborative learning and mutual support.

Since the introduction of *Kurahashi*-articulated kindergarten teacher education theory, we have focused on cultivating preschool teachers who continue learning through personal and collaborative *Shousatsu* and *Furikaeri* of the self and of ECEC practice.

References

Kurahashi, S.（倉橋惣三）(1965a) 倉橋惣三選集　第2巻 フレーベル館, 323–328.

Kurahashi, S.（倉橋惣三）(1965b) 倉橋惣三選集　第3巻 フレーベル館, 174, 185–187.

Ministry of Education, Culture, Sports, Science and Technology. (2013). 教職課程認定申請の手引き　平成２５年度改訂版

Ministry of Education, Culture, Sports, Science and Technology. (2013). http://mext. go.jp/a_menu.shotou/kenshu/1244827.htm

Otokuni, M. (乙訓稔) (2012) 倉橋惣三の幼稚園教育の理念　実践女子大学　生活科学部紀要第49号、65–80.

Schon, D. A. (1983). *The reflective practitioner*, New York, NY: Basic Books.

For all statistics, see below.

○教員の資質能力の総合的な向上方策に関する参考資料 http://www.mext.go.jp/b_menu/shingi/chukyo/chukyo0/gijiroku/__icsFiles/afieldfile/2012/07/24/1323733_4.pdf Also: http://www.kantei.go.jp/jp/singi/kyouikusaisei/pdf/dai5_2.pdf

○指定保育士養成施設一覧（平成25年4月1日時点）http://www.mhlw.go.jp/bunya/kodomo/pdf/hoiku_youseikou.pdf

○学校教員統計調査平成22年度　http://www.e-stat.go.jp/SG1/estat/NewList.do?tid=000001016172

For the kindergarten funding system, see below.

○平成25年度幼稚園就園奨励費補助の概要　http://www.mext.go.jp/a_menu/shotou/youchien/__icsFiles/afieldfile/2013/06/12/1336129_02.pdf

Minegishi, M.　峯岸正教（2011）学校法人の財務分析－幼稚園法人の財務状況－産業經理. 産業經理 *71(2)*, 産業經理協會, 147–154.

All the data and information on S Junior College is from unpublished college data and instruction materials. Some survey data of S Junior College is kept at Mikiko Tabu's office.

11

REFLECTION THROUGH STORY: STRENGTHENING PALESTINIAN EARLY CHILDHOOD EDUCATION

Buad Mohamed Khales

In this chapter, I examine the role of reflective thinking and teaching for early childhood preservice and inservice teachers' professional development and growth in the West Bank, Palestine. I discuss how Palestinian kindergarten teachers, who work with children aged 3–5, reflect on their beliefs and practices through interpreting and writing stories. The stories focus on the recent effort at my Palestinian university to adapt and integrate more child-centered and inquiry-based teaching in Palestinian education.

In presenting these teacher stories, I address key questions about the role of reflection in strengthening Palestinian education and creating a new image of Palestinian teachers and students as reflective, inquisitive, lifelong adult learners. What does reflective thinking look like for our teachers? What is the importance of reflective thinking in teaching practicum courses? What are particular features of teacher stories that promote new teacher voices and new practices? In addressing these questions, I present the work and voices of teachers with whom I have worked at Al-Quds University, at the Abu Dis campus, in the West Bank, Palestine. The preservice teachers were enrolled in the early childhood education (ECE) program at Al-Quds University and completed their practicum teaching in local kindergartens and primary grades under my direction and guidance.

Palestinian Education, Inquiry, and Reflection

Palestinian education continues to face significant structural and pedagogical challenges for improving children's education from kindergarten to grade 12 (Ministry of Education and Higher Education/MoEHE, 2007; Nicolai, 2007). Strengthening K-12 professional development is a critical goal at the Ministry, in teacher education, and at K-12 school levels (Al-Ramahi & Davies, 2002; Wahbeh, 2003, 2011). Palestinian policy makers and others are also advocating for educational ideas and practices that promote constructivist teaching, increased student and teacher agency, and student-centered curriculum (Wahbeh, 2003, 2011). Of particular interest is for teachers to develop their own teaching materials and effective teaching methods (Wahbeh, 2011) that are less didactic and rote-based (Al-Ramahi & Davies, 2002). The inclusion of inquiry and reflection in preservice and inservice professional growth has shown potential for moving beyond traditional rote and teacher-directed learning that characterizes the majority of Palestinian classrooms (Wahbeh, 2003, 2011).

Teacher Stories and Reflection

Stories—oral, written, and dramatized and in music and song—have a long and time-honored tradition in Palestinian society. Stories are central to the social and educational fabric of Palestinian life and are linked to a number of cultural and educational traditions. Family storytelling is one rich tradition, and many stories and folktales are adapted from other sources (Nuweihed, 2002) and are used as an important medium for socialization and teaching. Stories in Palestinian society also have connections to Arab children's literature and to traditional literature, contemporary realistic fiction, and historical fiction (Al-Hazza & Lucking, 2007). Palestinian society is seeking to preserve and promote traditional stories and children's literature, as stories are seen as "cultural products" that help ensure the "viability and continuity" of Palestinian culture and society (Fasheh, 1995, p. 71). For example, the Tamer Institute for Community Education (http://www. tamerinst.org/resource-center), based in Ramallah, publishes children's literature specifically for Palestinian schools and libraries.

The use of narrative has been shown to be a powerful influence for promoting teacher observation, reflection, identity, and educational change (Connolly & Clandinin, 1990; Eagen, 1986; Paley, 1981; Pushor & Clandinin, 2009; Ritchie & Wilson, 2000). Stories help teachers recognize and understand the often nonlinear narrative flow of young children's learning as they socialize, play, and discover. Several critical elements to teachers' stories inform teaching and reflection (Eagan, 1986; Jalongo & Isenberg, 1993, 1995; Renck & Joar, 1993):

1. A mental element for processing information and taking decisions
2. A critical element for ascertaining the impact of experience, objectives, orientations, and values
3. A narrative element for uncovering teachers' objectives

The most "effective" teacher stories focus on exploration and reflection and lead to new professional growth and personal insights. Stories help teachers uncover the complex realities of what it means to teach well as teachers take on active roles as listener and teller. Teacher stories also enable teachers to communicate with one another and "compare notes" about their individual practices and beliefs (Jalango & Isenberg, 1995) and to see the "truthfulness" of their relationships with students and their inner feelings and thoughts.

The Al-Quds University Teacher Education Program

The majority of Palestinian kindergartens follow traditional ways of teacher-directed and rote learning in a whole class setting. The kindergartens primarily adhere to a specific curriculum that focuses on skill development in literacy and numeracy rather than an emphasis on how children can understand and use various kinds of knowledge in multiple contexts. My colleagues and I are interested in new kinds of learning based on children's real-world experiences, and a new way of learning based on inquiry-based teaching and learning. Our traditional forms of teaching can be transformed by guiding our teachers to reflect and analyze how and why their teaching can become more child-centered. We want to promote reflection and inquiry as a mirror for teachers to gain new insights about who they are as teachers and to empower teachers to adapt and implement new educational ideas and practices.

Our work so far has raised several questions discussed in the literature on reflection and educational change. To what extent can reflection actually improve practice? Is there enough time for teachers to reflect as they are learning to teach? What types of discussions are needed to evoke reflection? What type of arguments or proof can reflecting teachers present to support their teaching? To what extent does reflective thinking motivate teachers to review their practices?

My colleagues and I believe that Palestinian teachers are capable of thinking and reflecting systematically about their practices, and we are adapting ideas and practices on systematic inquiry from primarily Western-based educational research (see, for example, McNiff, 2007; Rust, 2010; Stremmel, 2002). The integration of reflective practice in teaching and the professional growth of teachers has the potential to change teachers' personal and professional lives. It requires a great deal of courage to criticize one's practices and to listen to the advice of fellow teachers or supervisors and make use of findings from the latest research on reflective thinking. To overcome some of the challenges that teachers might experience implementing reflective practice, it is important to look for mentors who can help teachers express their individual fears, feelings, preferences, and interests freely. Preservice and inservice teacher professional programs can play a critical role in this process, helping teachers learn to teach with a disposition for reflective and inquiry-based teaching (Loughran & Russell, 1997).

The Al-Quds University early childhood program has recently emphasized an innovative linking of teacher reflection, inquiry-based teaching and learning, and curriculum and instruction based on children's interests (Khales & Meier, 2013). The preservice teachers engage with readings and assignments intended to adapt and implement more child-centered approaches to young children's learning. The program also introduces teachers to and guides them in learning practical ways to involve children in an emergent curriculum based on children's interests (Jones & Nimmo, 1994). Given the lack of existing child-centered materials and resources in the local Palestinian kindergartens, the preservice teachers prepare their own activities and materials as part of their coursework and use these materials during their practicum teaching.

The teaching practicum course at Al-Quds University is a central component of our teacher education program, and it allows student teachers to experiment with their new knowledge about child-centered teaching in local classrooms. To deepen the students' learning and teaching, I ask preservice teachers to write reflective stories about their teaching in kindergarten to address the challenges they faced in their teaching and to improve their practice. The teachers' stories also assist the university in developing other educational programs related to early childhood education.

In the fourth year of their BA program, the early childhood student teachers enroll in a practicum course and teach in Jerusalem, Alexaria, and local Abu Dis kindergartens three days a week for a full semester. They first observe, then participate partially, and then fully engage in teaching in local kindergartens. The preservice teachers featured in this chapter enrolled in a practicum course and taught in Alexaria and Abu Dis kindergartens. All of these students prepare, teach, and reflect on their child-centered activities in a practicum course that focuses on kindergarten as well as curriculum in grades 1–4. This is a new kind of teaching for Palestine, and it requires a new kind of thinking and risk-taking on my part as well as that of the students.

The practicum course guides preservice teachers in the process of asking young children about what their needs are, what their experiences have been, and what they would like to learn. All of our course readings and discussions are in Arabic, and the student teachers teach in Arabic in the local kindergartens. I also introduce a number of research and practical sources and materials such as children's literature books written in English, which I translate into Arabic for the student teachers. A few teachers are fluent in oral and written English and directly consult additional educational materials online. English is taught in Palestinian schools beginning in the first grade, and for those Palestinian teachers who want to teach English, they receive separate specialized training in English-medium instruction.

In their initial work with the children in local kindergartens, the student teachers draw a brainstorm "sun map" and title the project that the children have chosen. For example, Sabti, a student teacher, and the children created a sun map about their interest in butterflies (Figure 11.1).

FIGURE 11.1 Children's sun map about their interest in butterflies.

FIGURE 11.2 Interactive discussion with a small group of children.

FIGURE 11.3 Story matching game created by student teacher.

Sabti then carried out a series of hands-on and interactive activities with the children based on their butterfly interests. Student teachers are encouraged to talk with children about their family and community experiences and prior knowledge of the project. Sabti also varied the physical environment and groupings for the children, encouraging them to meet and talk about the butterfly project in small groups on the floor or around one large table (Figure 11.2).

In another example, another student teacher's project focused on birds, and the project's initial sun map recorded the children's early interests: bird sounds, songs, food, colors, flight, and varieties. Teachers and children then co-create and engage in several activities within each project. In the bird project, the teacher and children shared stories and discussions about birds, observed birds in flight, drew birds, and played games such as puzzles, matching pictures, and dominoes with images of birds.

The student teachers create their own beautiful and intricate hand-made educational materials and games to promote active student engagement with each other and the teachers. For instance, one student teacher created a puzzle game where children match sentences from a story with the corresponding picture in a puzzle format (Figure 11.3).

The student teachers learn to make developmentally appropriate and high-interest materials that not only encourage interaction and discussion with the children but also promote fine- and gross-motor coordination (Figure 11.4).

FIGURE 11.4 May, a student teacher, and the children create animal pictures.

To deepen their understanding and implementation of project-based and inquiry-based teaching, the student teachers read more about the project topics on their own and maintain a reflective journal of their teaching and inquiry journey with the children. They also use the journals to plan possible activities for the project and share and discuss this plan with the children. The student teachers write in their reflective journals throughout the practicum course and reflect on their implementation of child-centered activities, the children's reactions, and how their teaching can be improved. The reflective journals are a beginning road map for the student teachers to guide their teaching, and they use these journals for sharing their reflections in our practicum course discussions.

Preservice Teacher Stories—Encounters with Reflection

In a recent practicum course, I asked my eight students to write stories about their successes and challenges in their preservice teaching. It was not easy for the students to write stories about what they learned in their university program and in their work with children in the classroom. But our earlier work writing reflective entries helped the student teachers to believe that they had enough raw material to draw from for reflection.

Their journals helped the student teachers look more deeply at what their children truly wanted to do and learn in the classroom and to reflect on materials and practices to promote more child-centered teaching based on children's interests. Over the course of their first three years in our BA-level program, I provided students with the following core set of questions to guide their written reflections:

> Why do I want to teach?
> What does teaching children mean to me?
> What goals do I want to achieve?
> How can I start teaching?
> How can I engage children to think, judge, ask questions, and learn?
> How can I create a meaningful learning environment?
> How can I build good relationships with the children and their families?

In class, we discussed how to look back over their journal entries for key challenges and successes and to think about some of the small moments and critical feelings in their journals. General comments from the student teachers indicated the value of our emphasis on reflective practice and critical thinking:

> "I learned about learning strategies that work for me in my own learning."
> "I have discovered my talent for critical thinking."
> "I improved my teaching, and I started to have the passion to teach."
> "I now read articles about children's interests."
> "We did not memorize—we understood, we learned how to be reflective and effective teachers through real experience."

I now present three students who wrote a series of reflections at the end of their practicum. Duaa is especially interested in the arts and enjoys using art and music with children in her teaching. Haneen has a particular interest in reading and children's literature. May enjoys and has a special talent for creating her own educational games and materials.

Duaa—Internal Conflict

The first time I taught in the classroom, I wasn't afraid to teach the children. I heard from many of my colleagues at the school that teaching children was difficult, and when the head teacher left me alone with the children, I got their attention by singing, reading a story, and doing drama with them. They all listened to me. But after that, the teacher didn't give me a chance to work with the children alone. She always said that she was the teacher in the class and that she wanted me to do what she wanted. I didn't like what she did because her relationship with the children was not good. I felt conflicted—teaching in this kindergarten is not as free as I hoped it would be. I want to be a teacher who is inviting to the children, and not continue in a traditional, boring style and manner. I care more about the child in front of me than the vast amount of information we are supposed to teach. I hope to be a teacher who reflects on how to work with children and to use new teaching aids and educational games that have long been neglected in our schools. If I can engage children in meaningful ways, then they will not notice the passage of time. My goal in becoming a teacher is to discover and develop children's thinking and creativity. I want to use all my energy for the development of the children and my community because they are the future.

Haneen—An Open Mind

The first day I entered the kindergarten I felt afraid because it was my first time teaching. But day after day I started to love the children and to teach them in the ways I learned in my university classes. We started a project together on the four seasons, and I asked the children what they wanted to learn. This experience was strange and new for me as it also was for the children. We created a sun map together, and then we worked together through conversation, drawing, playing games, eating fruits, reading books, and matching words for the seasons. As I learned at the university, I tried to keep an open mind about this kind of child-centered teaching, and writing in my reflective journal helped me discover what I could improve in this kind of teaching.

May—Teaching in a New Way

The first time I started in my practicum kindergarten class, I was afraid because I had not taught children before, and when I saw how the teachers were teaching, I cried. It was traditional teaching, and they wanted me to teach this way; they do not believe that children need to learn through play and discovery. Preservice teachers like myself who are trying new ways of teaching need to be patient and to find support—the kindergarten was not what I hoped it would be like and what I learned at the university. But with support from the instructor of my practicum course, the children and I created sun maps about what interested them, and I discovered that they are creative and active learners. As I worked with them according to this approach, I began to learn and grow because I want to be a good teacher. The challenges in this first experience helped me see myself as a teacher in the future. I learned that it is not easy to work with children, but if we decide to change ourselves, we discover that we can be good teachers. Dialogue with children is very important. At first, the children were ashamed of speaking, but I learned that when I set up a dialogue through a story, for example, the children's responses were creative and we started to remove the barrier of shame and fear. Writing in my reflective teaching journal also helped me—I became more curious about where I stood regarding a certain teaching idea or practice and to understand why a certain child said or did a particular thing.

Taken together, these brief reflective stories give a "developmental snapshot" of the first generation of Palestinian early childhood educators to embark on expanding reflective practice in our schools. The stories focus on certain universal, global challenges that all new teachers face, but they are also about particular challenges pertaining to Palestinian education. The student teachers themselves grew up and experienced classrooms featuring mostly whole class, rote-based learning and they are the first group of new teachers to experiment with understanding and implementing more child-centered teaching approaches. At the preservice level, Palestinian universities and other institutions have the responsibility and challenge of providing our future teachers with a foundation and orientation toward new ways of teaching and learning.

Inservice Teacher Stories—Finding a Voice

A year later, at the end of their first year of full-time teaching in local kindergartens, I asked the same teachers to write new stories about the value of reflection in learning to teach. A few teachers, such as Duaa, were working alongside other recent graduates of our Al-Quds University Early Childhood Program. They are beginning to form a group of reflective inservice teachers, sharing their teaching ideas and helping each other plan their activities. Through Facebook and meetings at the university, I continue to provide guidance for the teachers on building their reflective practice skills and knowledge.

Duaa—Engaging Young Children

Now that I'm a teacher, reflective practice means more to me. Reflection has helped me revise what I experienced and learned from my university work and practicum teaching last year in kindergarten. I have learned many new lessons through reflective practice about how to base my teaching on children's interests and to help them be creative and active in their learning. I continued to write in my reflective journal, writing entries before and after my lessons to reflect on my objectives and if the activities I designed met children's needs. This year I worked with my children in a new way. I implemented many activities similar to what I did in the practicum course. We told stories, had discussions, played educational games, and I used technology in my teaching. I had 38 children in my class, and engaging all the students was a real challenge. It was not easy to work in such conditions, but I believe that teaching children involves sacrifice, patience, and cooperation. I started to think of activities that suit large classes. Today I am more confident in using reflective teaching and teaching based on children's interests. Now I find myself different. I feel free, and I can do many new things with my children.

Haneen—Challenging Traditional Beliefs

Looking back on my first year teaching children, I relied on the professional development through reflection that I gained in my practicum course at the university. It was very important to see the map of my own development and how we develop our practices through writing diaries. Reflection is new in Palestine. For this reason, reflection is very important. It's like a road map. Reflecting on my teaching helped me learn more about effective objectives and outcomes and what I really wanted my children to learn. It also helped me understand how children think and how to engage them through play, music, puzzles, and stories. This was all new for the children and for me. I also faced a big challenge in changing parents' beliefs toward the application of new methods in education. Parents need to realize that children are different from adults and need different techniques and strategies. They have different intelligences and learning styles. I was intrinsically motivated to use new and modern methods of education that I learned about in my university studies. I'm now very confident in using reflective teaching because I know what the children want and what they need in the kindergarten. I now see how the new ways of teaching give children the chance to play, think, discover, and work together. I now want to learn more about how to use learning centers and to continue to change my teaching in good ways.

May—A New Adventure

If anyone asked me about my first year of teaching, I would tell them that I learned how to create a good learning environment in my class that allowed my children to play, think, ask questions, and work as a group. I reflected on my teaching over the course of the year and continued to write in my reflective journal. At the beginning of the year, I still was not sure that the children could learn according to their interests because they are not aware of what they want to learn. But I discovered a different issue—children do know what they want to learn, but they need opportunities to discover and examine their interests. It was not easy sometimes when my administrator asked us to teach in traditional ways, but because we believe in new ways of teaching, we take responsibility for a new adventure to change our teaching. I hope to be an expert teacher through more inquiry and reflection on my teaching. It has opened my mind to understand children in a deeper way, and now I see new ways to become a better teacher.

Duaa, Haneen, and May reflect on their teaching successes and challenges and reveal the beginning stages of conceptualizing and implementing a new way of teaching and learning in Palestinian kindergartens. Their reflections indicate how much they relied on their preservice training for thinking, discussing, and writing about their teaching goals, materials, strategies, and ways of interacting with children and parents. This reflective foundation helped the teachers to persevere and overcome a number of personal and professional challenges in implementing a new form of child-centered curriculum in their classrooms.

The first-year teachers' stories also allowed them to release their feelings and emotions about the challenges and joys of their first year of teaching—emotions that they might hide even from themselves. The opportunity to write and express their feelings also helped them appreciate the personal meaning of their teaching practices and experiences.

I believe that preservice and inservice teachers benefit from a strong and confident voice and sense of agency through reflective practice. The teachers' stories indicate the degree to which they are motivated to critique their own teaching and to bravely confront their thoughts and emotions. This kind of self-reflection and self-critique builds a strong sense of a teaching self and professional voice. As one first-year teacher at an inquiry group meeting remarked, "Through reflection I am now able to identify my weaknesses and strengths and to change my thinking."

In a related way, this interest in reflecting on practice strengthened the voices of the children themselves. The teachers reflected on new ways to raise children's voices in the kindergartens, to encourage children to express their needs and concerns, to work in groups, to play and think, and to discover the world around them. One first-year teacher noted, "I learned how to put myself in the children's place to see if they can learn in many ways according to our new way of child-centered learning."

Closing—A New Way Forward

Palestinian teacher educators, policy makers, and teachers are in the early stages of strengthening the quality of Palestinian early childhood education. I strongly believe that the promotion of reflective practice, taking an inquiry stance toward one's teaching and learning, is effective for improving the motivation and teaching of Palestinian early childhood educators. I realize, too, that the inclusion of reflective practice on a larger scale, as well as changes in our infrastructure and school organization, will take time and dialogue. As one kindergarten teacher said, "It would be much more effective to implement a reflective approach if we had fewer students in our classes."

As the first generation of teachers to learn a new of way of teaching and learning, they were reluctant at first to engage in reflective practice, but became more confident later as they saw that becoming reflective teachers is part of the entire teacher development process. Palestinian kindergarten teachers are reflective and creative when provided with supportive opportunities at the preservice and inservice levels. I look forward to creating larger learning communities of Palestinian kindergarten teachers at the university and in local schools to increase our teaching excellence and improve children's learning.

References

Al-Hazza, T. & Lucking, B. (2007). Celebrating diversity through explorations of Arab children's literature. *Childhood Education, 83(3),* 132–135.

Al-Ramahi, N. & Davies, B. (2002). Changing primary education in Palestine: Pulling in several directions at once. *International Studies in Sociology of Education, 12(1),* 59–76.

Connolly, F. M. & Clandinin, D. J. (1990). Stories of experience and narrative inquiry. *Educational Researcher, 19,* 2–14.

Eagan, K. (1986). *Teaching as storytelling: An alternative approach to teaching and curriculum in the elementary school.* Chicago, IL: University of Chicago.

Fasheh, M. J. (1995). The reading campaign experience with Palestinian society: Innovative strategies for learning and building community. *Harvard Educational Review, 65(1),* 66–92.

Jalongo, M. & Isenberg, J. P. (1993). Teachers' stories: Reflections on teaching caring and learning, *Childhood Education, 69(5),* 260–261.

Jalongo, M. R. & Isenberg, J. P. (1995). *Teachers' stories: From personal narrative to professional insight.* San Francisco, CA: Jossey-Bass.

Jones, E. & Nimmo, J. (1994). *Emergent curriculum.* Washington, DC: National Association for the Education of Young Children.

Khales, B. & Meier, D. (2013). Toward a new way of learning: Promoting inquiry and reflection in Palestinian early childhood teacher education. *The New Educator, 9(4),* 287–303.

Loughran, J. & Russell, T. (1997). *Teaching about teaching: Purpose, passion and pedagogy in teacher education.* London, England: Falmer.

McNiff, J. (2007). My story is a living educational theory. In D. J. Clandinin (Ed.), *Handbook of narrative inquiry: Mapping a methodology* (pp. 308–329). Thousand Oaks, CA: Sage.

Ministry of Education and Higher Education (MoEHE, 2007). *A diagnostic report of the education in Palestine.* [Arabic]. Ramallah, Palestine.

Nicolai, S. (2007). *Fragmented foundations: Education and chronic crisis in the occupied Palestinian territory.* UNESCO: International Institute for Educational Planning.

Nuweihed, J. S. (2002). *Abu Imeel's daughter and other stories: Arab folk tales from Palestine and Lebanon.* Northampton, MA: Interlink.

Paley, V. G. (1981). *Wally's stories.* Cambridge, MA: Harvard University Press.

Pushor, D. & Clandinin, D. J. (2009). The interconnections between narrative inquiry and action research. In S. Noffke & B. Somekh (Eds.), *The Sage handbook of educational action research* (pp. 290–300). Thousand Oaks, CA: Sage.

Renck, J. & Joar, I. (1993). Teachers' stories. *Childhood Education, 69(5),* 260–262.

Ritchie, J. & Wilson, D. (2000). *Teacher narrative as critical inquiry: Rewriting the script.* New York, NY: Teachers College Press.

Rust, F. (2010). Shaping new models for early childhood teacher education. *Voices of Practitioners, 5(3),* 1–6. Retrieved from http://www.naeyc.org/publications/vop/teachereducatorarticles

Stremmel, A. (2002). Nurturing professional and personal growth through inquiry. *Young Children, 57(5),* 62–70.

Wahbeh, N. (2003). Teaching and learning science in Palestine: Dealing with the new Palestinian science curriculum. *Mediterranean Journal of Educational Studies, 8(1),* 135–159.

Wahbeh, N. (2011). *Educational reform and meaning making in Palestinian schools: An ethnographic study of six public schools.* Ramallah, Palestine: Qattan Center for Educational Research and Development. Unpublished research report.

EPILOGUE

Linda R. Kroll and Daniel R. Meier

This edited volume has focused on the role of teacher reflection in educational change and transformation in international early childhood contexts. The text is intended for teachers, researchers, policy makers, and teacher educators interested and invested in educational change and teacher development in early childhood on a global level. The book has focused on the particular forms and functions of inquiry and reflection in the international contexts of China, Japan, Finland, Guatemala, Italy, Kenya, New Zealand, Palestine, South Africa, and the United States. The authors have examined how reflection can be seen as honoring and continuing local as well as national or regional educational traditions, beliefs, and practices. The authors also show how reflection at local, national, and regional levels can adapt and make use of ideas and practices from other cultural, historical, and educational approaches and perspectives on a global level.

The chapters, written by early childhood teacher educators, teachers, and researchers, offer a cross-cultural and cross-regional set of perspectives on how reflection can elevate the early childhood profession, improve practice, and provide children with a brighter future. As the editors of this text, we strongly believe that country and regional educational change can be influenced by raising the status of the early childhood profession and teaching as a thoughtful, intellectual, and social pursuit on par with teachers of elementary- and secondary-aged students. In the pursuit of global educational and political reconceptualization for all children, teacher reflection and inquiry can play a new role in expanding and elevating the image, talents, and influence of early childhood teachers. Our belief is that this book contributes to a new international view of early childhood education as a scholarly, engaging journey for reflective, inquiring, and curious educators.

On the international level, we also seek a greater professional affiliation and level of dialogue among and between early childhood educators. This entails an in-country and regional dialogue—for instance, Scandinavian early childhood educators communicating and sharing certain common cultural and educational beliefs and practices as well as dialoguing about certain practices particular to their countries and approaches. We believe that this is a critical form of reflection and change for educators, as they cross physical and psychological boundaries to expand their ideas and mindset. We also envision a more distant form of international dialogue and exchange—for instance, Palestinian and U.S. educators exchanging ideas on reflection and child-based learning and New Zealand and South African educators communicating about new ways to include families in the early childhood curriculum and assessment. We believe that an interest in and commitment to a reflective stance will help initiate and sustain this kind of global dialogue and exchange of educational ideas and practices. It will provide a shared foundation and language. Our future goal, then, is for growth and development for the early childhood profession both "at home" and "abroad."

In light of the unprecedented global expansion of educational ideas and practices, we are at a critical juncture in the history of the early childhood field and profession. Long seen in most countries and regions of the world as the last area of education to be funded or resourced but viewed as critical for children's lifelong growth and well-being, early childhood education is now poised to lead the way on a global scale. It is in early childhood that we can see the basics and the fundamentals of what it means for adults to teach well, with passion and love, and for children to learn with confidence, motivation, and joy. The greatest structural, physical, and psychological inequalities at the global level can be seen during the early childhood years as our most vulnerable population continues to be deprived by governments, regional conflict, and other human-made factors of the dignity and human right to an engaging, meaningful, and positive start in life.

A new focus on the value of reflection and inquiry for early childhood educators—at the policy, research, political, and instructional levels—can foster a new generation of teachers capable of and passionate about an inquiring stance toward their own learning, toward the learning of children, and toward communication and dialogue with families. Making room conceptually and pedagogically for reflection and inquiry at the global level can open up new kinds of dialogue across physical, ideological, and political borders. In this process, we might begin to convince ourselves that what is really "effective" and of "high quality" about particular approaches and practices is more about the very process of international exchange, sifting through global ideas, testing and experimenting with new practices, materials, and perspectives.

In reflecting on the perspectives and ideas of the contributors to this volume, we invite readers to consider how they might adapt and apply those ideas on reflective practice that make good pedagogical sense for teachers and children in their particular social, cultural, and educational context. The titans of educational theory and change—from Vygotsky to Montessori to Freire to others—cannot alone solve global educational problems and challenges in early childhood. We can, though, use their ideas for reflecting on new ways to enact educational change and equity on a global scale. The way forward might just lie in the hearts and minds and bodies of teachers—their motivation and ability to change, to adapt, to ponder, to envision, to move, to act. We believe that the promotion of inquiry and reflection on a global level can move us along in this most human of learning processes and journeys. Based upon the kinds of forward-thinking ideas and frameworks presented in this volume, we invite readers to adapt elements of this book to expand their work as international early childhood educators.

INDEX